Praise for *(Her)oics: Women's Lived Experiences During the Coronvirus Pandemic*

"I'm a proponent of sharing our truth. These womens' stories are raw and real. They make me want to cry, or laugh, or call them up and say this sh** happened to me too! We've got this. These women really are the heroines of the pandemic: nurses, doctors, teachers, badass moms, women having a mental health crisis, healers, grandmas… I love this."

- Jennifer Pastiloff, best-selling author of *On Being Human*

"The homefront has always been inhabited by women, including anyone who identifies with and enters the space of "woman" – caretakers and home keepers and compassionate community builders. This collection reminds us how the heart warriors never give up or in, which is the only reason we have a chance. Where are the purple heart medals for these legions of women? Secular Blessings on every one of their stories, every single body."

- Lidia Yuknavitch, author of *Verge – Stories* and *The Small Backs of Children*

"This is a remarkable, kaleidoscopic record of a catastrophe that simultaneously struck us all. While physically isolating, we need emotional closeness and these essays are consolation for any reader who ever wondered, I can't be the only one feeling this, can

- Leigh Stein, author of *Self Care*

"These are remarkable times and call on all of us to become even more remarkable people. I bow to these women and hope all can read their stories of courage, failure, despair and love. In addition, these stories give proof to what some of us have known all along: that the challenges, deep service and heart opening of motherhood can be an enlightenment intensive. Motherhood in a pande

- Hallie Iglehart   *rt, Myth and Meditations of th*   *e to Women's Wisdom*

"*(Her)oics* is just the antidote our world needs right now. Here are the accounts of women—brave, fierce, unflinching—meeting head on the unprecedented challenges we are currently facing. Just holding this anthology in my hands gave me a sense of overwhelming hope and courage. Upon opening it, I found a polyphony of voices, each distinct and resonant, working seamlessly together to lighten up these uncertain times."

- Alex Espinoza, author of *Cruising: An Intimate History of a Radical Pastime*

(HER)OICS

Women's Lived Experiences During the Coronavirus Pandemic

Edited by Joanell Serra and Amy Roost

Pact Press

Published by
Pact Press
An imprint of:
Regal House Publishing, LLC
Raleigh, NC 27612
All rights reserved

ISBN -13 (paperback): 9781646031641
ISBN -13 (epub): 9781646031658
Library of Congress Control Number: 2020941109

Interior and cover design by Lafayette & Greene
lafayetteandgreene.com
Cover images © by AS photostudio/Shutterstock

Regal House Publishing, LLC
https://regalhousepublishing.com

Printed in the United States of America

Dedicated to the voices we lost in the COVID-19 pandemic

Contents

Dear Reader,

You've picked up this book and, in doing so, made a bold choice to travel, despite whatever travel restrictions may or may not be in the world today. Reading *(Her)oics* will take you on a journey, a long winding road trip around the U.S. from the streets of Manhattan suddenly gone quiet, to rural areas where writers find solace in the mountains and coasts. Along the way you'll visit with women who are holding their lives and their families' lives together, despite the worst pandemic in our living memory. You'll enter homes full of young children offering joy despite living in an aura of fear, adolescents who hesitate in the hallways of life, and parents navigating uncharted territory. Nurses and doctors will offer you a view inside the hospitals where they've rolled up their sleeves and waded into a sea of despair, trying to stem the tide. You'll catch glimpses of young lovers who can't believe their good fortune—quarantined with a new match! Meet lonely seniors who live to see their grandchildren's faces pressed to a Zoom screen across the country and old friends who mail each other mementos of happier times. Brave souls will open their worlds to you—as they head to a factory to test for Covid-19, to work in a call center despite dangerous conditions, to deliver masks to local nonprofits, or to hold the hand of a dying child. These women refuse to turn away. They see the gaping needs and offer love to those around them—love in the form of free virtual yoga classes, meals delivered, late-night phone calls, rushing to a patient's side, playing on the floor with a toddler.

Love—for others and for self—emerged as a central theme. In the course of the long months inside, women found peace—in meditation, in observing the beauty around them, in communing with animals, in touching their children. They found solace in reading voraciously, in cooking for their families and themselves—even when ill—in writing, art, and music. To dispel their grief they lifted their instruments, knitting needles, packets of yeast, and pens. They write of facing loss, pregnancy, health crises, financial devastation, unjust laws, racism, identity crisis, mental illness, and deep loneliness. All with grace. A pandemic, protests, politics—nothing stopped these women from sitting down and writing their stories.

My own journey with Covid-19 began in early March, when I found myself in what would become the epicenter, New York City. I helped my son and his partner buy canned goods and hand soap, stocking their apartment on 107th and Lexington before they would settle in for a few weeks (or so we thought), and caught a plane home to California. I had come east from California a week earlier, to see a short play of mine that was being performed in a local theater festival. There were no cases in NYC yet, but I did have the forethought to bring a mask with me. That was the extent of my personal preparation. My return flight was harrowing—every seat taken, a sticky toddler in the seat next to me, and fear in the eyes of my fellow passengers. My mask was no match for six hours of recycled air with four hundred other travelers. My cough and fever started four days later. After enduring weeks of a debilitating cough, overwhelming body aches, intermittent fevers, and low oxygen rates, I found that getting care, let alone a Covid-19 test, was exhausting and surreal. Despite many years of advocating for myself and my patients in medical settings, when I found myself alone in the ER waiting for a chest X-ray, with danger tape around my cot, I still could not get a Covid-19 test. This told me how dire the situation was for every ill person in the country that day. My determination to do something positive in the face of this crisis was born there, alone under those unrelenting fluorescent lights, wondering why one nurse wore a spacesuit and another barely tightened her mask. I knew I would need to write about this.

Amy Roost had already birthed one anthology (*Fury: Women's Lived Experiences During the Trump Era*), and I was devouring it one essay at a time through my weeks of convalescing. When she messaged me one morning to see if I'd like to write a proposal with her for an anthology about women's experiences during Covid-19, my hand flew to the keyboard. *YES.*

It bears mentioning that Amy and I met through a women's writers' group online, which led to her attending a three day writers' retreat at my home. In September 2019, we spent a magical fall weekend with twenty other women writers. Words, wine, and laughter flowed. Under the hot Sonoma sun, many things blossomed—friendships, poetry, plans for more adventures, a commitment to tell the truth, to share our stories, to grow. It fit that, as the pandemic descended and our worlds became very small, Amy and I decided to collect women writers again. This time, we could not sit under the canopy of redwood trees near Jack London's original home. But we could gather under the umbrella of an anthology.

Amy and I took all our fears and frustrations and threw them into a book proposal. I was still not fully recovered from Covid-19. As a mother with several immunocompromised young adult children, I was frightened. As a therapist, I was discovering my tools were no match for the horrors that my clients were facing. As a writer, I feared the fever had burned many of my hopeful words away. Amy was grieving the loss of her meticulously planned book tour for *Fury*. She was examining the risks to her family—one essential worker, a husband who falls into the "higher risk" age bracket, and her adult sons far away. Yet we both felt compelled to create this book, this holding space for stories from around the country.

When our publisher called to discuss the project, the question we grappled with was whether we had time to get truly diverse stories—to get beyond the boundaries and borders of our own bubbles and find voices from around the country. The pandemic was hitting all strata of society, albeit harder in certain areas and populations. Women's experiences would differ drastically based on location, age, race, and health. We needed to include voices of younger women facing an uncertain future, as well as older women, and women particularly vulnerable to the virus. Voices of women of many cultures, many religions, many states. We had a month to collect their stories.

We dug deep. We called in favors from friends around the country to promote the call for submissions. We reached out to professors and mentors we had known, writing conferences, non-profit leaders, healthcare professionals, and leaders in the indigenous and immigrant communities. We held free workshops and promised to support emerging writers with a story to tell. We urged women to write their stories whether they were likely to be included or not—simply to take back a modicum of control in their lives. This experience served as a reminder to many of the power in voicing their experience, owning and sharing it. Hundreds of writers took on the challenge—to take this dark time and painful circumstances and write something beautiful. Perhaps the most gratifying part of the process has been the messages back and forth with the writers as they polished their pieces. A few words pulled from their many emails:

"I'm just going to try to relax, so I can sleep tonight. Last night I was energized by your words of encouragement about having a voice…I'm overwhelmed, but in a good way."

"Already, I've learned a lot about how I have to keep decolonizing my own artistic process as I explored this topic…To be included in this important anthology is such a gift…and the timing of this is, well, wow."

"I'm not satisfied with my work, it's overwritten, and the ending is weak. I cannot make it work. The well is dry. :) Thank you for getting me started. I'll continue to work on it, and it is to your credit that I even started it at all." (She rewrote it. It's wonderful, and included.)

"I am actually in tears. This means more than any acceptance I've ever had." (From an experienced and published writer.)

"It is a good sign that so many submissions were received by you… creativity and strength always rise out of sorrow!"

While we worked feverishly (yes, really) to spread the word, select pieces, and edit, the world continued to slide downhill. Racial violence flared, finally getting some of the attention it has long deserved. States took on drastically different approaches toward the pandemic and the civil unrest. The federal government fanned the flames of illness, pain, and betrayal.

What became clear to me, as I read these stories and kept one sad eye on the news, were the absolutely unfair expectations on women. Women were expected to walk into hospitals and care for contagious, critically ill patients, wearing bandanas as protection, or sometimes not permitted to mask up at all. Mothers were expected to continue to work full time remotely, but also care for and educate their children in the home. Elderly women and women with underlying health issues were told to stay home so others could have their freedom, but few had food delivered to them, or medical house calls, and the experience of isolation threatened the mental health of the most vulnerable. Pregnant women were asked to give birth without their partners. Mothers were asked to wait months for financial support from the government after being laid off, but to feed their families in the meantime. Lupus patients were asked to delay taking their needed medicine and risk intense relapse of disease, because the president had decided to tout the same medicine as a "Covid treatment" without evidence. Nurses had to beg, plead, and cajole their providers to be tested for Covid-19 but avoid interacting with others until they knew their status. Managers were told to lay off their subordinates on Zoom, then turn around to be fired as well. Women of color scrambled to create safe nests for their children, knowing they were at risk of police violence as soon as they stepped outside—or maybe as they rested in bed. Older women lived with the fear of losing their healthcare coverage if they were laid off, or if their partner was felled by Covid-19. And many women faced the final expectation—to say goodbye forever to a loved one on a cell phone screen.

Our respect and admiration for all of the writers, with accepted stories and otherwise, grew along with our outrage. It became clear that while there are "essential and non-essential workers" right now, there are no non-essential stories. Choosing the selected stories presented here was challenging, at times painful, and probably ultimately flawed. One cannot capture all aspects of this pandemic across the country in one anthology, but we believe we gave you much to consider.

We are well aware that over 120,000 Americans have died as of the writing of this foreword, and none of them had the chance to write something for the anthology. We have the voices of survivors here, and loved ones, but the book is dedicated to the voices that are not here, the voices that our society has lost. That the world has lost.

Please don't hesitate to dive in—the journey you are embarking on is as much beauty, delight, and peace as it is the harsh reality of a loss and suffering. We hope you'll smile as much as you sigh, and laugh as much as you cry. We know you'll meet many women you admire.

These are fifty-two women's essential stories, each one heroic in her own way.

Joanell Serra
July 2020

❧

Joanell Serra writes novels, plays, and creative non-fiction. Her novel *The Vines We Planted* was published in 2018 by Wido Publishing. A licensed therapist, Joanell is also the founder of Impactful Path Coaching and leads writing retreats and workshops. Her work and events can be found at Joanellserraauthor.com.

Corona, Corazón and Other Stories from the Heart

Corona, Corazón

Judy Bolton-Fasman

The first time I had to socially distance, I was six years old with a severe case of strep throat. "Look at those pustules," the doctor muttered as he gagged me with a tongue depressor. To this day, I cannot stand eating ice cream on a stick.

I lived in my parents' bedroom that long spring, watching black and white television. I wanted company and wrote to my aunt forty miles away to send me a Barbie doll. My parents fought when my father wrapped me in a bedspread and sat me on the driveway in a beach chair "to take sun." My mother cried. She was sure that germs lurked everywhere. She was certain I would contract scarlet fever.

"Fresh air is good for her," my father bellowed.

My father wanted to cure me. My mother wanted to convalesce me. I acquired my fearsome, what-if imagination from my mother. Disaster and danger were as ubiquitous as grass and sky. Throughout my childhood, I rarely left the house without holding her hand. When I was sick, she told me not to leave her double bed. And for the most part, I didn't.

Now, my eighty-five-year-old mother lives in a nursing home. I don't tell her that there has been an outbreak of the coronavirus in her facility. I don't tell her that she's tested positive for COVID-19. Thus far, she's asymptomatic. On the telephone she tells me that her 100-year-old roommate, Sadie, coughed throughout the night, and then went away.

"Where is she now?" I ask.

"*En el cementerio*," my mother says matter-of-factly in her native Spanish. To think, only a thin curtain separated my mother from Sadie's mortality.

Illustrations of the virus look like demented tinker toys. Red pieces of wood that resemble golf tees are stabbed into gray pockmarked balls.

These invisible and viral tinker toys are on doorknobs, on the mail, on the credit card I hand to the cashier at the grocery store. They're on the steering wheel of the car.

I don't take my cell phone with me when I walk the dog in case an errant germ lands on my screen. On one of those walks I see my neighbor weeding in front of his house. He forgets for a moment and steps toward me. I stagger backward. "Yes. Sorry—of course," he stammers.

I am a few months shy of sixty—that boundary between the biblical sounding decree of "who shall live and who shall die." My husband, who is sixty, grocery shops during early morning hours designated for senior citizens. "Do they think old people don't sleep?" he grouses.

People talk about the "silver linings" of this pandemic. I imagine most of those silver linings have teeth like a buzz saw—a macabre toothy grin. Get too close, and that's how a limb gets severed. But I love waking up to my sweet husband. In normal times he works out of town during the week. Now, I love hearing his voice booming through the house as he conducts business on video-conferences. He's a scientist responsible for organizing coronavirus testing sites.

At the home, my mother's television is always on, broadcasting in the midst of her room's fluorescent dusk. She checks for pandemic news all day. At night she falls into a restless sleep listening to pandemic bulletins. But nothing on the news is as harrowing for her as the forced quarantine she endures in her six-foot by nine-foot room.

"*Estoy encarcelada.*" I'm imprisoned, my mother says.

It's been a very long time since I've wanted to hold my mother's hand. But right now, I long to do just that.

I'm anxious about being housebound. I'm terrified of becoming the agoraphobic I was in my early twenties. That's when I moved to New York City to teach myself to be in the world. My cover was that I went there for love and then for graduate school. But the truth is I found comfort in counting my way around the city. I memorized avenues and was mindful of the numbered streets. I ended up living in the city for nine years.

The news hammers away at me. New York City is the epicenter of the virus. So many people die—young, old, even children—no one is spared. Refrigerated trucks are converted into makeshift morgues. Fifth, Madison, Park—avenues that are tumbleweed empty now. Yellow police tape does the job of vacating playgrounds and parks. New York, where I taught myself to be free, is a deathtrap now.

In Spanish, *corona* means "crown."

In astronomy, there is the sun's luminous corona.

When I visited my son in Spain this past winter, we drove through *A Coruña,* the largest town in Galicia.

When I was a little girl, my mother told me a story about the time King Solomon took off his crown and placed it on his mother's head. There is even a Ladino song with the refrain, *Que el coronó, a el su madre, en día de alegría, de su corazón.* "When the king crowned his mother, it was a day of joy, a day close to his heart."

"That is how you honor a mother," said my own mother.

Corazón, corona.

When my mother calls today, I hear her panting on the other end of the line. I become terrified that she is finally presenting with coronavirus symptoms.

"When is this going away?"

It takes me a moment to understand she's okay, that she is talking about the virus in general.

"When are you coming to see me? *Te extraño.*"

On the surface *extrañar* means "to miss." Really, though, it's a deep longing for something one will never have again. It's a word my mother used whenever she talked about Cuba. *"Ay Cuba como te extraño."*

"I don't exactly know when we'll see each other again," I say to her softly, lovingly. "But we will get through this," I whisper, entirely unsure of what I have promised.

Judy Bolton-Fasman is a four-time winner of the American Jewish Press Association's Simon Rockower Award for her essays. Her writing has appeared in *The New York Times* (op-ed page), the *Times'* family and parenting section (formerly "Motherlode"), the *Boston Globe, McSweeney's,* and WBUR's "Cognoscenti" essay page. She has been awarded fellowships at the Vermont Studio Center, the Mineral School in Washington State (2018 Erin Donovan Fellow), and the Virginia Center for Creative Arts (Alonzo G. Davis Fellow for Latinx Writers 2020).

Essential: A Shopping List

Amy Roost

Champagne. Yesterday, when the stay-at-home order was issued, I was instructed to shop "only for essentials." Today, champagne is essential because today is the release date of my book. A book I spent two and a half years of my life compiling and promoting to booksellers, twenty-two of whom signed me up to do events in their stores. Events that were all canceled in the past week.

A haggard-looking manager wearing a Hawaiian shirt walks the line outside the entrance to Trader Joe's. Recognizing me, a regular, he stops to ask what I'm here for so he can check on availability for me. My response is unapologetic.

"Do you have good champagne?" I ask. "Because it's essential that I drink good champagne tonight." The younger woman in line behind me snort-laughs. I turn to her.

"Thanks," she says. "You just made my day."

"Champagne *is* essential," I explain. "How else am I supposed to celebrate the release date of my first book during a pandemic?"

She asks me the name of my book and I tell her. "*Fury: Women's Lived Experiences During the Trump Era.*" She nods and returns to her phone. I shift my focus to the string quartet of four red-haired children busking next to the shopping carts. I appreciate their tender rendition of "Sheep May Safely Graze," and am reminded of my first wedding when my bridesmaids walked down the aisle in front of me to this Bach standard. I also wonder why the dad—who watches over the spare change in the cello case—is allowing *his* sheep to expose themselves to germs. Could it be that this is how the family is getting through these hard times? Or maybe he's an exploitive parent? Or perhaps there's nothing for me or the dad to worry about because, as our president insists, this whole thing is just one giant hoax. My thoughts continue to bob and weave and eventually land on my own child, a son who lives outside of hard-hit Seattle and whom I'd planned to check in on during my book tour. I worry about him because he is cognitively impaired, resulting in his sometimes not registering illness.

"Is this it?" the woman behind me asks. I turn around and she's holding up her phone with a picture of my book on the screen. I tell her yes. "Wanted to make sure before I purchased two copies. One for me and one for my mom."

Her small gesture makes for great consolation.

Beans. Once inside the store, I figure I might as well grab a few other essentials. I've read that beans are a good staple during a pandemic. And even though I don't much care for beans—with the exception of refried—I roll my sanitized cart to the canned goods aisle only to discover they're all out of beans. Two crew members busy themselves spraying and scrubbing the empty shelves with disinfectant. This touches my heart somehow, and, as I stand there and study the industriousness of these two strangers working to protect me, I feel the prick of tears.

Toilet Paper. There is none. Fortunately, I'm well stocked at home and for the first time in my marriage, I appreciate my husband's apocalyptic tendencies.

Hand Sanitizer. Sold Out, the sign reads. I saw somewhere—maybe Pinterest?—how to make my own. I Google it. Looks like I'll need to resort to concocting a home brew consisting of the last of the Bacardi 151 rum I keep on hand for fire breathing, the bottle of aloe vera I keep on hand for burns (thus far unrelated to fire breathing), and the lavender essential oil I purchased from a multi-level-marketing friend. I can do this. One of the many things I will learn to do during this pandemic, such as replacing a cable splitter and snaking a drain.

Cat food. As I make my way to the cat food that isn't there, I flash back to that time in 1984 when I visited a grocery store in Moscow, astonished by all the barren shelves. It occurs to me that this experience feels like that one except I'm not in the Soviet Union. I feel that prick of tears again.

Chocolate. In my world, champagne without chocolate is not a thing, so—expensive brut in the cart—I head to the chocolate located on a shelf above the nearly empty freezer bins. As I reach for the last tub of dark chocolate almond butter cups, I glance at my watch and notice my ten-minute shopping limit is nearly up. There's more I need to stock up on, but I don't want to go through the sting of rejection that is another empty shelf, so I head for the checkout.

The woman in front of me pays cash for her groceries. The checker hands her change then pumps a puddle of sanitizer into his hand. Meanwhile a co-worker wipes down the counter where my items are about to be placed before bagging. "Want some?" the checker asks, holding up the sanitizer. I eagerly accept his offer, as if being offered some decadent dessert I can't resist.

As always, I make small talk with the checker, the friendly staff being one of the many reasons I shop almost exclusively at Trader Joe's. I inquire about the checker's stress level, and his long hours. In his thick Spanish accent he tells me the stress is manageable because of the metering of customers, and that the store pays time-and-a-half for overtime and has given everyone a $2/hour "hazard" raise. "Sounds like they're taking good care of you?" I ask. "They are," he says.

A robust woman appears out of nowhere to help bag. Her exuberance and beauty—the way her red lipstick matches her glasses and offsets her ebony skin—remind me of all that is good in the world. I tell her this; she blushes. I then turn back to the checker, who is holding out my receipt as he says, "Enjoy the rest of your day." Something that I couldn't have imagined possible only ten minutes ago.

I manage to say, "I'll do that" before choking on, "You too." Tears, now freed from their bubbles, flood my cheeks. I think, *This is what it means to "ugly cry."*

"You okay?" asks the checker, whose sweet nature I now realize reminds me of my son's. Not trusting my voice, I nod and smile, dip my head and make for the exit. There I'm handed a yellow tulip by another sunny-dispositioned employee.

Once outside the door, I pause to appreciate all the grace I just encountered. Then, I breathe a sigh of relief thinking once again of my son, whom I had hoped to visit next month, who is quite possibly, at this very moment, telling someone to enjoy the rest of their day. For he, too, works at a Trader Joe's—a business that was willing to take a chance on him and provide the extra training and accommodations he needed. My son, whom no one else would hire, is now considered "essential" not only to me, but to everyone.

❧

Amy Roost is an author, journalist, documentary podcaster, and 2019 Annenberg Health Journalism Fellow. She is co-editor of *Fury: Women's Lived Experiences During the Trump Era* (Pact Press, 2020). Amy's writing has appeared in numerous print and digital publications including *Ms. Magazine*, *Narratively*, *Talk Poverty*, and *Bitch Media*. She is currently at work on a memoir based on "Finding Rebecca," a Peabody-nominated podcast she wrote and co-produced for *Snap Judgment*.

Neighborhood Love Story

Christina Adams

I have an alcoholic neighbor. A bald, brown and rake-thin Mahatma Gandhi look-alike, his head is spattered with cancerous-looking sunspots from waiting at bus stops. Perpetually cheerful, his eight-toothed jack-o-lantern grin grows wider when he's spreading drunken cheer to strangers in the street. People edge away from him in our shared alley, avoiding his offers of food or a sip of beer from his take-out coffee cup. But I love him.

I didn't want to. When he arrived at the door of our new house with an expansive welcome, I kept him outside—a response he often evokes, even from friends of mine who know him. "I'll bring you food," he said.

"That's okay," I replied, waving him off.

"Don't worry, I'll be back!" he said, swinging his skinny legs over the fence. No gate for him.

"This guy is gonna be trouble," I groused to my husband. But he kept coming. I didn't want to be rude, so I accepted an herb-sprinkled Mediterranean beef and rice dish starred with pita triangles. It was delicious. I thanked him, and he came again and again. "He's using food to get in with us," I told my husband. I could feel myself trying to withdraw. I had a flash of intuition that he would worm his way into my heart and I might even end up having to take care of him. That I would refuse to do.

Then he started offering to watch our house when we traveled. "Don't worry," he said, waving his thin hand dismissively. "I'll make sure it's perfect, like you never been away." He was sitting in my side yard in his plastic lawn chair, smoking and reading the newspaper, his can of beer on the ground, as usual on his days off. I was perturbed at this odd stranger barnacled to our unlikely dream home, a '70s shabby French Provincial cottage near the Pacific Ocean. But since we'd been flooded once, it seemed both smart and risky to let him do it.

Will he rob us? Set our roof's carved wooden buttresses aflame? But everything was fine. It became our regular arrangement. We'd pull up and there he'd be, our very own house gargoyle, like a beachside Notre Dame. "Welcome back! Dinner at six," he would say.

He is, after all, a chef, as we first discovered at the boozy next-door yard party when a platter of ten lemon and garlic-capered trout fillets appeared. One taste and I was hooked. He worked for a well-known California chef then—he wasn't just "a drunk." Since then, in the few mornings I've seen him sober, I've glimpsed a polite, shy, even thoughtful person. We dined at his current restaurant and were shocked to see him work the grill like a battle commander, flanked by a dozen Hispanic co-workers who affectionately call him "abuelo"—grandfather.

As we got to know him, boundaries had to be drawn, mostly conversational, such as telling him to stop saying something offensive or leave. But he's courtly, asking, "Are you home, mi amor?" but rarely entering if my husband isn't present. His frayed sense of propriety is one of the few Muslim traits he retains (he scoffs at religion).

Before alcohol took over his life, the Iranian boy who loved pigeons and bikes came to America to study architecture in the seventies, but his college money dried up during the Islamic revolution.[1] He's cooked in top restaurants from Canada to California. Yet his profession shames him. He let his family think he was a restaurant manager for forty years until a visiting relative learned the truth. In her last year, his mother begged him to return—"You can have a car, a place to drink your beer, just come home." She hadn't seen or touched him since he left. But he didn't. He cannot travel without ID, nor endure such a trip without incessant cigarettes and the thin stream of watery beer that feeds his veins like an IV drip, from morning till night.

Maybe I'm blunt about him, but I have a history with elderly alcoholic male adoptees. Like me, my parents moved their family into a new neighborhood and two attached themselves to us, helping my father raise tobacco and other farm chores. Like him, they refused money, seeking only a ride to town and alcohol—beer for one, liquor for the other. One became my friend, while the other died in a trailer fire after exposing himself to a local teen. So I know such men can be risky and off-putting. But they're humans with histories, even if their personalities are misted in beer fumes. Still, my friend's calling out to strange women in the street makes me uncomfortable. I shush him as they turn away. But he's being "friendly." "What?" he says, his arms wide, shoulders shrugging. Sometimes I leave him there.

It's around beer eight that things shift. His eyes get unfocused, his lips droop, and he picks fights. He's banned from most bars, so at least he doesn't drive. Even on a good day, he can be infuriating. The famed chef he once worked for "hired me eleven times and fired me twelve," he says with the laugh that stops only for periods of morose self-loathing. He's repetitive, telling his '70s stories and yesterday's incidents over and over again. He can't bear conversations about the vast category of things he has no knowledge of, so he shouts out party songs or scrapes his chair back and leaves. Few dinner guests can tolerate him, unless he's cooking. Yet many people love him. His landlord drops off cases of beer between times of wanting to strangle him. Iranian friends who made it big pop up to share their upscale problems. "They're asking *me* for advice?" he says. He's unwisely generous, giving an inherited house in Iran to a relative, cash to "the Mexicans" at work, and food to the neighbors, accepting only the T-shirts and gifts I buy him on my travels or food.

"I love me!" he sings daily, capering around the living room, the alley, his yard, anywhere, with a beer. "I love *this*," he says of the Modelo Light fused to his hand. Inside his untidy single-room-occupancy-style apartment during our brief evening visits, I notice there's another pointed tooth gone from his smile.

Once he gave up beer when a doctor told him his smoking and drinking would kill him in a year. But he resumed in days. "I'm bored," he said. "I'm lonely."

"You have so much to offer others," I said. "You can cook, you're funny. Go meet people—the city has classes, or you can volunteer."

"I have this," he said, pointing to his Modelo. He won't hear of rehab or counseling. He carried his beer cup to court-ordered AA meetings.

Three years later, he's still alive. But he's higher-risk for Corona virus than most older people[2] . He eats only once a day. His frame has dwindled so badly his skinny '90s-style jeans appear to walk on their own. His smoker's cough now drives him from our house to recover. But at age sixty-seven, he produces $12,500 worth of meals a day, at least before the pandemic. Maybe he's impossible to kill.

[2] alcohol use disorders can impact immune function: https://www.alcohol.org/resources/coronavirus-and-alcoholism/

When the virus entered our lives, he was initially angry at social distancing, eager to hug and kiss me and my husband on the head as usual, Iran-style, huffing off when I tried to explain. He still brings food but I accept only what can be reheated, adding the disinfected plate to the growing pile that normally travels between us. And how can I distinguish his normal cough from something more virulent?

"Not hungry," he texted me yesterday. "Made beautiful food. No taste. To eat it."

"Can you still smell and taste?" I texted back. I'd read that could be a coronavirus symptom.[3]

"No worries, miss scientist," he replied. "I see what you. Doing." He is just lonely, he says.

But now it's me who lies in wait for him. I ask him to Facetime—he won't. I peek across our alley, hoping to spot him. "Come join me in. The garden," he texts, but it's too small to be safe. "Want white bean salad?" he texts. It's a cold food, so I say, "No thanks. I have to drive somewhere." I do have to drive somewhere, but we know it's a lie.

All these years, my friend wants only to be loved, to know we are here. He feels better, less anxious, when we're home. Yet now that we're always here, we're divided.

Will I take care of him, if he gets this illness? I'll bring him food, although he barely eats. I'll call the doctor or read medical records, urge him to take things he won't. What else I might be called upon to do, I don't want to think about.

"I'm not gonna get it—the virus will see this and run away!" he says, hoisting his Modelo when I catch him taking beer cans to the trash. "You think it can survive in there?" He points to his stomach, concealed by a grimy V-neck sweater, and grins. He is as immutable to change as time. I hope my worry is useless. Because if this virus is anything like me, it doesn't stand a chance.

Christina Adams is the author of *Camel Crazy: A Quest for Miracles in the Mysterious World of Camels*, which won a Nautilus Book Award, and *A Real Boy*. Her work has been featured by the *LA Times*, the *Washington Post*, NPR, OZY, *Ravishly*, CBS, the PLOS Blog, and international media. She has an MFA in Creative Writing.

---

[3] https://www.statnews.com/2020/03/23/coronavirus-sense-of-smell-anosmia/

Two Too Wet Lilies

Joni Renee Whitworth

Of course, lesbians have dreamt of this for years: sleeping in late, reading to each other, fretting over the cat, cooking, stretching, listening to jazz in silks. No parties to attend. A breeze scented by western red cedar lifts her hair to my mouth. I shouldn't pull away from what is good and true, but I do, just to check real quick. Yes, the morning media is personal, tragic, assaulting from all angles. I've been instructed to breathe. Most days I mute the phones and kneel before her at the only thing still known and nameable. "Be here with me, baby. Be right here."

We've been working our way through a twenty-five-pound bag of flour. If epigenetic theory is true, my ancestral Irish brown bread and hearty colcannon should serve us well now. What got us through the famine should do just fine today.

We've been spring cleaning and un-cleaning, wrist-deep, gliding slick from room to room—that smelly, transcendental sex. Frankly, the end of the world makes me horny. From my quarantine window, I can see tawny brush rabbits nibbling and tiny Pacific wrens singing their flowering songs. I've worked two jobs as long as I can remember. I've never been home to hear them. I take her in both of my hands and feel certain, mashing my slit onto hers, we could make something if we tried.

I went out. I did the dance with neighbors and at the curbside, this new choreographed veering that scuttles us in the aisles harsh lipped or with empty, apologetic half-smiles. Even back at the trailer park and later, on food stamps, I never saw an empty shelf. The reek of privilege is White and hot through my veins. I look to the loading dock, repurposed and triaged, and take in what authors and mothers have been telling us for years: these systems are untenable.

We did it! We halved global emissions overnight. Some reports allude to a net reduction of deaths. Is it true that by lessening pollution and workplace accidents, the industrial slowdown is sparing lives as well as taking them? I can't follow that logic to its reasonable conclusion. I only know what it felt like to start a garden, how it healed me to run at sunrise six feet behind strangers on the marshy, muddy earth, and how trillium, wet on the hill, burst to greet us. It's the season of re-creation, renewal in the bud. I find myself milling around the apartment, asking, "What else can burst?"

I called a trusted older friend who's lived through the worst of the worst: wars and threats of atomic bombs, devastating losses, not to mention the sexual abuse, both specific and generalized, that attends femmehood. "I've never been through anything like this," she said. That was the first time I felt the sting.

The most prolonged eye contact of the week is with my cashier, who skips his usual compulsory greeting and instead just looks at me. I want to ask him something real. As an autistic person, I've fantasized about a culture of direct speech, free from vague, meaningless niceties. No more, "How are you?"; "Fine, and how are you?"; "Fine, and how are you?" His eyes are storybook brown, New England copper brown, gleaming Appalachian chestnut brown, twine baling the Missouri hay for America brown, brown like cocoa chips in the banana bread I made this morning. Everyone's doing it. I admit I want to be a part of something. If the predictions about global food supply chains are true, these might be the last bananas we'll eat for some time. "Are you okay?" is what I eventually manage to ask him. I've stopped turning things up like a question at the end; the new world is flat and declarative.

"No state, no metro area, will be spared."

"This is a refrigerated truck for the bodies."

"War-ravaged Syria just reported its first COVID-19 death."

We're here. We're here. We're here now.

A few weeks before quarantine, I steamed and pressed pale peach twin-sized sheets for the first guest room I've ever had. It was supposed to be an artist residency. Our city was among the earliest to pass an eviction moratorium so, for the next six months, I am housed and physically safe. With so many of my friends in other states unhoused and desperate, I wonder how the nature of this residency will change. Home as shelter. Survival as art. If and when they need to roll into town, I want to be there to receive them. By then, will I have to kiss them with my eyes, stand twelve feet away? In kink, there's a theory of fluid bonding: what you do with one, you do with another, and with their others. Who knew kink would show us the way? We could stuff a few more twin-sized beds in here. Endless sleepover. The ultimate residency: actually moving in.

Some friends have returned to their parental homes and holed up with cartoons and mom's cookin'. For me, and for so many other queer kids, there has been and will be no homecoming. Home is the one I've scrimped to arrange here with the girl with lithe fingers. I close my eyes as she braids my curls. Of course I am afraid of what lies at the bottom of this bag of flour. Of course I am.

There will come a Monday. We are jobless artists in a nation that hasn't paid for art in years, if ever. Will society rise to meet us? Will there be a place for us in the new world order? Will I make something with both of my hands?

&

Joni Renee Whitworth is an artist and writer from rural Oregon. They have performed at The Moth, the Segerstrom Center for the Performing Arts, and the Museum of Contemporary Art alongside Marina Abramovic. Their writing explores themes of nature, future, family, and the neurodivergent body, and has appeared in *Tin House*, *Lambda Literary*, *Oregon Humanities*, *Proximity Magazine*, *Seventeen Magazine*, *Eclectica*, *Pivot*, SWWIM, *Smeuse*, *Superstition Review*, *xoJane*, *Unearthed Literary Journal*, *Dime Show Review*, and *The Write Launch*.

Phone Calls from My Son

By Janet Johnson

It's a breezy spring day in warm Arizona. In my covered courtyard, I water my geraniums and notice new buds opening. My phone rings, and TJ's smiling face lights up the small screen. It's a treat to see my blond, blue-eyed son. Since the COVID-19 outbreak, TJ's group home has been on lockdown. His nightly calls have become grounding touch-points for me.

TJ is my thirty-two-year-old son with disabilities and the youngest of my three children. He is the size of a ten-year-old and will never grow any bigger, due to a growth hormone deficiency. He struggles with cognitive challenges, such as knowing who can be trusted and when to cross the street. For ten years, he has lived in a group home—a decision he made on his own.

In pre-COVID times, we spent our Saturdays running errands and sharing a meal at the Olive Garden where TJ always ordered macaroni and cheese. After paying our bill, TJ would type in a request for our next reservation. On March 14, 2020, TJ submitted a reservation request for March 21, 2020. The following day the restaurant closed.

I think back to our last outing. At the dry cleaner, TJ used my credit card to pay our bill while Julio, the store's manager, supervised. At Fry's Marketplace, TJ helped me shop for groceries and gently placed Red Delicious apples, Happy eggs, and Kerrygold butter into our cart. Despite already knowing the location of everything, he smiled and asked the clerks for assistance by pointing to items on his list. Although it can be difficult for others to understand his speech, TJ loves to interact with people. At the Olive Garden, TJ asked the waitress which manager was on duty before ordering our meal. As we waited, he played games on his iPad. Halfway through our meal, Chris, the restaurant manager, greeted TJ. I wonder if I would have done anything differently if I'd known this might be our last time together?

I have two sons with disabilities, who both live in separate group homes. When the boys asked to move away from home in early adulthood, I wasn't sure if they were ready. I certainly wasn't. But I knew I had to honor their choices as young adults.

When we arrived at a potential group home for TJ, we saw children playing across the street and neighbors walking their dogs. We were greeted warmly at the door and took a tour of the facility.

"How do you handle safety?" I asked. "TJ has no understanding of stranger-danger. He will open the door to anyone."

The group home manager explained their safety protocol. Comfortable with their answer, we moved on. Helping my sons find the right group home was, as a parent, one of my greatest acts of advocacy on their behalf. Right now, it's also my greatest source of distress.

According to the *New York Times*, people in group homes or similar facilities in New York City are 5.34 times more likely than the general population to be infected with COVID and 4.86 times more likely to die from it.[4] While my sons' homes are not located in New York City, the danger is spreading to group homes nationwide.

Scott Landes, an associate professor of sociology at Syracuse University's Maxwell School of Citizenship and Public Affairs, was recently interviewed on NPR's *Morning Edition* about the death rate for people with developmental disabilities.[5] "They're more likely—four times more likely, we're showing—to actually contract COVID-19 than the general population," he says. "And then if they do contract COVID-19, what we're seeing is they're about two times more likely to die from it." He elaborated upon the higher chance of pre-existing conditions among individuals with developmental disabilities and the concerns regarding community spread in group homes. "When you reside with multiple roommates, with staff coming in and out," says Landes, "your chances of actually contracting COVID are high. And then if someone in your home gets it…there's nowhere you can go."

Will those with intellectual disabilities receive adequate hospital care? I worry. Will they get ventilators?

As a seven-day-old newborn, TJ took what could have been his last breath. Concerned about his shallow breathing, I rushed into a hospital emergency room in the middle of the night. By the time we reached the

---

[4] https://www.nytimes.com/2020/04/08/nyregion/coronavirus-disabilities-group-homes.html
[5] https://www.npr.org/2020/06/09/872401607/covid-19-infections-and-deaths-are-higher-among-those-with-intellectual-disabilities

registration desk, he had turned blue. A nurse quickly pushed an alarm button. Red lights flashed and a siren went off—my son had coded. Doctors and nurses in blue hospital gowns ran toward me. Someone took TJ from my arms, and as I was ushered into the hospital's chapel, I felt total despair. They only put you in the chapel, I knew, if your loved one wasn't going to make it out alive. In another room, a ventilator helped TJ breathe.

Every time I remember that gut-wrenching time, I pull the blanket over my head and let the tears flow. When this doesn't work, I visualize TJ and me in a calm, peaceful garden. I remind myself that TJ survived, that he has since become an adult.

Every night, TJ calls me from his room on the group home's cordless phone. As he tells me about his day, I imagine the striped bedspread I bought him and the Special Olympic medals hanging on his wall.

"I miss my day program," TJ says, then adds, "I miss you."

My heart aches. I know he loves his day program. COVID-19 lockdown is hard for all of us to grasp, but particularly difficult for someone who doesn't understand what a virus is. I try to explain these changes in his routine. I remind TJ that when I go back east for a summer vacation, he gets by fine without seeing me. I tell him that when the lockdown is over, he can resume his day program and we'll keep that dinner reservation at the Olive Garden.

"Okay," he says, downcast. The next night, he again mentions how much he misses his day program and how much he misses me. I feel sad for him. I am an action-oriented person and feeling helpless, for me, often leads to anxiety and sometimes actual terror. Before COVID-19 hit, TJ and I both looked forward to our Saturday outings. Now, however, I can no longer be with him, and each passing day brings more worries. What if he has to go to the hospital and I can't be with him? What if he is dying and I am not allowed to be with him? Who will be with him if he has to go to the hospital? What if he takes his last breath without me by his side? This is my greatest fear.

If I had kept him safe at home with me, would it have changed anything? Then clarity hits—I still wouldn't have been able to sit by his hospital bed.

At eight p.m., my cell phone rings. "Hello, hello…" Silence. "TJ is that you?" I hear throat-clearing.

"Yes, Mom, I'm here. I'm okay."

❧

Janet Johnson has a Ph.D. in Learning and Instructional Technology. She created the first online teacher training program to train teachers around the world. She is the co-founder of New Directions Institute for Infant Brain Development and serves on the Board of Directors for a non-profit organization called SEEDs for Autism. In addition, she serves on The Guerrant Foundation Advisory Board which helps women in developing countries start businesses to support their families.

"Breathe Through the Pain": Pregnancy Amid a Pandemic

By Kit Rosewater

Just breathe. Go inside yourself.

I'm lying on my couch in early January 2020. Your dad is playing a birthing meditation recording. The woman's voice soothes and guides. My eyes are closed. My breathing is slow and deep. I visualize wading into an ocean, staring at an island far away where you are waiting to come to me. The waves are strong, but steady. Knowable. Foreseeable. I am entirely at peace as I imagine giving birth to you.

I have not yet heard of COVID-19.

Breathe in. Hold. Breathe out.

I'm sitting in a waiting room at the bloodwork lab in early February. I hate the waiting room. Children are running back and forth across the seat aisles. Mothers crouch over their bassinets protectively. I'm called back for my gestational diabetes test. The lab technician is sick, she tells me. A cold she cannot shake. She sneezes on me while drawing my blood. I hold my breath until I can escape from the chair. I'm shaking with frustration and fear in the car on the way home.

That afternoon, I read about COVID-19 rampaging through Wuhan, China. I ask your dad if it's something we should be concerned about. He shakes his head. "Probably not," he says.

Imagine your lungs inflating like a balloon. Let the balloon inflate to its fullest capacity. 1, 2, 3, 4.

I'm reading an email from my writer friend in early March. She says she can't make our writing retreat. She won't come to the next town over—my town—due to COVID-19. I conduct some research on the web. There is no mention of any cases of COVID-19 in our state. I'm hurt and sad and angry. I vaguely wonder if this will affect my book launch in three weeks. "Probably not," I tell myself. I remember that you're supposed to somersault this month into birthing position. I can't let the stress get to me. I have to stay calm for you. I have to relax.

Hold the balloon of breath inside you. Cradle it lovingly. 1, 2, 3, 4, 5, 6, 7.

The following days of March crash around me like shattered porcelain. One day I finalize plans for the last trip of our pregnancy—the launch and release party for my debut children's book. The next day I slash the plans in half and encourage anyone traveling out of state not to attend. The day after that, I cancel the whole thing. A few days later, the entire bookstore venue closes. The world is slipping through my fingers. I am scared that now is the wrong time to be pregnant. I decide not to leave the house anymore.

Let the breath flow out of you. 1, 2, 3, 4, 5, 6, 7, 8.

I'm shaking as I tie my shoes, leaning over my growing belly on the last day of March. My fingers fumble as I strap my mask on. I have another prenatal appointment. I don't want to go to the doctor. I don't want to go anywhere. I want to curl around you and keep you safe. I don't want this world for you. The panic attack takes over quick. Your dad stoops by my side. He whispers close to help me calm down, calm down, calm down.

1, 2, 3, 4.

I'm counting the diapers in the nursery again in early April. Enough for one month. It's not enough. I read stories on the internet of shortages in diapers, in wipes, in formula. I order more diapers. I take an online breastfeeding class. I cry when I can't find any baby thermometers for less than hundreds of dollars. I tell myself crying is okay. I tell myself I'm releasing the stress hormones from my body. But nothing seems to empty out. The waves keep crashing over me. I can barely see you on the distant shore.

1, 2, 3, 4, 5, 6, 7.

I'm washing a window for the umpteenth time in late April. It's the window we've chosen to use for you to meet your grandparents. I want it to be as clean and clear as possible.

It's still a window.

Halfway through, another wave of grief presses me down. I lean my forehead against the glass and cry. I have to start over. I sing a song to you as I scrub and wipe. I bounce my knees and try to sound happy. I want you to be ready for this world. I want to be ready for you in this world.

1, 2, 3, 4, 5, 6, 7, 8.

Your dad and I are holding hands in early May. We're walking in the moonlight and singing softly together at the park. We wear masks here every morning when we walk the dog. But now it is dark and quiet. No one is around. I breathe deep, remembering what it's like to inhale the outside air without three layers of fabric. You shift inside me. "We can make it," I whisper to myself. "We can do this."

Exhale fully. Your baby loves you. Your baby is so happy you have carried them this far. They are ready for their journey to you.

I'm sitting in an uncomfortable chair two days before your due date. Your heart rate is dropping. Your heart rate always drops at the doctor's office. I suspect it's because I am holding my breath nearly the entire time I'm inside. I glance out the window, trying to see your dad waiting in the car. I wish he could be here. The fetal monitor bands are stretched taut over my belly. Your heartbeat is faint. The alarm on the machine punctures the air.

A nurse comes in and glances at the graph paper. Frowns. She complains that her mask is itchy. I try not to think about how my own mask feels. The nurse tells me we need to see the baby move. "Relax," she says. "Breathe nice and deep." She leaves and I'm alone again.

I look down at you, to the place where I know you are curled up tight, held in close by months of tension in my body. I inhale and exhale one, two—the fabric of my mask gets stuck in my nose. I want to cry but I'm too exhausted, too empty. I adjust the mask, try inhaling again. I send my mind back to January, a world now far away and dreamlike. I twist the waves back into waves of labor. I push away the staggering riptides of panic attacks and grief. I peer into the distance. I try to see you on the horizon.

The machine ticks and whirs with your heartbeat.

I close my eyes, disappear inside myself, and *breathe*.

৶

Kit Rosewater writes books for children. She has a master's degree in Children's Literature from Hollins University. Books one, two, and three of her illustrated middle-grade series, *The Derby Daredevils*, release in spring 2020, fall 2020, and spring 2021 respectively through Abrams. Kit lives in Albuquerque, New Mexico.

The Boy with the Checkered Pants and Other Stories of Remembrance

Reflections on my Grandmother's Costume Shop while Anxiously Making Masks

Melissa Hart

Step 1. Cut two fabric rectangles, 6½ by 9½ inches, for the mask. Researchers have found that a blend of cotton and silk or chiffon is most effective at protecting against droplets and aerosols responsible for spreading the coronavirus, Covid-19. Cut four fabric strips, 1 by 16 inches, for straps.

The scissors are Fiskars, the only brand my grandmother would ever touch. A bouquet of them bloomed, orange-handled, in a jar beside her sewing machine. Weekends, I fled my college dormitory with its endless margarita parties and slept on the daybed in her sewing room next to the dressmaker's bust, size 12, and the plastic bins marked "sequins," "fringe," and "faux fur."

Once I had to hoist a full-length gorilla costume from the bed and drape it on a door hook. Other evenings, I exhumed Egyptian togas or Renaissance dresses heavy with embroidery and glass jewels. The masks on the top of high cabinets—a Chewbacca mask in for repairs, a terrifying foam-and-cardboard Easter bunny head—gave me dreams so vivid and strange that I'd awake unsure of both where I was and *who* I was.

Whole minutes, I blinked at the weak coastal sunlight streaming in from the window and illuminating the silver blades of the Fiskars. Ronald Reagan had just passed his torch to George H.W. Bush. AIDS was ravaging the country, and my grandmother's gay male friends lived in terror of night sweats and sarcomas. Outside the sewing room door, my grandmother's slippers tapped; I imagined her fingers twitching to get to her sewing, the one way she knew to calm her own fear.

Step 2. Fold in raw edges; sew straps down the middle. Pin straps in the corners of one rectangle. Place other rectangle on top, and pin with right sides together.

My fingers fumble with the pins, ancient and rusty, stuck into a three-lobed pincushion that must have once resembled a flower and now boasts the color and texture of a cat's hairball long after the expulsion. I haven't sewed in earnest for years, but I come from generations of seamstresses who passed down the art of stitching fabric together to create something useful and resilient.

My grandmother grew up in the Great Depression, daughter of circus performers turned vaudeville comics and jugglers. Hap Hazard the Careless Comedian, her father called himself, with his wife Mary, his sidekick, "who cares less," according to their promotional posters. When she was a toddler, Hap and Mary lost my grandmother for hours. An acrobat finally discovered her napping in the elephant barn.

They were aviators; summers, my grandmother flew with them from theater to theater on Mary's lap in a biplane painted with their show business names. The rest of the year, they abandoned her to a great aunt in Kansas City so she could attend school, which she loathed. On the family farm ninety miles north, which she also loathed, a trio of other aunts taught her to sew crazy quilts—heavy blankets made from worn-out clothing scraps and pieced together with wild, multicolored chicken-scratch embroidery. I have one, chaotic pinwheels patched across a yellow background, spread on my bed. I imagine it reflects the state of my grandmother's teenage mind as she sat in a run-down farmhouse, wild to get back to her parents and the theater.

My grandmother graduated high school and worked for a time as a secretary, then—with her parents overseas on a USO tour and unavailable for comments—she married a handsome and fastidious World War II soldier who left off commanding liberty ships and commenced commanding her and their two small daughters. She was not allowed to work. They were not allowed to cough. For years, he bound my mother's left arm to her chest, telling her southpaws were the work of Satan.

In the early '50s, my grandmother had no savings, no home of her own. She was stuck with two small, sad children—pinned in a beautiful house in the hills above the Monterey coast. Her husband permitted her to volunteer as a costume seamstress for a community theater company on Fisherman's Wharf; she never dreamed that those first silk and satin assignments would change her whole life.

Step 3. Sew around the perimeter of the mask, ½ inch from the edges, leaving a 2-inch gap on one side. Turn the mask right side out.

My grandmother's round brown wicker sewing box is embroidered with faded pink roses. It holds a jumble of old needles and stitch-rippers and stray rhinestones and gold tassels, along with her smallest Fiskars, sharp enough to cut to the truth of any matter.

After her parents retired from their work as USO entertainers and moved to Monterey themselves, her mother, Mary, shook her head at the domestic disaster my grandmother had gotten herself into. "I raised you to live in a big world," she said. "What the hell are you doing with your life?"

My grandmother filed for divorce in 1954. She became a single mother, purchased a building on Lighthouse Road with a check from her parents, and opened up a costume shop. These weren't the cheap paper-and-plastic outfits bought in drugstores the day before Hallow-een; they were handmade, hundreds of them, researched from history books and pop culture magazines and sewn by machine in an alcove between the shop's lobby and the dressing room.

An exuberant and kind-hearted actor from the Wharf Theater—a former chorus boy in MGM musicals—purchased the space adjoining hers and opened up a dance studio. They maintained their properties and their romance for forty years. Each time he proposed, she refused to marry him. He could stay every night in the beautiful house with her and her girls, but she would never again commit herself for life.

Step 4. Pin three folds on the front of the mask. Topstitch all around, 1/2 inch from the edges.

My grandmother owned numerous sewing machines over the years. She left me the last one, a five-stitch Singer. I use it now and think about how, a few years before she purchased it, Hap and Mary retired from show business and built a small house in her half-acre backyard. He built a homemade airplane in the backyard as well, and flew it up over the Salinas Valley with a younger pilot. The year I turned four, it exploded in midair and both men died.

"They gave Hap a twenty-one-gun salute," Mary said proudly to me, when I was a child, while she showed me how to sew crazy quilts at her kitchen table. My grandmother said nothing. Hap and Mary, after all, had forbidden her to cry, even as a toddler, so as not to disturb rehearsals and performances. I imagine her tight-lipped at the funeral, spreading her father's ashes in Monterey Bay, then returning to the costume shop and the silent salvation she found in sewing for other people.

On road trips to Monterey, my mother and I stopped in our VW bus at the costume shop and greeted my grandmother at her sewing machine beside a glass display case of fake mustaches and latex cigars and false eyelashes, and the *piece de resistance*—a battery-operated light saber before anyone else had them. She embraced me awkwardly, with her characteristic bemused groan instead of a kiss, and then I was free to try on her costumes.

Racks of them lined the back room, organized by era. Leopard-print loincloths and latex caveman-clubs hung at the start, progressing through Cleopatra sheaths and Renaissance gowns and capes, and Victorian hoopskirts and pioneer calico, and roaring twenties flappers and poodle skirts, all the way up to aliens and Chewbacca and a white Princess Leia dress complete with a dual-bun wig.

In costume, I slipped into the empty dance studio and paraded past the wall of mirrors. In the next room, bursts of stitching punctuated anxious conversation between my grandmother and my mother, who had left my abusive father and come out as a lesbian. My mother borrowed money from her, again and again, to fight a homophobic judicial system that declared homosexuality a mental illness and forced me to live with my father.

My mother wept but not in front of me, but I could hear her tearful voice on the other side of the wall whenever the whine of the sewing machine ceased. I wept, but not in front of her, and never in the costume shop and dance studio where I could be anyone at all, and never a girl who had lost her mother.

My grandmother didn't weep. She wrote my mother another check, and took orders for Smurf costumes and Ninja Turtles. She bemoaned kids and their gum, adults and their cigarettes, declared the weeks before and after Halloween her own personal hell. She kept her head down and sewed. When I finished with the costumes, she taught me to sew, too.

Step 5. Iron the mask, pressing folds down firmly.

I inherited my grandmother's iron, as well, broken on one side and revealing the inner workings of the machine. When I was thirty, a stage four cancer diagnosis elicited my grandmother's bemused groan from her hospital bed. With our family around her and no costumes in sight, she performed an E.T. puppet show with the red-lit pulse monitor on her index finger. What a gift to sit with her—a present more profound now that so many people, in the midst of pandemic, can't accompany their loved ones on this final journey.

My grandmother navigated the final months of her life alternately tight-lipped and laughing. True to character, she didn't cry. In the years since I'd graduated from college, she'd witnessed the death of her mother at the kitchen table and the dissolution of her forty-year romance with the chorus boy. She sold the costume shop and the beautiful house and moved to Southern California to live next door to me. The sunny alcove downstairs, surrounded by backyard roses, became her sewing room, and then her hospice room.

"You do the work you know how to do until you can't do it anymore," she told me, "regardless of what life throws at you. You provide entertainment where you can."

She left me her sewing machine and her iron. I turn off the news and set up the ironing board, my best weapon against Covid-19. I gather fabric scraps in leopard-print, hippie tie-dye, and garish plaid. I thread my needle and sew.

છ

Melissa Hart is the author, most recently, of *Better with Books: 500 Diverse Books to Ignite Empathy and Encourage Self-Acceptance in Tweens and Teens* (Sasquatch, 2019).

The Avocado Plant

Jo Varnish

After a summer lunch, my former husband shows me his avocado project. He's been told they're difficult to grow from seed, and he can't resist the challenge. Each time I visit his home, it's there on his kitchen island. Suspended by skewers, the pit balances over the top of a water-filled glass hurricane. As summer turns to fall and then on to winter, his pride shines as a tangle of roots reaches down into the water and a small stem spouts up. He plants her—for the avocado plant is a she—in a large bright-red pot.

Our eldest son, Cameron, texts his father—my former husband—and me in a group chat from his university in England. He has been reading about this virus, and it's looking serious. He cautions us, *I think it's way worse than we know.* On the news, in coffee shops, in chatter with friends, the hum of the virus grows louder each day.

It's mid-February. Our daughter, Grace, turns eighteen in a whirl of laughter and candles and best friends. The following day, my former husband dies in an accident. I can't prepare my words, my most important words, for Grace and our younger son, Luko. They arrive home from high school just twenty minutes after I get the news. They see the state of me and immediately they know what, they just don't know who.

The house fills with flowers and homemade dropped-off food and the smells of banana bread and lasagna, tulips and roses. Cameron flies home. Teardrops and questions spill onto every surface. The days fill with appointments, arrangements, decisions and nausea, checking on the children and emails, calls, texts, cards and caring wishes and kindness. After the funeral's white flowers and hundreds of mourners, my heart threatens to crack open again as I put Cameron on a plane back to England to finish the final months of his degree course. At twenty-one, he is the age I was when I met his dad. Cameron's first official act since turning twenty-one was to sign off on his dad's funeral arrangements as his next-of-kin.

I bring the avocado plant home and put her in the back room, where she can bathe in the sunlight. She's by the sliding door, and I plan to water her when I let the dogs in and out. She's not the prettiest of plants, a thin stem and three small leaves, her two-inch height lost in the oversized bright-red pot.

More minutes of my life were spent with my former husband than anyone, more moments, more experiences, more conversations. We left England for a new life in America when I was twenty-four, and he was twenty-seven. At a twist of the kaleidoscope, another set of memories gain clarity. Reading *The Liar* and *'Tis* aloud to each other, the perfect bacon sandwich he made me one Christmas Eve, watching our boys learn tricks at the skate park, blasting *Where Have All The Cowboys Gone?* as we drove through London, feeling invincible. Are all those memories just minutes now that he isn't here to breathe them to life with me? His text messages to me, *You think that's bad...*, or *Slovenia*, and myriad other private references, are meaningless to anyone but us. I worry they are simply words now, because he isn't here to send them, to hear them, to say them.

The New Jersey schools are closing due to the virus. Grace and Luko had just started to settle back into full-time classes, but tomorrow, March 13th, one month since the day their father died, will be their last day for now. The routine that was coaxing them back, the distraction they craved in seeing their friends, has dissolved. Cameron calls me from England. His classes are all going online. I am on hold with the airline as Pence announces that the UK is to be added to those countries with limited travel to the U.S. starting on Monday. Cameron arrives home Sunday night. He didn't see his friends to say goodbye, he didn't pack up his apartment. He left, one small backpack in hand.

On his first night back, Cameron and I sit on the sofa until the half-light before dawn. His face lit by the muted news channel on the television, he laughs through his tears at his dad's jokes, we share text messages from him, pore over old photographs. We don't talk about the pandemic sweeping the globe. We talk about his dad.

Within a couple of weeks of the schools' closing, New Jersey enters lockdown. I can't see a grief counselor, nor can the kids. We can't sit and talk with friends. I watch the news on repeat. I see the death toll rise in the top left corner of the screen. I imagine the agony of not having a funeral. At least we had that.

Lacking any semblance of a green thumb, I'm worried about the avocado plant. I need to keep her alive, at least until she bears an avocado. How long will that be? Luko Googles, then turns his screen to show me: it will take eight to thirteen years. This is Dad's final prank on me, I say.

The days roll on a loop and I wonder how I might have spent this lockdown in different circumstances. As it is, I go through my photos, my letters, my keepsake boxes with an obsessive thirst. My then husband was an eloquent writer. He gave me letters, notes, cards, scribbled missives on scraps of paper and on pictures. I am comforted, though scraped by nostalgia's rough edge.

My former husband's dog, Copper, who we adopted from the Newark Shelter many years ago, lives with us now. She is a little old lady, a spaniel mix, light brown fluffy fur that sheds tumbleweeds around the house daily. She was incongruous next to my former husband's tall, broad frame, but he loved her dearly. Copper has had a wound on her face for a year. The vet told my former husband it was likely a spider bite, but months of wearing a cone and keeping it clean didn't help. I take her to my vet, for a pandemic vet visit. I call from my car to announce we are here, and put on a mask as the vet technician collects Copper. Ten minutes later, my vet calls me from inside. It wasn't a spider bite. The wound is from an abscess in her mouth. With antibiotics and surgery next week, she will be fine. And then, a strange sensation. There is a pulse of a moment, not long enough for words or movement, just a pulse, a feeling of satisfaction in having the mystery of her discomfort solved, and being able to share that with my former husband. I drive home with my mask soggy from hot breath and warm tears.

I don't experience waking up and having a few seconds' peace before reality shatters it. I know when I am asleep. My dreams—whether he is in them or not—are knowing. Night and day, my body is pulled tight by wires under my skin, and my mind is fragmented. Grace tells me her friend said I am not the same, I don't look okay. Grace's friend is right. I make a mental note to seem more okay.

There's a game I have played for years, where I reveal the modern world to my mother, who died when I was eleven. I imagine myself describing post-1987 life to her: cell phones, the Internet, cloning. Now I imagine explaining today's new world to my former husband, who passed just weeks ago. Working from home, businesses closed, limited access to food shops, masks and gloves and sanitizer. I picture him returning to this reality where coyotes hang out beneath the Golden Gate Bridge, and socially distant lines form outside Trader Joe's, and I want to hear his thoughts.

Grace comes to me in the night. I am awake. Her face is strewn with pain's wreckage and her words are thick with tears. I'm just so sad, she says. Like her dad, Grace keeps her emotions in check for the wider world, saving her breakdowns for private moments with me.

The pandemic affords time. I stop watching the news. I can't focus on reading. I decide to watch *The Sopranos*, having put it off for years. The opening sequences stun me. Filmed in 1999, it is the same scenery, the same New York and New Jersey landscape that greeted my then husband and me on our arrival in 2000. I am back in our Manhattan apartment, those early nights when jet lag and adventure woke us both in the small hours. We'd lie in the darkness, whispering as we listened to the Goo Goo Dolls album he'd bought me for the song "Broadway." Giddy independence coursed through us. I need to talk to him about that time. I have lost my co-rememberer. Watching *The Sopranos*, I shift in my seat. Suddenly I am struck by the foreignness of where I am. I have no one from my English past with me anymore. English blood runs through my children's veins, but there is no mistaking they are American.

Among the text messages I read and reread are those sent in hurt, needling exchanges, jabs from times of miscommunication and stubborn disagreement. And yet, the pattern is clear. They are never far from a friendly, *remember that time*, a funny meme, or *you have to watch this show*. Reading his words, I hear his voice and his being gone just doesn't seem possible. In recent months, we were at the point of deep introspection. We prodded old bruises, we took a scalpel to scar tissue and sliced it wide. Through tears and honesty and generosity, those wounds healed quickly, leaving just a spidery trace, a faint reminder of the importance of understanding and growth.

Cameron is worried. The leaves have fallen off the avocado plant, he says, I think it's dead. I find tiny new leaves shooting at the top. I think she's okay, I say, maybe that's just how avocado plants are.

There will be no ceremony for Cameron's graduation from university. Luko's junior prom is canceled, and he won't be getting his license

on his seventeenth birthday. Grace loses her senior prom, her graduation ceremony, and her entire second semester as a senior—those
weeks of little responsibility and much fun, the culmination of a school
career. Grace's friends' mothers text of the understandable devastation
their daughters feel. I check on Grace. In her room, her long, navy
prom dress hangs from its straps on the side of her floor mirror. She is
disappointed, but losing her dad has recalibrated her reactions, just as
losing my mum did for me.

My friends and family text or call to ask, How am I? And the kids? I
don't say, we aren't ourselves, or that seeing my kids' pain is eating me
alive. I don't say I bite back tears so often during the day that I have a
welt on the inside of my mouth. That when one of the kids opens up
to me, I am thankful for their love and trust, and I do all I can to help
them through this, but I also know that nothing can erase their pain.
I say, we are taking it day by day, we will be okay. I say it will be easier
after the pandemic. I don't say, when things are back to normal. There
is no back to normal.

In the closet by my bed sits the pile of gifts my former husband
gave me for my birthday eight weeks before he died. A throw-blanket, a
cushion, and a stack of books, each selected for its particular meaning,
a nod to our history. I figured you'd wrap yourself up and read them,
he had said. I touch the blanket, smooth my palm across the spines of
the books, and close the door.

Luko, sixteen, is my easygoing kid, thoughtful and compassionate.
Since lockdown, he is largely nocturnal: he does his online schoolwork,
he plays video games, he talks with his friends from the isolation of his
room. This evening, he sits with me. I was thinking about when Grace
gets married, he says, and that Dad won't be there to give her away. We
cry for the many levels of life this loss has cut through. I know grief.
I know how it settles in, makes itself at home. I tell Luko it won't stop
hurting ever, but it will become less sharp. I can't tell him when that
might be.

The avocado plant has a routine. She grows bigger leaves now, and
as she focuses on the new bright green ones emerging near the top, so
those beneath turn brown and fall. She has five leaves at a time. I don't
know if that's typical for avocado plants, but she seems well.

Grace and I start walking. We leave our house and walk four, five,
twelve miles. We walk past our old houses, including one her dad and

I designed and built. We stop and take it in: the handsome house, bay window and balcony, on the hill, our home for a few years until our separation. Five and a half years ago, we divorced without seeing lawyers. No one does that. We were told we were crazy not to seek legal counsel. Someone told my then husband that if getting divorced without having lawyers were possible, then we clearly shouldn't be getting divorced. When he told me that at the time, I had no words. When he mentioned it since, the words flowed. Grace and I start walking again, up the hill, possibly the steepest in town.

He texted me a couple of years ago, saying, *I always thought if I had met your mum, the whole fucking world would have been different.* Unusually for me, I hadn't probed him or excavated his exact meaning. I loved the way that message read, its words of love and power were a balm requiring no specificity. When you share your life with a partner who didn't know your parent, there's a loss for you both. In knowing my love for my mother, my former husband knew what he had missed. And now he is on the other side of that equation.

Copper heals quickly after her surgery, eating well and being playful. She's so much happier now she's out of pain, Grace says. The boys agree. She could only be happier if Dad walked in, I say. We are silent. None of us says the implied, *and so would we.*

I have to write an essay for my Masters. I spend a day reading academic papers and books from my own collection. One such book falls open to a United Airlines napkin. I had discovered this "bookmark" in January as I collated materials, the essay in mind. On the napkin, pressed flat from six or seven years, my former husband's idiosyncratic writing: *I will probably let you down again, but I will never stop loving you. Sorry for those times in advance.* I had never finished the book back then, so the note remained unseen. I took a picture of it to show him back in January but then it slipped my mind. Now, the day after Mother's Day—a day he always marked for me, both as a mother and as a motherless daughter—rediscovering this note feels like a sign. It is a reminder of what matters and what doesn't, and of what remains. I trace my fingertip across the embossed dents of the words and tuck it inside the book, just as he had.

Exactly three months after his death, I am awake the whole night. I message with Luko, sleepless in his room. At around three a.m., Grace sends a picture of her dad from a trip to North Carolina. He is smiling, skin tanned, in swim shorts in the darkness, a cigar in his mouth. I remember taking the picture. He had been kayaking on the ocean in the glow of the moon, the crashing black waves issuing that challenge he could never resist. It's a gorgeous picture, and Grace has written across it, *Forever the Coolest Ever.* She sends another. She is in her dad's lap, her hand curled around his arm. On this one, she has written, *I wish I could hear his laugh and feel his presence one more time*, and, *We all miss you every single day.* I stare at the pictures. The birds start singing. No one told them to do anything differently.

The avocado plant has seven leaves and is eight inches tall. According to Google, she can spend the summer months outside. I have chosen a spot where she'll be shielded from any wind by my potted lavender and hydrangeas, but it's not reliably warm enough just yet. For now, the avocado plant stays in the back room, on the inside of the sliding glass door, until it's safe.

ॐ

Originally from England, Jo Varnish now lives outside New York City. She is the CNF editor at *X-R-A-Y Literary Magazine* and CNF contributing editor at *Barren Magazine*. Jo has work in many venues, including *PANK, Jellyfish Review, Pithead Chapel,* and *Al Jazeera*.

Sacred Story Stitching

Nako Joanna Mailani Lima

"Paulie needs me different. You know that, right?" My nana held both of my hands in hers as we sat together on my aunt Pattie's beige sofa.

"I love you the same," she added, squeezing harder. "But Paulie needs me different."

I nodded solemnly. Though I was only five or six, I understood that my cousin Paulie was different because of a botched surgery he had had when he was only a few days old. The surgeon was supposed to correct a stomach obstruction but loss of oxygen during the procedure caused permanent brain damage. That's why Paulie didn't know my name or how we were related. Nana taught me to love Paulie by being kind and patient with him, even if he sometimes behaved in ways that were strange. She also instructed me to pray for him and for his mom, dad, and sisters. Throughout my life I've brought my hands together to do so.

As the Covid-19 pandemic rapidly worsened and nursing homes began closing to visitors, I thought often of Paulie, now a dependent adult living in a group home. I prayed for him and for all those who are less visible to the rest of society and thereby more vulnerable.

With Paulie on my mind, when friends were organizing projects to sew face masks for local care facilities, I wanted to contribute. I assessed my supplies and set up my machine, starting with a few masks for family members. My skills were rusty, but I felt confident enough to make offerings for others. I determined that I could make forty masks with "fat quarters" of quilter's cotton, and I laid out a plan to efficiently construct them from start to finish.

I'd barely started this project when Aunt Pattie called to tell me that Paulie was in the ICU in a New York hospital. He had contracted coronavirus, probably from an asymptomatic care worker.

"Oh no," I whispered, clenching my phone. While Aunt Pattie spoke hopefully of Paulie's stubbornness, I feared the worst—that this would be the second child she would bury in her lifetime; the second child that she wouldn't be able to hold in the end.

I hate that I was right. On April 15, 2020, after more than a week on a ventilator, Paulie died.

My sewing project took on new meaning. I decided to sell the masks to raise money to make a donation in Paulie's name to the organization that manages the home where he lived. When I shared this on Facebook, my friends were so generous that I quickly sold out of the first batch of masks and had many requests for more. I dug deep into my fabric stash and my energy reserves to make a second batch, bringing the total number I sewed over two weeks to eighty-five, and I raised $650.

The front-page headline of the Sunday *New York Times* on May 24th read, "U.S. Deaths Near 100,000, an Incalculable Loss." They were not simply names on a list. They were us. Yes, Paulie was us, the Peter and Webb families, a baby who survived, a man who lived. We loved Paulie the same and he needed us different.

When I was a little girl, Paulie's other grandma sewed a blue felt poodle skirt for me. She swiftly measured me, wrote down numbers, and then let me watch her work. Confident and unhesitating, she was a magician with scissors and thread, my first taste of this alchemy! I wanted to learn this craft. Eventually I did, during a time when I was recovering from a serious infection that nearly rendered me blind in my left eye. Sewing, grieving, and renewing are intertwined in my body.

The best part of sewing, for me, is the hum and rhythm of the machine as the needle punctures the textiles and stitches the thread. Carefully controlling the pace, I guide the fabric toward the feed dogs and under the needle, trusting my Brother to transform the pieces into a new whole.

As a hula dancer, I use my hips, hands, and heart to tell stories. The basic movement in hula is called *kaholo*. It's easy to demonstrate, and not so easy to describe in words. A *kaholo* is a lateral movement—side to side. Four counts to the right: step, together, step, tap. Then retrace four counts to the left: step, together, step, tap. Back straight, knees bent, hips swaying. Step, together, step, tap. That's what a *kaholo* is.

The word *kaholo* means "to stitch." The dancer is stitching the story into the ground, creating and living history in the present moment. One definition of the word *kapu* is "to make holy or sacred." *'Aina* literally means land but carries the metaphoric meaning "that which feeds." Put these together and *kapu ʻaina* means "sacred ground." Or, "that which feeds and is holy."

When I dance, many stories converge—the story of the *mele* (song) and the intentions of the composer and the musician; the story of the choreographer and their vision for the music; my story as a dancer and the interpretation of the music by my body; and your story, as the recipient of this gift, and the way the story lands in you at the moment it is shared. Each of these stories carries *mana*, spiritual energy of power, strength, and healing. If I do my job as a storyteller, my *mana* affects you, and becomes embodied in you. Together, we create *kapu ʻaina*, sacred nourishment. This is how we tell and receive stories in languages we don't speak.

And so it is with sewing: into the fabric, I stitch many stories. The unknown and mysterious story of the fabric and thread and their long journey to my hands. The story of my eyes, the colors they see, and the deep well of saltwater they can be. The story of my Hawaiian ancestors who created a distinct and stunning style of appliqué quilting, and of Paulie's family lineage held in his sister Pam, in our cousin George, and in me. All of these stories converge with the story of you, when what I've made comes to be held in your hands.

In Hawaiian, the word *lima* means hands, so my offerings are Nako Joanna Mailani Lima, literally a byline and also "From Joanna Mailani's Hands." Without touching, there is *pilina*—connection—and my *mana* is with you.

When we were kids, Paulie had a Count von Count hand puppet. The Count was Paulie's favorite Sesame Street character and he loved hand puppets. While I was writing this, Paulie showed up for me when I suddenly thought of my favorite Count von Count song, which is called "Hands."

This is *mana* and *kapu ʻaina mailani*. From Heaven.

༄

Joanna Mailani Lima is an emerging writer and this essay reflects her exploration of the healing power of expressive arts.

The Boy with the Checkered Pants

By Amy Schnieder

I arrive on a Monday morning in March to the clinic where I am a nurse for children and adolescents with cancer. Normally I am happy to get there, even in the pandemic. I love caring for my patients and their families; easing their burden has been my life's work. But today my tread is slower and my heart is heavy as I think back to the prior Thursday afternoon and the call we received in the nursing office.

A patient's mother called our office to tell us he was "breathing funny" and had a fever. This nineteen-year-old young man had been our patient literally from infancy; he was originally diagnosed with retinoblastoma, cancer of the eye, which necessitated removal of his eye and chemotherapy. Then, as a young boy he was diagnosed with osteosarcoma, a bone tumor in his left leg. After limb salvage, he walked with a crutch. A few years later, a new osteosarcoma was found in his left arm, necessitating amputation at the shoulder. Our patient endured extensive additional chemotherapy over the years. He had significant late effects, including very diminutive size and a seizure disorder. Most recently he was found to have metastatic disease in his lungs. He had further chemotherapy, radiation, and surgery. Imaging scans just two months before this phone call showed stable disease. Because of his medical history and the fragile nature of his lungs, our patient would be very vulnerable to the insidious COVID-19.

We encouraged his mother to bring him so his alarming symptoms could be evaluated. We reassured her she would be able to stay with him.

Upon arrival, he was short of breath, complaining of chest pain; he had very low oxygen levels, and a fever. His chest X-ray showed a lung that was completely "whited out" and his heart and mediastinum were deviated to the left. This could have been due to infection. His labs showed multi-organ dysfunction. He was admitted to our pediatric intensive care unit for symptomatic management and further work-up.

He tested COVID-19 negative. We were not sure whether or not to be relieved. Even though the testing at our hospital is purported to be very accurate, what if it was a false negative?

I had taken care of our patient from day one, some nineteen years ago. In my current role as Thriving After Cancer Case Manager and Survivorship Coordinator, he was not part of my caseload, but he was mine in another way. I am a facilitator of our adolescent and young adult peer support group, SOMBFAB (Some of My Best Friends Are Bald). We provide adolescent cancer patients and their teen siblings an opportunity to get together for fun and age-appropriate activities. In addition to connection, the hope behind SOMBFAB is that the peer socialization will make it easier for participants to assimilate back into normal activities post-treatment; or in the event that a patient will not survive their disease, they will have had a place where they could experience all kinds of things teens should be able to do—mostly parties, truth to tell.

Our patient dreamed of being a fashion designer and was very particular about his wardrobe. He loved making friends, parties, Snapchat filters, and Beyoncé. It was hard for him to get to our events. His single mom worked long hours, there were transportation issues, and his health was always a concern. But in 2019, he was thrilled to be able to attend our annual Disneyland trip.

The buzz in the air is palpable when loading eighty teens affected by cancer onto buses headed to The Happiest Place on Earth. We leave behind lonely hospital beds, harsh chemotherapy, difficult side effects, and suffering. For the patients who are undergoing treatment we have RN chaperones who provide that extra layer of care. I keep the most medically fragile kids in my group. Naturally our patient, missing one eye and one arm, with his crutch and his seizure disorder, was with me. At the beginning of the day, we rent wheelchairs for whoever needs one. He said he was fine without, but I told him I had gotten an extra one and he would be doing me a favor if he used it. He did not say no. I gave our patient his permission slip, telling him he was my Disneyland Ride or Die. The day was perfect.

While waiting in line for the Guardians of the Galaxy ride, formerly Tower of Terror, I asked him to hold my hand as the hand grips are almost nonexistent and the drops are wild and unpredictable. He took my request quite seriously. He settled himself down, fastened his safety restraint, and held out his hand, not letting go until the ride was over. Afterward we were breathless and laughing, boosted by fun and adrenalin. I thanked him for holding my hand when I was scared. Looking at me sideways, he grinned and stood a little taller.

Our patient participated as often as he could in SOMBFAB activities. For instance, he attended the 13th Annual Friends of Scott Unforgettable Prom. He'd strutted down the Red Carpet and promptly had a seizure after entering the venue. Word rippled through the crowd. I rushed over to tend to him in the aftermath until he was sufficiently recovered to carry on with the revelry. An hour after that, he was interviewed for the news. Half an hour later, he was crowned our 2019 Prom King. When they asked him to say a few words, he'd surveyed the crowd and earnestly said, "Thank you! I am just SO happy!"

The day after he was admitted with what we thought was COVID, a Friday, he developed more respiratory distress. Saturday he was intubated and placed on a ventilator. His lungs were not full of coronavirus. They were full of tumor. His cancer had come roaring back through his small frame: a wildfire. This was the last word I had heard about him over the weekend.

On Monday I push the door to our office open and our social worker is waiting for me. She tells me that on Sunday our patient's mother made the excruciating choice to compassionately extubate him and allow him to go to heaven. He remains in the ICU. His mother has asked for me to come and the social worker is heading up there. I set down my things and go with her. Masks on, we make our way upstairs. As an outpatient case manager, I do not venture into the world of the ICU often; it's a foreign landscape, made more so in these tense and uncertain COVID-19 times. Our patient remains on contact isolation, as fevers continue to ravage.

The stack of personal protective equipment, or PPE, is on the isolation cart outside his room. We are all worried about a shortage of PPE. Although it has not seriously affected our hospital, we are all being careful; we think of our colleagues in other places, without this very gear to keep them safe. The ICU nursing director stands behind me as I eye the isolation gowns, uncertain whether it's right to take one. Rumor has it, the gowns are in shorter supply for our hospital than masks or gloves. She looks at me for a moment and nods toward the cart: "Go on."

Our patient's mother's voice is low. "He was asking to see you. There isn't much that I can do for him now, but I can honor these small last requests." I tell her I am grateful to be there. Our patient is asleep. He is heavily medicated. He is breathing on his own—deeply, albeit a little uneven. I stop at the foot of his bed. His mother and the social worker and I reminisce. About prom and how excited he was to be crowned our King. About Disneyland and how he had to know the color of our group sweatshirts for the trip, so he could coordinate his outfit. The first year he attended, the sweatshirts were red. His black-and-white-checkered pants were all the rage with everyone, becoming part of the legend of our group. His mom shows us a photo of him and another patient sharing a hug in front of The Magic Kingdom, his screen saver since the trip.

She tells us that "after," she will bathe him and dress him in an outfit chosen by his brother. She reminds us he always likes to look "perfect." We nod, we know.

They will transfer our patient down to the oncology floor, or as his mother calls it, "home," where we will make him as comfortable as possible, away from the sound and the fury of intensive care. We have a family bed on our unit that we use at the end of life. It is wider and more comfortable than a regular hospital bed and allows parents to lie alongside their child and hold them.

His nurse is gowned, gloved, and masked, her hair tucked away under her blue bonnet. All that can be seen of her is her kind eyes; a world of compassion and strength greets us as she assures us she will take impeccable care of our patient and do everything she can to help him make the transfer to oncology. Her competence and her empathy soothe the tatters of my broken heart and I am comforted.

I approach our patient's bed and let the words of the social worker and his mother melt away. I take his hand into both of my gloved ones. it feels warm even through the barrier.

"Hey you," I whisper near his ear, "it's me, your Ride or Die. I want you to know that for forever, Disney will be about you, for me. Thanks for holding my hand when I was scared. I'm so glad I get to hold yours now." I stroke his fingers and squeeze his hand again, the blue of my glove bright against his palm. I know he knows I love him, but I tell him anyway.

It is time for us to go. Instead of hugging his mother as I normally would in non-Covid-19 world, I look at her over my mask and pat my heart several times. She returns my gaze. She nods.

Outside the room, the social worker and I tear off our gowns and throw them away. We dispose of our gloves and rub sanitizer into our hands vigorously. Our masks remain in place.

Back in our office, I clutch a tissue that one of my colleagues had ready for me upon my return. I sit down, my mask wet from tears. I feel a twinge of guilt about needing a new one, but it is a small twinge. My phone rings. I replace my mask, square my shoulders, and go to work.

Our patient is moved down to our unit that afternoon, but I do not go see him again, knowing there are others who would like to say goodbye. He was ours for a lifetime. Although his life was fraught with suffering and loss and pain, it was also full of love and it had times of great joy and laughter, some of which was directly because of SOMB-FAB. What an astonishing privilege and comfort it is to know his life was richer and happier because of our group.

SOMBFAB is on hiatus for the pandemic. I am hard-pressed to imagine how we will reconvene in its aftermath, but I remain hopeful.

Our patient dies that night. On our unit. In our family bed. Unlike so many during this horrible epidemic, he is in the arms of a loved one—his mother's. She is able to bathe him one last time, and she dresses him in one of his favorite outfits. An outfit that indeed includes his famous black and white checkered pants.

಄

Amy Schneider, BSN, RN, CPHON, is the Case Manager for Cancer Survivorship at The Peckham Center for Cancer and Blood Disorders. In addition, she is the founder and facilitator of SOMBFAB, a support group for adolescents and young adults who are affected by pediatric cancer.

AIR

Mary Powelson

My mom died ten years ago, and her stuff is still in my basement, next to my dad's stuff which arrived three years before hers, my brother's stuff which showed up just before my mom's did, and even stuff of my ex-husband's which, shoved next to the back door, remained a dusty reminder that all the death that preceded our divorce was not the end-all, but the be-all.

Before now, it was easy to ignore the basement, ignore how long it had been since I changed the oil, ignore the time since my last haircut or confession (*wait – confess what? And why start now?*) Before now, I put on foundation and eyeliner and spent too much time deciding which pair of sexy ankle boots would not hurt my feet at work. Before now, I merely threatened come *this* spring, all boxes go to the dumpster without one look inside (*because I just might want to spend my free time with a man I've yet to meet*).

But now, all this family stuff has to go because I need somewhere to put my new stuff: jars of peanut butter, cans of pinto beans, tomatoes, cat food, way too much pasta, not enough bleach, and bulk paper products that are as exhausting to talk about as they are to find.

And now, I'm unemployed and need a mission.

Speaking of the Mission, I drive my housemate to and from his shop at Fourteenth and Valencia. (*The drive and drop-off reduces our exposure; it's my new job.*) He raises live things that require tending, so we schlep daily to the Mission District the back-road way: up Lincoln, over the hill to Roosevelt, and through shaded lanes between Noe and Sanchez, each alive with lush trees, homeless camps, and ghosts.

Speaking of ghosts, I now teach *Hamlet* online with teenagers. One girl's Zoom name just became "hell yawning contagion." (*Find that in Hamlet.*) I prefer: "There is nothing either good or bad but thinking makes it so."

It's an early April Friday night, and I'm waiting for a nine o'clock call from a man I met on Match. I didn't really *meet* him; I recognized him. From childhood. He lived across the street from me in Colma, a suburb known for its windy fog and abundance of cemeteries; my hometown is where San Francisco keeps its dead. His younger sister was my best friend until fifth grade when our family moved to San Bruno for a larger home and better weather (*wasn't better*). Though his profile crossed my filter boundaries (*moderate politics, no kids*), I was curious. I swiped right; we connected, made a phone date to talk for the first time in fifty years—or ever, because what little girl wants to speak to her best friend's older brother, especially when he's cute? So, to allay all thoughts, good and bad, I bide my time by cleaning.

Out of a decomposing box falls yellowed newspaper. Packing material? Maybe. It was ripped in half, torn with age, but originally folded and tucked neatly between black heavy paper, the skeletal tissue of an old brown scrapbook. Seventy-five years old, almost to the day. Front side, "Woman's Body Examined for Rare Poison!" (*Hamlet!*) The other side, a full-page obituary: "President Roosevelt." (*Hamlet!*) The loving nod to FDR's death is both an easy distraction and a worrisome wonder: where would our current situation be with a president like Roosevelt instead of the Other? (*Enough said.*)

Sometimes I read the beginning, then the end, then the whole story, to see how the dots connect.

Open last page: FDR.

Check first page: "Happy Easter. Your Classmates. 1945." (*Perfect Palmer handwriting.*)

Turn next page. (*Never mind, the phone rings. It's him.*)

With immediate ease, as though we had talked that morning, he and I talk about our day, comparing respective basement plumbing problems. (*Strangers in our houses!*) The next two hours, we jump in and out of each of our timelines, comparing our lives in LA (*I was an actress, he dated an actress*), giggling about childhood (*not all of it was funny*) and the current chaos (*some of it is funny*). I tell him things I rarely tell people and he tells me about his father who just died. (*Hamlet!*) I text him a 1968 picture of his parents. (*Found it in a box.*) We like talking to each other. (*We text that.*) It is a good Friday.

My mom and I always talked a lot. (*But we didn't tell each other much.*)

I knew my mom had TB as a kid. (*I got TB tests as a kid.*)

I knew my mom had a good friend who died of polio. (*Bad vaccine. His picture always hung in our family room.*)

I knew my mom wanted me to go to church. (*I didn't.*)

I knew my mom worried too much about things. (*I couldn't cross the bridge on prom night.*)

I knew it angered her when I challenged Catholicism. (*Once I referred to her beliefs as myths; she was furious.*)

When I was six, I knew *not* to tell my mom that the school bus driver asked me to stay on the bus after the other kids left so he could give me a present. (*It wasn't a good present.*)

I didn't know how desperately she wanted me to be hers.

At eight, halfway through an underwater swim test, I pulled myself up the side of the pool to catch a breath; mom quickly jumped from the bleachers, met me at the edge, and comforted me: "That's all right, you're not strong; you're like me." (*But I am strong! I'm just coming up for air.*)

When I was thirty, my aunt—Mom's older sister and a nun—decided I needed to know something about my mom. My mom and I had grown apart, and my aunt thought if I understood what Mom had lived through, I might uncover patience and find compassion. So, my aunt told me this (*minus the parentheticals*):

In 1943, the landlord subdivided the family flat on Henry Street, a shaded lane between Noe and Sanchez. A man moved into what was once their living room. He had a bad cough. (*Stop thinking about coughs.*)

In January 1944, in the middle of her fifth-grade year, my mother got tuberculosis.

My mom was hospitalized, isolated with strangers, in the TB ward of San Francisco General Hospital until 1949. (*A little girl. Five years in lockdown. Think on that.*)

Sundays were visitor days: she could see one parent—usually her mom—in the ward and the rest stayed outside in the lot below. Mom saw them through a window, several floors up. (*Physical distancing.*)

In 1949, she moved back home to a new family flat: they had since moved to Seventeenth and Sanchez. In 1950, she returned to school for the first time in six years. (*She had a part in the Notre Dame Senior Class play. Mom watched me work on stage for forty years and never once mentioned she did a play. I just found the program: my mother played the mother of a girl who only wanted to be an actress.*)

After graduation, she attended Lone Mountain College, worked in an office, and after three years, relapsed. (*Diseases come back.*)

She was hospitalized again for eighteen months, this time at Arequipa, a TB sanitorium in a small woodsy canyon on the back of Mount Tam, across the Golden Gate Bridge. Her father took the Greyhound to visit on Sundays; the rest stayed home. (*I went to Arequipa: once as a Girl Scout and once as a teacher. Both times, my mom commented: "Oh, I've been there!"*)

Mom's second round of TB demanded invasive treatments, including a thoracoplasty. Several ribs were removed, her diseased lung was collapsed, and she was left with one good lung and a scythe-like scar on her back, stretching from shoulder to waist. (*I stared at it when I was a kid. Never asked.*) A scar that embarrassed her when wearing dresses. (*Her sister covered it with makeup.*) A scar that disheartened her about marriage. (*There's a story there.*) A scar that warned her about pregnancy: learning she was getting married, her doctor advised Mom against rushing to have children—too risky. (*But, Doctor, we're Catholic, she told him.*)

❧

When I was about thirty, my therapist thought it might be the right time to tell my mom that I was molested on my sixth birthday. So, in session, I told her (*like a reporter*). Silence. Mostly. (*I made my mother cry.*) "What now?" said I. "I won't tell anyone," said Mom. "Good," said me. My therapist leaned in, saying firmly, "I think family secrets suck." Mom's eyes widened: "Oh, so do I!"

March 1944. One Sunday, my mom waved out the window to her father and sisters below. Waving at her three sisters from the ward had become a Sunday ritual. That day she noticed one sister wasn't there.

"Where's Carol?" she asked about her seven-year-old sister. And she kept asking, and each week, her mom kept explaining: Carol stayed home, at Auntie's, in Sonoma visiting Grandpa… (*Mom learned to stop asking.*)

One week, as she awoke from a nap, in that space between sleep and wake, Mom could make out a conversation. The mothers were chatting while their girls slept. To the question, "How many children do you have?" her mother replied: "Four, but one died."

That's how my mom learned that her sister was dead. She never told her mother what she'd overheard. (*Me: "Why NOT?" Mom: "Because I didn't want to make my mother cry."*)

In 1949, she was released and returned home to meet two new siblings: her youngest sister, age four; and her baby brother, age two. No one mentioned Carol.

In 1951, she finally asked her sister what had happened.

One Friday, Carol had struggled to keep up with her older sister as they marched home from school, up Sixteenth to Noe.

Her nose was bleeding.

She died within two days.

Meningitis brought on by tuberculosis.

The whole family was tested for TB, they were all positive, and they remained so for the rest of their lives. No one else ever got sick.

The scrapbook. Since that Friday night, I never bothered to look inside, assuming it was merely full of children's handmade cards to an ill classmate. Because teachers like to do that kind of stuff. (*Make a card! Draw a picture! Not too much paste! No, Johnny, you don't need scissors.*)

So, I'm thinking of tossing it but hesitate because last week I found eighty dollars in an old envelope in another box. (*Four old-school twenties—germ free.*)

I open the scrapbook.

Read the end: Six pages of news clippings about a president with polio who "….did not die in vain, who left no task undone, and gave his all and lost nothing but gained the fulfillment of deeds and dreams."

Read the beginning: Happy Easter. Your classmates. 1945.

Open the middle: Four pages of faded sepia-toned photos, neatly placed.

Steel bunk beds in a row.

Large-paned windows.

Sun pouring in hot and light.

Shadows on walls and faces,

All seemingly behind bars.

Girls, ages about eight to twelve.

White gowns, white pinafores.

Holding on.

Holding hands.

Holding up.

Classmates.

I find her. She is standing behind a girl. Her pointy chin. Her long black braids falling off her shoulder. That smile. Her arms wrapped around the shoulders of the girl, two or three years younger, like a sister.

I text the hospital images to her sisters (*not Carol*). They had never seen them, never knew they even existed. (*She knew they would upset me, my aunt says.*) Mom saved her sanitarium self in a scrapbook, stored behind shoes in the back of all her closets in all her homes. No light to reveal, no air to diminish, their weight keeping them submerged.

My mom had four children. (*But one died.*)

Every year when she went in for her chest X-ray, Mom made her younger sister promise to take care of us. (*If the news was bad.*)

(*The scar story my mom never told me.*) My mom told my dad that she was worried about getting married. She didn't want him to see her scar. It became an issue when discussing the wedding. One night, my dad reached over and pulled up the back of her sweater, quickly put it back, and said, "There, I saw it. Now we don't have to talk about it anymore."

Beverly married Donald and got pregnant immediately. Doctors had voiced concerns about respiratory failure. She had been receiving monthly air injections since Arequipa. Pregnancy was a risk. But she was young, in love, married, Catholic; it was the sixties, there was a polio vaccine, and an Irish Democrat was running for president.

It turned out Mom didn't need injected air. She could breathe just fine. Inside her, I held up her lungs. (*It's all right, I say. You're strong. Like me.*)

❧

Since April, I've chatted a few times with my childhood friend's brother. (*Okay, his name is Tony.*) He says we should meet up when the smoke clears. He makes me laugh. I tell him things. I tell him that my friends stopped by to deliver presents on my fifty-ninth birthday. I tell him that I stayed at the top of the stairs and they stayed at the bottom. I tell him it was all good—we waved at each other (*in masks*).

Why, he asks.

Because! Duh, say I.

You're overthinking this, he says. He may be right.

❧

Mary Powelson is an actor, director, playwright, and teacher. She holds a B.A. and M.A. in Theatre from San Francisco State University. Mary created and ran a San Francisco youth theatre company where its community tended artistry and humanity. She taught algebra and playwrighting and led story workshops with young women. Her son, her people, and the theatre are her deepest joys.

The One that Hurts Less and Other Stories of Serving in the Front Lines

Scrappy—An Essential Worker Reluctantly Tries to Help Mend Her City's Supply Chain

Joyce R. Lombardi

At first, I was too vexed to help. After lockdown, two of my Facebook friends launched a site to connect local essential workers with protective gear. They knew what was coming. Our city is famous for heroin, murder, and crab cakes. We are still recovering from what our Black majority call "an uprising"—and our white minority call "a riot"—to protest police brutality. Our mayor and one of her predecessors had been convicted of fraud and graft. Our town was struggling before the pandemic hit. After? You can imagine.

I could imagine too, but I was busy panicking over being an "essential worker" myself. I work at a child abuse center, where trauma professionals surround a child with warmth and expertise after the child discloses some heinous thing an adult did to them. We are assuredly not closed in a pandemic. We are open because when kids are stuck at home, sickos have unfettered daily access.

I know this, I feel this, but I was still terrified of going to work. We didn't have masks for everyone and the CDC was recommending them only for those who touched people or were sick. My fellow managers were not as conflicted as I. We are an all-in, can-do outfit, staffed by social worker types who would run into a code blue without hesitation. I am not a social worker type. I am a lawyer/lobbyist prone to anger and anxiety, and Covid was provoking plenty of both. Masks were coming, but when? Shouldn't we cut the back-up staff from our skeleton crew? Can't we close the elevator? Are Ubers sanitized? I was the person on the Zoom calls in the early days snapping, "People will die." I meant me.

My Facebook pals also knew people would die, especially friends of theirs who were nurses and correctional officers. Especially women.

Especially women of color. We are a city of workers, of single moms, of bus riders. Hospitals are our largest employers. Inspired by similar sites around the country, Lisa and Kim jumped in. I'd seen them both in action in the state capital. They are young fireballs who get stuff done. I joined the site when invited, but then went back to fretting.

My two teenaged children and I hunkered down. They barely left their rooms. I left the house only for a nerve-jangling trip to the grocery store or when I was put on the work schedule. I armed myself with a bottle of disinfectant and a homemade mask. I looked crazy.

Forget masks, I fumed. What about rights? Could essential personnel refuse to work if they don't have PPE? I reached out to my former colleagues in employment law. Short answer: not really. If bosses are following current CDC, OSHA, and state guidelines, the employee doesn't have a chance. No surprise there. I know the power belongs to him who writes the rules.

Back to masks. My employer, a large hospital system, came through in spectacular fashion. They created a sterile mask and gown factory equipped with brand-new sewing machines, staffed by eager volunteers and (less eager) repurposed hospital staff. They knew what was coming, too.

Soon my workplace had masks. We had disinfectant wipes and hand sanitizer, though not much. The CDC finally came around to widespread masking. We had a rhythm going. They figured out how to do some tele-health. My co-workers and I were sterilizing the elevator buttons, door handles, and clipboards. Our little haven felt relatively safe. At least for us. The detectives and social workers who are in and out of our building, and in and out of dire situations in dire homes, were not so lucky. As expected, our city did not yet have masks. Or much PPE at all.

I reached out to my Facebook pals. "How can I help?"

"Administration," said Lisa. She sent over their spreadsheets and links to how other sites had set up their mask-making ventures. I cobbled together some forms.

The requests started trickling in, precautionary at first:

They are screening patients who come in and we are an ENT department. There is a chance for a possible positive patient to be seen by us. Surgeons, nurses, CMAs, front desk staff.

Today I went grocery shopping and observed that no employees had masks. The employee told me they'd run out. I spoke with the manager, who noted that they are in need of donations.

We are handling the mail all day and interacting with customers

After a few days, the requests were pouring in.

...a med-surg floor that recently turned into bio mode for...Covid-19 patients with direct contact. We have had positive patients on the floor.

We are a unit that treats Covid+ patients every day at the hospital.

...medical as nurses taking care of inmates.

Homeless shelters up to 200 people living in congregate care.

Ten days in, Covid was having its way with us.

...1000-bed hospital. To date we currently have approx 12 Covid-only units.

...inpatient unit for symptomatic covid patients in their final days.

More than sixty different requests came in the first two weeks. They asked for thousands of homemade cloth masks—up to our maximum of 100 per agency—but also hand sanitizer, face shields, surgical masks, gloves, surgical caps, and disinfectant. The seekers ranged from world-class hospital systems to city government to tiny nonprofits. They all had one thing in common: they couldn't protect themselves or their clients, for any price.

We had stumbled into what life looks like when the global supply chain breaks down. Like the rest of the privileged industrial world, we were figuring out how to live beyond the reach of money or influence, in that zone of scrappy self-reliance when you realize no one is coming to save you. At first it was terrifying. But then it was galvanizing.

Because while these requests rushed in, so did offers to help. In the first two weeks, almost fifty people—overwhelmingly women—signed up to help. They offered to sew, donate fabric, use 3-D printers to make face shields and mask extenders, scrounge for materials, or make deliveries. A few offered money, but at that point, there was no time for money. Cash is not always king. We weeded out the opportunists who came to hawk their wares and focused on the doers.

Kim promptly organized a small army of committed sewistas (please note, the word *sewers* looks like a drainage system—hence *seamsters*, *maskers*, and *sewistas* popping up in our collective new PPE lexicon). She had donated fabric, which was cut by a local sail factory, packaged into kits with elastic or ties, and delivered all over town. When local stores ran out of notions, she stayed up late to manufacture long, tedious ribbons of bias tape. She drove to a remote, deserted warehouse to collect bolts of shirting material and suddenly precious elastic donated by a retired factory owner. "So this is how I die," she recounted to Lisa and me later, "in the basement, surrounded by fabric with one titty hanging out." I could not stop laughing.

Lisa, the captain, not only met demand, she trolled neighborhood listservs and the now-huge Facebook site to drum up more. Between breaks in her full-time policy work, she made sure everyone in her grassroots and political networks knew that we were there, at the ready. She found a comedian-turned-altruist cranking out free hand sanitizer by the gallon. A mayor's deputy texted her about food distribution gloves. She never let up. *I haven't eaten yet today*, she'd text at three p.m. *Couldn't sleep last night*, she'd text. She started to feel better after she adopted a foster dog. "Now at least I go outside," she said.

The sewistas, meanwhile, churned out hundreds of masks each week. They'd finish one batch and then sign right up for another. Some had lost their jobs, some were retired, others were sewing around full-time work and mothering. Some were health care workers themselves. They posted memes of wine glasses, coffee cups, and sewing machines. They posted photos of their creations, rows upon rows of vibrant quilted soldiers awaiting deployment. Inevitably Rosie the Riveter images popped up. We admired each other's stitches and swatches. "This site is my favorite part of the pandemic," wrote one of the sewistas, "I needed to do SOMETHING."

Sometimes it felt like we were winning. Like when hospital workers started posting pictures of themselves, thumbs up, wearing our masks. Or when one of Lisa's contacts, a developer-turned-savior with connections to China, donated 10,000 disposable masks. Within twenty-four hours Lisa and Kim dispatched a tiny fleet to deliver boxes of these imported gems around the city. In your face, supply chain.

But sometimes it felt like recent American wars, something only a few people really noticed. Like the weekend a nail-salon owner got a team of her friends to sew 100 masks. The masks were intended for a residential substance abuse treatment facility in desperate need. The salon owner had been asking for fabric for over a week. We scrounged scraps, old curtains, and pillowcases from porches and stoops around the city. Some of the fabric came from a friend of mine up north, who was surprised to learn that our local shops had run out of everything. As the salon owner was dropping off the masks, one of her manicure clients—who sported a highly coveted N95 mask while walking her pooch—intervened on the sidewalk and asked if she could have five, for her friends. The owner graciously complied and waved away offers of payment. Lisa and I seethed.

Seething is familiar territory for me. Outrage has fueled most of my professional life. But several weeks in, I was questioning my motives. Why exactly did I take this PPE project on? Aren't my own family and full-time trauma job enough?

My children were struggling. My fifteen-year-old daughter would sob on the phone in the deep night. My nineteen-year-old son, yanked home from college, smoked alone on the midnight stoop. After an eruption with their dad and new stepmom, the kids came to live with me full time. My own response was to cook: bbq pork sliders, apple crisp, fresh iced tea, yet another loaf of banana bread. I cordoned off nights to spend time with them, in whatever state I found them. This, to me, was bliss. *Be the light,* I told myself.

Outside of home, I felt my own light dimming. I started to dread my phone. Every time it pinged, it was because someone out there needed something: nursing home workers needing a mask, or an isolated mom needing legal advice during a custody battle with an abuser. When my work colleagues started strategizing new ways to support our clients— groceries or text check-ins—I fell silent. I had nothing left. I had hit my wall of compassion for the world at large.

But somewhere around week eight, or 80 or 800, something happened. Supply almost caught up to demand. Rather than a hundred unclaimed mask requests clamoring on our sign-up form, we were down to our last twenty. One of our seamsters could polish that off in a weekend. Lisa and I went back to the spreadsheets to see what I might have missed. We opened supply up to patients, not just workers. And then we breathed. Or at least I did.

It was a tipping point. The surge was flattening out just enough so that the supply chain of materials had time to catch up a bit.

At work, we each got an N95. It was like getting an emerald necklace. It reminded me of when I was in the Peace Corps and an Italian suitor sent a box of little jams and Kellogg's corn flakes to my thatch-roofed hut. I had not seen such riches in over a year and I swooned to have them.

Maybe that's how our city's workers felt to get a batch of our hand-sewn masks, this bouquet of scraps and ribbons. Cared for. Seen. Valued. As if someone is coming to save them, even if it is just a scared stranger, sitting up at night with her demons and her doubts, stitching away, thinking of the nights her mother and grandmothers did the same thing, simmering the stock, righting the wrongs, and being the light in whatever lives they could touch.

⤔

Joyce Lombardi is a writer who lives and works in Baltimore, Maryland with her two children. Her award-winning work has appeared in the *Village Voice*, Salon.com, the *Baltimore Sun*, and other publications.

COVID Chronicles

Babs Greles

I spend my working life as an RN in the surgical intensive care unit of a large urban teaching hospital in upstate New York. When the Covid ICU unit opened in our hospital, I volunteered work in the unit. The ground beneath me began to shift and crack. I wrote the following raw journal entries as a way to cope with the heartbreak and sorrow. We are still in the eye of this storm together. Our stories will heal us.

April 11, 2020

At the start of my shift, I make sure to fill out the online health survey daily to see if it's safe for me to report to work. Green check mark. I'm good to go.

My fellow nurses and I huddle at the start of the shift. I stand there in my scrubs, wrinkled as an elephant's knees. I'm hoping my shield has a little life left in it. I'm imagining the scene from Shakespeare's *Richard III* where he gives that great rousing pre-battle speech.

A thousand hearts are great within my bosom:

Advance our standards, set upon our foes

Our ancient word of courage, fair Saint George,

Inspire us with the spleen of fiery dragons!

Upon them! victory sits on our helms.

I'm teamed with a pediatric intensive care nurse who looks like she's afraid to breathe. I give her a quick tour of the massive unit, explain the negative pressure doors, show her the drips running on the in-poles outside the rooms of our patients. I set her up with a walkie-talkie, and then we gown up for four straight hours in a room with a fresh Mercy-flighted patient while three different doctors try to place an arterial line.

I stay connected with her through the talkie. "You okay? Go up on that propofol if you need to, twenty mcgs."

The motor on my head makes it impossible to hear the mumbling interventional radiologist. He finally shouts, "You can't hear a word I'm saying!" *Duh*. I told him that seven times. *Speak the hell up*. I finally give up and just assist him by trying to anticipate his next move.

My throat is getting scratchy, my varicose veins branching out and making friends with my plantar fasciitis as I stand there holding my patient in position with one hand, stroking her sweaty hair from her face and telling her to hang on. She is very close to my own age. I imagine her being born, riding her first bicycle, telling her first joke...

I am getting dizzy, probably rebreathing my own CO_2.

When I was around seven or eight I contracted chicken pox during the summer. I was quarantined with a high fever, and my mom cooled me with calamine lotion and cherry Jello. My older sisters brought me gifts, books, and Colorforms. I experienced a new pain, like someone trying to cut off my arm with a spoon—hearing my friends playing in Michele's oval swimming pool that sat between two garages in a tiny city yard. I loved that pool. I was sure I would never see it or them ever again. I lay there, surely dying, burning, itching, feeling sorry for my pathetic self.

One day my girlfriends gathered on the sidewalk in front of the house. I put on a play with my dolls for them. I remember the feeling of connectedness with these sweet girls that brought me back into the world again. I wonder if they remember. Michele Davenport, Colleen Galiotti, her sister Valerie, Terry Malone Young.

I think of them as I stand there telling the person in the bed to hang on. Trying to connect through the shield. The nurses outside the door, connecting through the walkie-talkie. I look out at them. I see these people with their great hearts working so hard , and here I am getting irritated that I've been in this room for far too long. I'm such a cranky bitch, they have no idea how much I love them. How did I get so lucky to work with these people? I wonder.

I see myself and the road that led me to this moment. My sisters teaching me to dance on a table to "I Wanna Hold Your Hand." My first red bicycle. My first best girlfriend. Falling in love with a boy. That side street in Manhattan with the weird old Hungarian bookstore that I loved to spend hours in. The shattered heart that mended bruised and tender.

I look out at the brave PICU nurse. So courageous. I admire her. I look out at the charge nurses and the attending physicians and the med surge nurses and I think that because of this shift in the ground beneath us, everything will settle better than it was.

April 14, 2020

You are off the ventilator, breathing on your own, asking me for apple juice. I ask you where you got that unusual, stately name. "My father," you are proud to say. You are gentle and polite, and you give me hope in an ocean of despair. I tease you that I want to give you a bath so I can read all of your tattoos. Your sister calls twice every shift. I am happy to tell her that you are watching ESPN and looking good. She cries with joy and I knock on the window to get your attention. "Your sister!" I yell, pointing to the phone. You smile and wave and I tell you that she loves you. You gave me a thumbs-up and I tell her, "He knows." She laughs and thanks me. I can hear the lightness of relief in her voice.

My friend calls me the next morning to tell me that you had died. That the nurse held up an iPad so your mom and sister could see you and say goodbye. My friend doesn't want me to find out when I returned to work. He wants to give me the time and the space to grieve you.

I grieve you.

I will never forget you.

I'm so exhausted.

I want social distancing to last forever so I can hide away from the ignorance.

I was social distancing before it was a thing because of people.

It's snowing. I watch a surreal sunset from the eighth floor through a blizzard. In April.

The nurses are all over the hospital, moved to wherever they're needed. They are unsettled, afraid, angry, sad.

I hold the hand of a woman as she lays dying. I communicate with her nurse via walkie-talkie when she needs more pain medicine because the pump is outside the glass door. I wait with her until her breathing becomes easy and gentle. I notice that someone has painted her fingernails bright pink. They were chipped, probably done weeks ago. I imagined her then, maybe laughing and joking and blowing on the polish impatiently to make it dry more quickly.

She cannot get the sacrament of Last Rites because the diocese was swamped with a backlog of sacrament orders.

Admissions were down this week. Because keeping one's cooties to oneself works.

I hope that the "liberated" states will have someone to care for them when their time comes. Without a vaccine this liberty has a steep cost.

In Buddhist philosophy the concept of liberation is for all sentient beings to be mentally free of delusion and ignorance.

I'm so exhausted.

April 19, 2020

I've always taken an interest in history and literature so that I can put your own existence into perspective.

Anne Frank lived in a crowded attic in Amsterdam while being hunted by Nazis. She was thirteen years old. She wrote about the inherent good in people. The hunters found her and she and her family were murdered. She and her sister Margot died together in Bergen Belsen of typhus two weeks before the camp was liberated.

Native Americans were driven from their lands and banished to remote reservations and their culture stripped from them.

African slaves provided free labor that built the wealth of their owners, and the disparity in opportunity and wealth persists today. A Black man who sells weed will spend years in prison while a white frat boy who rapes a girl gets off with a slap because he suffers from "affluenza."

There is a cosmic butterfly effect to all of this.

We do not live in a vacuum. You don't need to board an airplane to see the world. Read about the humanity that has contributed to your very DNA and think about how you can improve upon it. Nothing is about you. You were born to serve. When you see that you will know true freedom.

It's not us and them. It's us. And us.

April 26, 2020

It's getting curiouser and curiouser. Mark drops me off at the official drop site—the children's hospital lobby. It looks like *The Jetsons'* living room. I stand there for a minute, centering myself for the night ahead. I want to just curl up on that lime green sectional that's shaped like a boomerang and sleep for a week.

Old friends have come back to the hospital to work in our ICUs. We struggle not to hug.

I'm working with young nurses whose names I can't always

remember but they treat me like a respected elder and/or old goofball.

We're starting to see glimmers of hope; she waves back through the glass, he squeezes my hand for the first time in weeks.

Human touch. Human voice. Human compassion. Sedation. Time. These people are terrified. The virus gives them red eyes that look like a million fiery tears have run through them.

A new nurse, brave as any child soldier, calls me over. "He's gagging on the tube! What should I do?" She's trying not to panic, because anxiety is the most contagious germ. I gown up and mask up.

I focus on the patient. I take his hand and meet his eyes. He squeezes so hard my fingers go numb.

"We will get you through this. Okay? You just hang on. You are safe here with us. We won't leave you alone." He nods and squeezes harder.

I show the new nurse all the things to do. She is open, grateful to learn. She is a wonderful nurse.

His wife is on the phone with his other nurse. We talk through the glass. Charades, yelling, writing backwards on the window. I tell his wife that he is my new boyfriend. He is smiling now and gives me a thumbs-up.

His fight to live is only beginning.

I take a cool washcloth and hold it to his reddened forehead. He sleeps the strange sleep of the body under massive attack. Only my respirator mask can be heard in the slowly dimming room. Outside the window the sun is melting down the side of an indifferent sky.

"We are right here with you." I tell him. "We've got you."

Babs Greles is an emerging writer who also works as a nurse at large medical center in upstate New York.

What Is Enough?

Raluca Ioanid

Every workday I get up at 6:30 a.m. and drive to my clinic in Hendersonville, North Carolina, from my home in Asheville. The commute is a straight shot through the Blue Ridge Mountains, along Interstate 26, a major artery of the South that runs from Tennessee to South Carolina. As I drive the twenty miles between artsy, cosmopolitan Asheville and the orchards and farmlands of Hendersonville, sporty SUVs give way to tractor-trailers and pickup trucks with deer carcasses tied onto them and MAGA and "Jesus Saves" bumper stickers. Our clinic, a federally qualified health center for uninsured and low-income folks, is a cluster of simple but handsome two-story brick buildings sandwiched between Walmart, the Lost Sock Laundromat, Ebenezer Baptist Church, and Moore's Grove United Methodist Church.

When I arrive at the clinic, I meticulously change into clean scrubs and retrieve the N95 respirator mask I have been reusing all week from a paper bag inside my desk drawer. Now I am ready for the day. For patients without COVID-19 symptoms, most visits are now done via Telehealth. While video limits my ability to adequately examine and accurately diagnose patients, it has offered rare and intimate glimpses into the homes and lives of my patients—to the inside of double-wide trailers shared by multiple families, the cool shade of covered porches, threadbare favorite armchairs, Virgen de Guadalupe statues, cameos from kids playing in the background, cats, dogs, chickens, and even pet lizards.

In the clinic parking lot, sick patients with possible COVID symptoms wait in their cars until we can screen them by phone or video call. If they meet the CDC's stringent testing criteria, I don a paper gown, latex gloves, N95 mask, and a plastic face shield and conduct the medical visit through the patient's rolled-down car window. As I approach one dented, dusty, once-white Ford minivan, I see that the patient, Ms. O., is a middle-aged woman who has her elderly mom in the passenger seat and two teenage kids in the back. Both Ms. O. and her mother, recent immigrants from El Salvador, are still wearing their uniforms from the local nursing home where they work as caregivers and where several residents and employees have just tested positive for the virus. Everyone in the car looks uneasy. I try to smile with my eyes above the mask and make polite conversation in Spanish before I poke nasopharyngeal swabs deep into the nostrils of each family member and drop them into carefully labeled specimen jars to be shipped to a lab in the state capitol.

This "no touch" approach to caring for patients feels invasive and distant at the same time, and it runs counter to everything I know about being a good nurse. I can offer no real answers or reassurances for this anxious woman, her frightened kids, or her vulnerable, elderly mother. There is no treatment or cure, and the lab is so overwhelmed, test results can take seven to ten days to come back. I try to convey kindness and compassion through the thin sliver of my face that can be seen above my N95 mask as I hand them flyers on "CDC home isolation instructions" and "What to do if you get sicker," and I ask them to wear masks and self-isolate until we know their test results are negative.

At first, the threat of pandemic seemed low. The total cases in Henderson County were few, and for a while, not one of the hundreds of COVID-19 tests our clinic sent to the lab came back as positive. We've had access to more tests and protective equipment than many other healthcare facilities in the country, and that feels like a luxury. But as the first positive tests started coming back, I began to face the possibility of getting sick—or worse, becoming a carrier of this virus. Every time I return from doing a COVID-19 test, I peel off the thin, easily torn, permeable yellow paper gown and the week-old N95 mask, and I wonder if this protection is enough to stop the virus from seeping into my skin. There still aren't enough tests to know who is carrying the virus and who isn't. I am afraid of the day the protective equipment fails and I become "radioactive," unknowingly infecting more patients, coworkers, family members, friends, and neighbors.

Often my patients who test positive for COVID-19 confront a whole different set of challenges that amplify the risks. Many are low-wage workers already at higher risk for COVID-19 because they cannot work from home, cannot afford to stop working, and have "essential" jobs (farmworkers, packing plant workers, home health aides, janitors, nursing home staff, construction workers, food delivery workers, and grocery store workers) that require interacting with others at close range, often without adequate protective equipment. Some are migrant farmworkers or undocumented immigrants from Central America who don't have safe spaces to quarantine, no opportunity for paid sick leave, and no access to stimulus checks, unemployment benefits, or health insurance. On top of that, some fear that accessing medical care or testing positive for COVID-19 will lead to deportation.

As I toggle back and forth between worlds, from the farmer's market in rapidly gentrifying, middle-class, and mostly white Asheville to the trailer parks and factories and farms that my patients inhabit, I wonder if my neighbors are aware of the struggles that those who pick and pack our food are facing. It's an unprecedented time in our lives of forced physical distance, isolation, and economic shutdown. I worry for those who are already living at the margins. This virus has further unmasked the hypocrisy and dysfunction of our nation and shown us to be a country unwilling to care for its most vulnerable citizens or protect the "essential workers" who provide us with food and keep us alive.

A few weeks ago I joined my colleagues from the clinic's outreach team and went to a tomato packing plant where there have been several confirmed COVID-19 cases. We set up a mobile clinic inside the plant, known also as "La Tomatera," and tested all 220 workers. For my colleagues, it was just another day on the job, but for me it was my first experience going inside a factory to care for the needs of assembly line workers. I was struck by the enormity of the plant, a large aluminum-sided box the size of a football field, surrounded by a vast parking lot lined with row upon row of sixteen-wheeler cargo trucks. Inside the plant there is a constant deafening roar of conveyor belts and forklifts as workers wearing hairnets and cloth masks work elbow to elbow to sort and package thousands of pounds of tomatoes at a breakneck speed. Almost all of the workers are Latinx, many of them middle aged and even elderly. Some are stout and stooped with age, the packing plant being a welcome respite after decades of work in the fields; others are lithe and strong young people, wide-eyed new arrivals to the area who form part of the seasonal Eastern migrant stream from Florida to Vermont.

The workers handle thousands of pounds of tomatoes shipped

from Florida; they pack the individual tomatoes into plastic packages, stack them into cardboard boxes, and load them onto trucks that crisscross the country to supermarkets, where consumers cringe at the prices and want cheaper, fresher produce. The workers earn $7.25 an hour and are on their feet working the assembly lines for ten to twelve hours a day.

My role at the mobile clinic was to physically examine each person who had symptoms of COVID-19 and anyone with abnormal vital signs to determine who had to be pulled off the assembly line and sent out on a fourteen-day quarantine. Each worker suspected of having the virus had to be reported to their supervisor, a stocky gray-haired white man with a trucker hat who would snap a photo of them with his phone "to keep track." He spoke a few words of Spanish but mostly relied on a young bilingual, bicultural Latina manager who explained to sick workers that they would be paid for the fourteen days of forced quarantine. The workers were incredulous, having never had access to paid sick leave before.

The tension between a worker's ability to keep earning and their health is a frequent paradox in my work, especially when caring for low-wage and undocumented workers. The workers I examined looked at me with fear and pleading in their eyes. They asked questions I could not answer like, "Do you think I have the virus?" "How will I support my family if I am off work?" "What will happen to me if I get sick?" "How can I protect my babies?" The vulnerability behind their questions, and my inability to protect them from COVID-19 or bring fair wages and working conditions to the tomato plant, underscores that I am definitely not a hero. I do not have the answers, and I do not have a treatment or a cure for this virus. Instead, I stand by impotent as the virus disproportionately ravages communities of color and the working poor. What I can offer is my presence and my willingness to be here in this with my patients, bearing witness.

Raluca Ioanid was born in communist Romania and raised in capitalist New York City. By day she is a UCSF trained Family Nurse Practitioner working at a community health center in Western North Carolina. By night she is a trapeze-flying writer of stories. She is a founding member of the Reverie Writing Group and has published her work in several anthologies and literary journals.

The One that Hurts Less

Kristen Marinovich, written with Dawn Marlan

I am a registered nurse at a large hospital in downtown Minneapolis. Our unit specializes in end-stage heart failure. Our patients are at high risk of complications, so when it became clear that Covid-19 would reach our hospital, the administration planned to place Covid patients in another unit.

Initially, we were told that we would take "airborne" precautions with Covid patients, treating them in specialized negative-pressure rooms by staff with the proper PPE. We were supposed to have either a PAPR (powered air purifying respirator), a CAPR (controlled air purifying respirator) or a fit-tested N95 mask, along with a gown, gloves, and a face shield.

I was at work one night in early March, just as we were beginning to see patients we suspected of having the virus, when we all received a startling email. It stated that effective at seven a.m. the next day, confirmed or suspected Covid-19 patients would be placed on what they were calling "advanced droplet" precautions. That is, most hospital staff would be required to wear only a simple surgical mask, gown, face shield, and gloves rather than the full protective equipment we were expecting.

I remember the charge nurse reading the email aloud at the nurses' station while a number of us gathered around, listening in disbelief. The Center for Disease Control (CDC) had just updated its guidelines to suggest that if N95s were unavailable, we could use bandanas or scarves, "protections" that were wholly inadequate. The hospital administration took the CDC's lead. This was the moment when we realized our safety was no longer a priority for our hospital administrators and our trusted CDC.

We knew there wasn't scientific data to back up the revised guidelines. In fact, an article released soon afterwards in the *New England*

Journal of Medicine showed that the virus could remain in the air for up to three hours, contradicting the assumptions under which our hospital was operating. It was possible that they weren't acting with mal-intent, that the shifts in policy could be attributed to inadequate data. But lacking adequate data, we expected them to err on the side of caution. We wanted "airborne precautions," because that was the gold standard. It wasn't what we got.

With constantly changing hospital guidelines, doctors and nurses attempted to protect themselves personally. The response was surreal. We were told that if we attempted to bring our own masks into the hospital, we'd face disciplinary action. They quickly enforced this—an internal-medicine MD wore a surgical mask to work and was asked to remove it. If she refused, she would no longer be allowed to practice at the hospital. It's worth pausing for a second here to take in the terrible irony of their message. We would be punished for trying to stay alive. *By the hospital.*

When the hospital reversed its guidelines the next week, now requiring all staff and visitors to wear surgical masks at all times within the hospital, rather than find it reassuring my trust dwindled further. All the decisions about safety were being made by highly paid management employees who did not work at the bedside but safely at home. It seemed obvious that these changing guidelines were based not on science, but on the lack of sufficient PPE. I realized during those brutal weeks that we were dispensable, that they were more concerned about "managing us" than about keeping us safe. I felt fury at the callousness of the people making these decisions. Anxiety about having so little control over my own safety. Sorrow for myself and all those who weren't being valued. Grief, the deepest grief, for a world turned upside down.

After work I spent hours on my computer, trying to research proper safety protocols. In countless videos and photos, I saw healthcare workers from other countries dressed in head-to-toe Tyvek suits, booties, head covers, long gloves, goggles, and either N95 masks or PAPRs. I came across a video showing a nurse in China gowning up to go into a Covid unit. She wore multiple layers of protection and had no exposed skin. Taking off personal protection equipment—or doffing, as we call it—has to be done meticulously and carefully in order to prevent the virus from spreading during the process. Some workers in China were working in four-hour shifts without eating, drinking, or using the restroom to maintain the integrity of the PPE. Others were wearing adult diapers so they did not have to disrobe. Nurses were quarantined together away from their families to prevent potential spread within their households. They were given sleeping quarters. We were told to expose ourselves and then go home to our families.

The thought of going to work began to make me sick to my stomach. I was filled with dread. I started seeing my patients differently, almost as threats. It wasn't their fault, but there was a real possibility that they could kill me.

Our heart failure team had begun to discharge as many patients as possible, including some who had been waiting for months for new hearts. With our patient census dwindling, our nurses had begun to float off our unit to staff the newly created Covid units. One described being at a bedside taking a patient's temperature when he coughed. She turned her head away from him, but she could feel his warm breath through the sides of her mask.

With a growing shortage of disinfecting wipes at the hospital, it became harder to fall asleep at night. I stayed up wondering about all the ways I could carry this virus home—on shoes, hair, pens, paper. Doctors and nurses were talking about how to protect their families. Some moved out of their houses, setting up tents in their garages. Many nurses were stripping down naked in the garage, putting their scrubs in plastic bags and walking immediately into the shower. I considered getting a hotel room, which made no fiscal sense. Instead, my husband set up a decontamination zone in the garage so I could strip down before stepping foot in the house.

Our fears and concerns became a publicized battle. We wanted to change into hospital-issued scrubs at work and leave them there to be laundered after our shifts. It wasn't a huge ask, but we were nearly fired over it. After the media got involved, there was yet another policy reversal, finally allowing those working in Covid units to wear hospital scrubs during their shifts.

It was astonishing how hard we had to fight to get appropriate protection for ourselves and our families. It felt as if we were soldiers being sent to a war without guns, or firefighters being sent into burning buildings without a breathing apparatus. My husband pleaded with me to resign. But I didn't want to leave, I wanted protective equipment. We contacted our legislators begging for the appropriate PPE. They told us, "We're doing all we can do."

At some point we won the right to wear N95s while caring for active Covid patients. But what "one hand giveth, the other taketh away." We had the masks, but we were forced to wear them for multiple shifts until they were visibly torn or soiled. We had to store them in paper bags. We had to use them in ways that went against everything we were ever taught as nurses and against the manufacturer's instructions for safe use. There is just no way to keep microscopic contaminants contained when taking masks in and out of paper bags. These sorts of masks were always designed for one-time use.

This became the procedure. At a "masking station," we could exchange old masks for new ones. But only after inspection. We wore the same masks for weeks. They became disgusting. With every breath, they grew moist, polluted. They captured every cough. Every sneeze. The damp, clammy cloth was a constant sensory reminder of the danger we were facing. We were trusted to save patients' lives every day, but not to know when to replace our own masks. And we could tell that they needed to be replaced by the sheer feel of them. It made no sense.

As I oscillated between intense sadness, anger, and anxiety, I had an impossible decision to make: stay home and protect my family, or stay at work protecting my patients and coworkers. I was completely torn. I was furious that I was being put in a position to have to make such a choice. Shamed and embarrassed for even considering walking away.

Then my mother was diagnosed with breast cancer. I was the only one who could help her through this process. She was about to become immunocompromised and at an increased risk of complications if she were infected with Covid. My stepfather had just gotten out of the psych hospital on a legal hold and my mom had been his caretaker. He was negative help.

I called my nurse friends to talk through things. One of them said, "You're not going to feel good about either decision; you just need to choose the one that hurts less."

Another friend and I talked over my love/hate relationship with nursing. We are constantly being asked to do more with less. We feel dispensable to our employers. We are often verbally, physically, and sexually harassed by patients and their family members. Somehow this is one of the only professions where this type of treatment continues to be tolerated. But I *have*, because I love caring for patients and I love the adrenaline that comes with it. My friend said, "I know. It's like being in an abusive relationship."

Like being in an abusive relationship, I had an enormous amount of guilt about the mere thought of leaving, and having the luxury of being able to choose to stay home. For most, that's not an option, because they are the main breadwinners in their households.

When you work together for years in such stressful situations and are constantly performing as a team, having each other's back, it is incredibly difficult to walk away while they are left risking their lives. We rely on each other every single shift.

In the midst of agonizing over this decision, I went on Facebook, where I felt barraged by people who actually shamed nurses.

Under the comments, one person wrote, "It sickens me. I've already seen posts from nurses saying they are refusing to help COVID patients because of their own health. I ask, why are they even a nurse? It this not a known fact that nurses can and do put themselves in harm's way every day? COVID or not? This is not the time to be selfish. Nurses from WW2 would be embarrassed."

But what was even worse was the post from a hospital director who publicly called us out for "running from the challenge" or for being "afraid of risk." She ended by telling us to "get educated" about how to keep safe because "the community is relying on you."

I am educated. That's what keeps me up at night. The director offered no explanation as to why nurses were refusing assignments. Were they immunocompromised? Were they being asked to perform direct patient care without an N95? And, no, we were not well prepared to deliver.

It stung to read the comment from a man who wrote, "My experiences in the military are that yellow-bellied cowards rarely become anything else...."

A yellow-bellied coward. That's how some people will think of me. Because I'm currently taking a leave of absence. And I don't even know if it's mainly because of my mother, or my husband, or my son, or because I have the audacity to want to live and to claim my own life as valuable. I don't know if it's because I'm so incredibly angry about the lies and deception and shaming, or because we have to fight so hard for necessities that they exhaust us before we even get in the room to fight for our patients.

With all of the years I've dedicated to caring for others, I've bought myself a little time. But it won't last forever. Here's something I've realized. Critical-care nursing becomes a part of who you are. You get used to discomfort. You get used to tragedy. You run toward these things, not away from them.

I absolutely want to be there using my skills and helping to save lives. I thrive in this adrenaline-high atmosphere of hyper-focus. So I understand why some people are saying that this is what we signed up for. This is what we do. But in calculating that choice, we believed in a shared core value that in this world of health care, all human life is valued. My own included. Being treated as dispensable was not part of the bargain.

Throughout my years as a bedside nurse, I've witnessed, with increasing frequency, how our healthcare system exploits our altruistic qualities. This pandemic has only unmasked what was already happening, silently and malignantly, in health care more generally.

Our profession is predominantly composed of women who are raised and then trained to be caregivers. The hospital administration and the healthcare industry at large capitalize on this. They know that we won't let our patients or our coworkers down, no matter the cost to us personally.

Somewhere on social media, another nurse said: "I'm afraid all this talk of nurses as heroes is priming the public to accept our deaths as casualties of war rather than a public heath failure."

I didn't sign up to be a soldier. I'm not interested in heroics. I simply want to use the skills I've spent so many years honing without worrying that it will be my last act. Soon, I will have to make a decision about whether to go back. Will I be able to face my coworkers again who have been risking themselves daily while I'm safely at home with my family?

I'm still reading, learning, listening, and watching the progression of this virus. The regulatory agencies (OSHA, JCAHO) have remained absolutely silent. They are the ones who inspect the hospitals to make sure we have no uncovered drinks at our stations, no tape on the walls, no carts in the hallways. Their reason-for-being is to protect everyone in the hospital. Where are they now?

Kristen Marinovich is a registered nurse currently practicing and living in Minneapolis, Minnesota.

My COVID-19 Gratitude List

Isobel Rosenthal

After four years in medical school and two years in graduate school, I'm finally an intern on my way to becoming a psychiatrist. But like so many doctors of other specialties, I'm on a detour, working as a primary provider for COVID-19 patients in the epicenter of the pandemic, at a New York City hospital.

The experience for every medical professional, from veteran physicians down to young interns and residents, has been overwhelming. I have never seen such a concentration of raw emotions from staff, patients, and families of patients. In this sort of environment it's easy, even natural, to despair. In my days off, my family and friends call me often, asking about all the horrors I have seen and experienced. They're well-intentioned calls, but they just end up adding to my sense of dread, as I know I have to return to the wards the next day.

But I've also figured out an antidote to the stress: a gratitude list.

The idea came to me just before my first twelve-hour shift in a seven-day stretch. While I was chatting with my co-resident, another budding psychiatrist, he told me that in an effort to avoid public transit, he planned to rollerblade from his apartment to the hospital. I began imagining him gliding down Madison Avenue in his scrubs—a sort of goofy, roving COVID superhero—and realized I was laughing to myself. Sitting alone the night before that first shift, beginning a self-quarantine in my empty childhood apartment far from my family and friends, this laughter freed me. I felt immense gratitude for that moment of humor. It reminded me of a story my mom used to tell me when I was a little girl—the story of a very sick woman, lying on her deathbed, who decided to watch a comedy movie daily to brighten her final weeks. Eventually, the story goes, she wound up curing herself through laughter. It's a story that I've often returned to in times of fear and stress.

I made a pact with myself right then and there to look for the humor, or for the good news—for something, anything, to be grateful for—every day of my shift.

One day it was the surprise birthday celebration that our attending held for my senior resident, who had expected the day to go unnoticed by our team. Other days I was struck by unexpected moments of generosity from the community, like when I left work to find half a dozen fire trucks parked outside and dozens of firemen clapping for everyone leaving the hospital. I felt a stir of New-York-specific emotion as I remembered clapping for *them* back in 2001, visiting firehouses as a child. It took me back to 9/11, a day on which my family had waited for several terrifying hours to hear from my father as he walked up from Wall Street to our apartment uptown without cell service.

The greatest sense of gratitude came when we discharged patients to their homes. It's so difficult seeing patients gasping for oxygen, having something they'd always taken for granted become a punishing physical trial. My team had been clapping for patients as we discharged them, and we soon had an idea for something more we could do. After we finished rounding, I ran up to the administrative assistant at the front of the unit and asked if we could play music when patients were discharged. He explained to me how we could page music from our phones into the units. We began brainstorming about songs that would give patients hope when they could hear one of their newly recovered neighbors leaving for home. I sent a text asking for ideas to my family and friends, and immediately suggestions poured in.

From that moment on, as we discharged patients we began blasting tunes, from "Eye of the Tiger" to "New York, New York" to "Here Comes the Sun." And when I get home at night exhausted, ripping my clothes off in my hallway so I can run to a hot shower to disinfect myself, I play this music in the background—theme songs to my strange new pandemic life.

At night, alone in my childhood apartment that my mother has evacuated—and facetiming with my boyfriend across the park, whom I cannot touch—I try to focus on these moments of gratitude before I go to bed, so that I can wake up and return to what have been the defining weeks of my young professional life.

Most of all, I feel gratitude for the kindness of my colleagues— bringing chocolate bars for each other and talking others through their tears after a patient codes, unable to reach out and hold them. As I wake up, push my finger into a small machine to test my oxygen saturation, and stick a thermometer down my throat, hoping that I am healthy, I try to think of these moments and focus momentarily on gratitude, so that I can get back in there and do my job.

❧

Isobel Rosenthal MD, MBA is a psychiatry resident in New York City. She is a graduate of the Icahn School of Medicine at Mount Sinai Hospital, Columbia Business School, and Yale University. Her interests are in behavioral health technology, the treatment of serious mental illness, and physician well-being.

Lost Woman and Other Stories of
Finding Ourselves in Isolation

On Isolation

Hannah Keziah Agustin

It hurts everywhere.

Crouched over like a wounded animal protecting its insides, I am sobbing on the toilet seat as I watch a video of Corporal Winston Ragos being shot dead at a COVID-19 quarantine checkpoint in Manila. He had fought the war in Marawi a few months prior and suffered from post-traumatic stress. I do not know him but I know the look of innocence. I've seen the surveillance footage. The cops were doing rounds while he bought cigarettes and a bottle of Coke. In broad daylight, they interrogated and cursed him for doing so. He reached inside his bag, but he had no gun. *Bang. Bang.* Because he violated the community quarantine, two bullets were planted in his chest and a .38 caliber gun was planted in his bag. He survived the war only to be slain in the hands of another soldier. Another victim of the pandemic.

It is the first time I've cried in weeks. Death is the last plague of Exodus and it is knocking on every door of every house in every country once again. All creation cries in pain, and there is no other way to respond to it than to grieve. There is no beauty in the hurting. No cathartic release. No symbolic self-penitence. Nothing. Just agony, a deep ache that pierces from flesh to bone. Sundered. This may be the reason why I try not to cry; some part of me knew that the spiraling sadness would overflow once the lightest blow touched it. It's a curse to feel everything so deeply.

Do all artists suffer the most? Back in the Philippines, I met Ate Byu in the mountains of the Cordilleras. I first laid eyes on her when she sang a stripped-down acoustic version of Up Dharma Down's "Oo" at a school event, rocking a bleached-white pixie cut. I applied to join the music organization she belonged to, and then soon found out that we were both Christians. Her voice was that of an angel. Her Christ-likeness bled into everything she did: from art to activism, to creating music, to her presence—a light that touched every corner of the room. She was a fine arts major who enjoyed sunflowers, cats, fashion, black chokers, and Paramore. She was an activist who spoke out for the plight of the masses but stayed silent when it came to her own plight. Most importantly, she was my friend. On the wall right by my closet, I still keep her painting of two hands reaching out to each other but never quite touching. I am now in America, but this print still hangs. This is how it feels to say, "I'm here for you," when you are not physically there. This is the only thing I have left of her.

When the news of Ate's death arrived at my door during quarantine, I wept in the bathtub while the water ran for half an hour, half a world away. I was there with her again. The silence oscillated and rang, and her voice oscillated and rang in my head as a memory. That's all she'll ever be. Right now, her soul rests suspended "between heaven and earth"—that's what her name meant. She chose, in her anguish, to say, "It is finished." We didn't check up on her. We will carry this for the rest of our lives. If only humans had the capacity to show love in tangible and straightforward ways, maybe we could've kept her here a bit longer; but love is messy and chaotic, hidden, difficult, and selfish.

The danger of loving so many is having so much to lose. During quarantine, my workmate lost her husband to disease, and I lost a friend to suicide. What's a better trigger to depression than loneliness? All the demons must be out during this quarantine, keeping us company, weighing down our feet like wet sand. It's safer at home, but still not safe at all. The worst fear for me about having the coronavirus is dying alone. This gnaws at me whenever my mother leaves to work at the nursing home. She might never come home. She might bring the virus back. This is why, when she returns, she purifies herself.

Like Moses taking off his sandals in the presence of the burning bush, my mother takes off her rubber shoes before coming into our house—a good Asian—then enters into the sacred space—our home. Before she leaves for work, she places her bath towel inside a gray Walmart plastic bag and sets it near the door. Then, at 10:30 p.m., she takes off her brightly colored and patterned nursing scrubs and wraps the towel around her body like a half-naked human burrito. She does this every workday. A ritual. She is a sacrifice to the shower head. I can only hug her after this routine. Sometimes she doesn't even let me touch her. She only waves at me and tells me stories about her work through the crack in my door. We both know that Lysol can only protect us from so much.

Being immigrants has taught us to live in fear. In a white man's country, we live together alone. My mother gets mad at me when I go out of the house without a mask. My father brings home unused N95 masks from his cleaning job. My sister offers herself as a tribute to weekly trips to Walmart. In the car, there is an empty bottle of glass cleaner now filled with isopropyl alcohol. We need to do this.

We are far from home. This is why my mother prays in lamentations. In the morning, she mourns as a way of purging the self before God, as if this, too, is necessary for cleansing. She mourns over our dogs, her sisters, our churchmates; she is triggered into crying by the most mundane of things. I am the same. Because she is my mother, I carry even the parts of her that I do not like: the anxiety, the constant tossing and turning at night, the groaning. I've inherited even her melancholia.

Because the biblical meaning of death is separation, coming to America for me has been one long funeral. This isolation isn't new to me. I've been trained for this: for a month, none of us went out of the house because we didn't have insurance; for a semester, I taught myself how to cope with writing and therapy checkups that nobody knew about.

I, too, have prayed in lamentations. I metaphorically put a sackcloth over my loins and dust over my head when I'm sad. I would throw away the rocks of my altar when I feel He hast forsaken thee. We aren't designed to be alone. In moments of great despair, His goodness is shrouded by sorrow, and I refuse to be comforted. A year ago, I stumbled upon an email I apparently wrote to a mental health website. The subject line: *I want to die.* I do not remember feeling that way, because when I'm sad, my body goes into autopilot. Self-destruction. For a moment, death becomes a deceivingly enticing paradise, a place of rest. As a writer obsessed with the lethargic, I have wrestled with this desire for years, like the troubled psalmist wrestling with so much anguish in the valley of the shadow of death.

I couldn't vivify death's sting even if I wanted to. I cannot pin it down. When I try, the words merely tread in circles around the black hole of grief. I am simply not brave enough to relive the trauma I experienced in my retelling. This is why I do not write about my grandmother. It took me a decade to break the silence of my sadness. I chose not to remember even the good moments, of trips to the wet market, buying fresh tilapia in my slippers and white sando. I chose not to remember the flower-patterned duster dress she wore from when I first remembered her until her last breath. I was sleeping on the night that she died. Before the doctors gave up on her cancer treatment, she was isolated. *Nanay* was so happy when she died, so full of life. Although our family grieved for forty days, she was so sure of where she was going. I choose to remember this, even if writing about the dead pins them to my pages. Maybe it is selfish to not let them go.

So I put down my pen and raise my eyes in a moment of silence. For the two men who died in Manila from drinking a mixture of paint thinner, toothpaste, and vinegar because of alcohol withdrawal since the citywide liquor ban. For the Filipino nurse in London who died alone in his flat while in quarantine, whose lifeless body was found on the floor days after he had passed away. For the two-year-old Asian American boy and his family who were stabbed at a Sam's Club in Texas because of a virus-fueled hate crime. For the fallen health workers. For Ate Byu. For the unnamed dead with bodies stacked in cold trucks as morgues overflow from so much death. It is everywhere, and we are all locked up in our own houses dealing with the aftermath of it.

I have done everything to try not to deal with this pain.

But it still hurts everywhere.

There is no easy answer to the difficulties of this isolation. The problem goes beyond simply being alone. We spend our energies on a billion tasks, pulled as we are in a billion different directions, battling the antagonists in our personal stories. At the end of the day, when the lights are off and our doors are locked, when we are left alone in the danger of our own headspace, I believe that most of us want to stay alive but not to feel the agony of separation.

My words still lie heavy on the paper as I write my way out of grief. But I try. Every day, I try. The act of surviving is to choose to live over and over again. I will forgive myself for not being a better friend, for not being there when I was needed most. I can only do so much. This is a testament to my remembrance. I will hold on to this as I scroll through Twitter and see "Rest in Peace" flooding my timeline as the shortest and most impersonal eulogy.

It will be over soon, but at such a great cost. On the other side of this pandemic, we'll be written down in history as survivors, maybe even victors. But the grief will remain, as we face the tedious and painful job of burying our dead. The loss will haunt us, even as we step outside to the waiting world. Death is intrinsic to the life we've signed up for. But outside, we live again. Out of nowhere the air rushes into our lungs. The only remedy is to hold one's breath, and hope.

❧

Hannah Agustin is a Filipina writer and undergraduate student majoring in Film Studies and English Creative Writing at the University of Wisconsin-Whitewater. She immigrated from the Philippines to the U.S. in 2019.

Newly Sober in the Time of the Coronavirus

Sari Caine

God/Goddess/WhateverWorksForYou, Grant me the serenity
to accept the things I cannot change, the courage to change the things
I can, and the wisdom to know the difference.

–The Serenity Prayer

"Stay:
    1: to stop going forward; pause.
    2: to stop doing something; cease.
    3: to continue in a place or condition; remain stayed."
When everything is fight or flight, *stay* is in between. The opposite
of trying to escape.

March 19, 2020. Kentucky.

The train whistle blows early Thursday morning. That's all it takes for
you to want to sneak out of bed, put your running sneakers on, and run
down to the tracks. Your hand picks up your phone, because seeking
help has become automatic, and phones are all you pick up now. You
know someone will answer, because helping you helps them—helps us.
Your sponsor, busy with her own life in Brooklyn, hears your inability
to speak and calmly says: "We'll start the same way we worked together
at the beginning."

Starting from the beginning feels like defeat, and you can barely
remember that far back.

"It's not one day at a time," she says, "it's one hour. From nine to
ten you will eat food. From ten to eleven, you will get caffeine. From
eleven to twelve, you'll take a shower. And we'll check in at the end of
every hour. Remember your one word mantra: *Stay.*"

Keep passing the open windows, John Irving wrote.

Right now none of them are open; you are scared of rain.

Tuesday, November 12, 2019, is your sobriety date. It is when you stopped, or rather, your life stopped for you, and you could not go on. At first, you assumed you had gotten this information wrong. You could, of course, "go on." Samuel Beckett's quote, "You can't go on, you must go on," was one of your favorite, clever things to say. But the months, weeks, days, hours, minutes, went on, and you did not. You did not go anywhere beyond the one unending thought, which was that your head was trying to vomit out your brain and you did not feel so clever now.

The morning you finally gave up, gave in, and stopped trying to "get out," you found notes scattered across your apartment. Some were crumpled, some were large and some were small. They were all in your distinctly scrawled, illegible handwriting.

"The tsunami is coming," they said.

And finally the last one, the one that made you admit defeat, found underneath your pillow: "The tsunami is here."

Four p.m., Thursday March 19. You wait anxiously on the veranda swing of your boyfriend's porch in Louisville, Kentucky, for a woman you've never met to bring you a book. The book is called the Big Book and the woman is called Alex, except that is not her name. You have no doubt Alex will come, because Ken told you so. You have never met Ken either; that is also not his name. Welcome to anonymity.

For the last four and a half months, you have depended on the kindness of strangers. At their suggestions, you have called two a day, every day, and your sponsor. You have sat in multiple meeting rooms daily, shared walks, shared coffee. You have taken phone numbers, house-sat, pet-sat, and opened your home and heart to strangers, who open their homes and hearts to you. And the only thing you know, more than you know your own (actual) name, is that they will not let you down. This is how you begin to learn optimism, defined by Merriam-Webster on Google as *a doctrine that this world is the best of all possible places.*

This sounds like the serenity prayer they say at the end of your meetings. It sounds like what you are starting to understand about reality. Most of all, it sounds like Leibniz. In fact, it is. "This is the best of all possible worlds" was his Enlightenment-era phrase, what is now called Leibnizian optimism. Historically, you've sided with Voltaire, who lambasted Leibniz: "Candide, stunned, stupefied, despairing, bleeding, trembling, said to himself: If this is the best of all possible worlds, what are the others like?"

You left your own Big Book in the back of your Uber on the way to LaGuardia Airport, and you want to believe this is the best of all possible worlds too; in the midst of a global pandemic, you never know who might need to find a Big Book in their car. It seems you agree with Leibniz now.

On November 12, 2019, when you stopped, the largest fear you had was that the world had kept on going. It is currently Thursday, March 19, 2020, and part of you is the smallest bit pleased to report the world has stopped; it has hit its "bottom" too. Admitting your powerlessness is Step 1. It turns out we are all powerless over something, whether it is our addictions, behaviors, or the coronavirus.

You are an addict in a 12-Step program, anonymity prevents you from saying which one. Before recovery, you had many lives, simultaneously sometimes. Jung said: "I would rather be whole than good." After months of recovery and outside therapy, whole is starting to feel good.

Not so long ago, you would have been delighted to lock yourself inside your apartment and go AWOL, writing the next Great American Novel. Social isolation mixed with chaos was irresistible. Society insisting *you may not leave your house* was a fantasy you've had for a long time. Neither you nor the Great American Novel would have made it through the quarantine intact.

There is a group of people currently scattered anonymously throughout the world, uniquely suited to handling today: individuals of 12-Step programs. The very qualities that make addicts and alcoholics so good at finding any substance anywhere at any time make us some of the most resourceful, resilient people you'll ever meet. As obsessively and intelligently as we once sought chaos and destruction, we now concentrate on creating discipline and peace.

Where you once sought escape, you now focus on being present. Where you once sought a fix, or to be fixed, you now question your understanding of broken. Quarantine makes your world smaller, more manageable, bite-sized chunks. And when the questions come, you are prepared to respond with calmness in the face of uncertainty, *How long will you be in Kentucky? How is it going with your boyfriend? Aren't you getting too old to have kids? What's happened to your apartment? Your cat? Family? Job?*

But practice takes practice, and sometimes we all just want things to be better *now*. When a Global Pandemic comes, they can't be.

There is a saying in the rooms: "Don't just do something, sit there." And as everyone, including the whole world, wants *this*—the virus, the economy—to be "fixed," you think about how hard it is to just sit still. *Stay*. You do, and slowly, as everything external gets stripped away, what you value comes into place.

Addicts also want "right now" to be fixed; that is why we use. But sometimes "right now" can't be. This time, the "right now" is shared by the entire world. This is Step One every day for each of us, admitting you have no control. You are right back in November 2019. *Stay*. And suddenly, after four and a half months of practicing love, strength, and hope daily, you don't feel so behind. You don't feel ahead either. You feel exactly where you should be, and equipped to meet the world—the best possible world there can be—as it is.

12-Step programs are a communal program and so is the internet. By the time the virtual world took hold for the rest of the world, yours had already formed. No one was left behind; even eighty-year-olds Zoom, waving at you during meetings, with one-dimensional hands.

Stay, they say. If only to find out what happens next. It gets better.

In Zoom meetings, trappings of anonymity are still present but small boxes of home behind your strangers' heads brings a strangely intimate feel. Men who had always looked so tough are suddenly re-vealed cradling cats. You are grateful for the technology that keeps you connected to your Brooklyn strangers, most of whom have scattered, like you, across the country.

Some people from your meetings disappear. Some reappear, some don't; they die. Most stay. Newcomers appear, individuals who have never been to any room in person, never met any of us at all. Zoom 12-Step meetings are the only recovery they know. One had three months yesterday.

"Your faces are my rooms," she said, and you smiled because her face is your room too, and right now it is glowing.

Stay, they say at the end of meetings. *Stay,* they say when you are getting off the phone. *Stay,* you think, looking at your running shoes by the door.

You watch the strangers in your 12-Step meetings facing the pandemic with humor, and resilience, and courage that you don't see elsewhere. You memorize the Serenity Prayer, and look up the word "courage" with your sponsor and discover that it must be learned; only bravery is innate. You realize distance (even virtually) counts; you need to find strangers in Kentucky, too. Even if you never get to meet them in real life. Even if it feels like you would rather step on a rusty nail. You do it. Ken is your first Kentucky stranger. He picked up the phone when you called Louisville's 12-Step office. Alex will be here soon, he says; her face will be your room.

Sitting on your boyfriend's porch swing in full-blown panic mode, you're trying very hard not to run away because after all, it is March 19, 2020, and other than Kentucky, where would you go? You don't run from things anymore; there is no actual getting away. As you sit with your discomfort, you don't feel so serene; if this is what Leibniz meant by "best possible world," you would like another now. But instead you call the even-newer-than-you newcomer, to offer help.

"What's the point?" she says.

The point is change, the gift is willingness, you could say, but instead you just listen. She tells you she is originally from an Orthodox Jewish community and has trouble with the "higher power thing," because she left her own God behind. You never had one.

"Is there anything you kept?" you ask.

She is silent, then. "There's something called *Hishtadlus.* It means your place, what personal action you must take in the world. *Bitachon* is your trust in and acceptance of the universe. The night I reached out for help, that was my Hishtadlus. I must have had some trust in the universe if I did that."

You smile because you realize you understand Step 2 now: A belief that something outside yourself will restore you to sanity. Faith. In this case, her.

"Stay." You say.

It is 4:30 when Alex arrives, as you knew she would. (Step 3: A belief in a power greater than yourself.) Alex is a sassy woman in her fifties with twenty-eight years of sobriety and a voice impossible to miss, even from ten feet away. She's also the last person (besides your boyfriend) you will see in real life for the next three months.

"Are you doing the dishes?" she says. "What step are you on?"

You are used to these personal conversations with strangers now. Are you sleeping? Showering? Eating? Drinking water? Remembering to pause?

"Step 3, and, yes, I'm doing the dishes."

"Every morning I get up, do Steps 1, 2, and 3," she says. "I have to resist, give up, surrender, and start again new, every goddamn day. But all that Step 3 asks of you is a willingness to try. Now, honey, I was never the suicidal type; I was the homicidal one, but as long as you're desperate in either direction, the willingness is there." She squints at you. "You look pretty damn willing."

You force yourself to meet her eyes. She puts the book down. *Stay.*

That night, you are desperate—or willing—enough to try your first Louisville 12-Step meeting, via Zoom. You decide to leave, no one will know, then you hear a familiar voice—Ken. "She's new, came here from New York City."

"Stay," the strangers say.

Women's phone numbers fill the chat. You will write them down before the meeting ends and call two every day. It will be awkward and slow-going at first, but you'll find an online women's meeting that will once again save your life, and you theirs. When it's time to read from the Big Book (courtesy of Ken and Alex), you can read along, too. You wonder who has yours?

"We are people who normally would not mix. But there exists among us a fellowship…We are like the passengers of a great liner the moment after rescue from a shipwreck when camaraderie, joyousness, and democracy pervade the vessel from steerage to Captain's table."[6]

In the front of the book are their phone numbers, Alex's and Ken's. And underneath, another word: "Stay."

So, Earth, take what you like and leave the rest. Thank you all for

---

[6] The Big Book (Alcoholics Anonymous), page 17. Alcoholics Anonymous. 2014. Alcoholics Anonymous: big book reference edition for addiction treatment.

joining me in my new sobriety. I'm grateful to find us both working simultaneously on Step 3. Get ready for Step 4: Taking Inventory. I'll see you on the virtual side.

Stay.

❧

Sari Caine is an award-winning writer and performer, and co-Artistic Director of Slightly Altered States. A native New Yorker and former scholastic chess champion, Sari has taught chess in NYC schools since she was thirteen and has specialized in teaching in schools for special needs children for the last seven. SariCaine.org

A Shelter of One's Own

Syd Shaw

"Mostly when people write about the trauma of gender violence, it's described as one awful, exceptional event or relationship, as though you suddenly fell into the water, but what if you're swimming through it your whole life?"
    —Rebecca Solnit, *Recollections of My Non-Existence*

I have a shelter now, though that wasn't always the case. I spent most of last year the way many of us are spending our lives now: trapped in an apartment in a constant state of fear. For me, the threat came from inside the house. I walked on eggshells around my partner from day one, cooking and cleaning and doing everything I could to make the one-bedroom apartment feel like my own. It hadn't begun that way, of course: In the beginning he was kind and charming, overly confident that it would all work out. I had just graduated from college, and when he suggested moving in together, it seemed like the perfect antidote to my lack of direction, a sort of storybook romance. It was seamless for the first few weeks, but once our families had met and the lease was signed, once our lives were too entwined for either one of us to escape, he changed. I thought at first that he was morphing into a different person, though I realize now that the charm was a cover; his true self was cruel, more horror than romance.

I left him and returned, then left and returned again. When he was away on an errand, I would sit in my same little corner, waiting for his return with bile rising in my stomach. If the dog barked, he screamed at me. If the house wasn't spotless, he called me worthless. When I went out with friends, he called the police to report me missing, determined to know where I was at all times. When I was with him in public, I never took my eyes off him, had to respectfully wait for his permission to speak, because to speak to a stranger equated to cheating on him. It didn't matter whether it was a waitress, an acquaintance, or a passenger on the train. He kept me within a bubble where he could mediate every interaction I had with the outside world. Every time this barrier was removed, he saw it as a threat. It was a mark of how worn down I was that I stopped questioning this. I hated the person I had become, the person I had let him turn me into. I worried that this was my true self and became trapped in the idea that we deserved each other. Now I see the ways he manipulated me and realize how he set me up to blame myself.

Virginia Woolf understood the inherent threat in a lack of space, the fear that women experienced while writing furtively in drawing rooms, constantly looking over their shoulders to make sure the coast was clear. In her essay, "A Room of One's Own," she argues that without their own space, women were not free to create. The inhibitions of the material world weighed on their right to self-expression. Her focus was not on domestic violence, but the everyday demands of the household, which left little time for anything else, and a lack of privacy, which constrained women's creativity. In abusive situations, the pressure is increased exponentially. *I thought how unpleasant it is to be locked out*, Woolf writes, *and I thought how it is worse perhaps to be locked in*. Indeed, it's a circle of hell familiar to many, but one that can't be fully explained if you haven't been there. Woolf's "locking in" is a metaphor for the adherence to gender roles, but her words resonate with me in my situation. I tried to write but none of it was good. I kept scattered diary entries, deleted paragraphs he might disapprove of, hid bits and pieces of poetry in journals and along the bottom of mundane documents, concealing my most intimate thoughts in folders labeled "cover letters" and "winter college essays." When I read these now, I see that a painful desperation permeates every word. The one coherent metaphor I used in these notes was that of a selkie, calling myself a sea creature "who burned her own pelt to remain on the land." I blamed myself for staying and pushed friends and family further away.

I thought I had no right to survive that winter. We had adopted a dog that fall, a brown-and-white spotted mutt named Jace. For two weeks, my ex bragged about what an excellent dog trainer he was. At the end of the two weeks, when Jace was still barking and not yet potty-trained, my ex demanded that I give the dog up. With Jace gone, the days began to blend into each other. I was depressed without understanding the illness, so when he called me crazy I believed him. Again and again, he threw bottles at me and I swept up the glass and blamed myself.

Eventually, I stopped going outside because it simply wasn't worth the fight. I gained weight, something he talked about mercilessly, and spent most of my time in front of the television. Only when he left for work could I breathe more easily. I frequently broke out in hives from the stress, and I apologized for everything from talking too loudly to not having dinner on the table immediately after returning home from a full day at my job. Eventually, I missed work because of him, so many times that they fired me.

"I am going to throw myself onto the third rail," I told the cats one morning, and they stared back unblinkingly as cats do. I wrapped myself in warm clothes, wanting my last walk to the station to be comfortable. Allie, the kitten, sat in the window. I remember turning back for him, taking my coat off with deliberation. "If he finds me gone he will probably give my cat away," I thought. So I stayed.

A month later, I left him for good and took the cats with me. This time, I had a foolproof plan, a friend's place to stay at, a plane ticket to get us all out of Chicago for good. I packed everything I owned into a storage unit during the few hours he was at work. I still dream about that morning sometimes, the way I threw everything into cardboard boxes and watched the clock. I left behind the things that belonged to both of us equally because I feared his anger. My getaway ride was five minutes late and I stood in the hall, eating a breakfast of dollar ramen and looking at the time, half expecting him to come home early, my phone already buzzing with his anger at unanswered texts from that morning. I hid at a friend's house while he and his family took turns calling me, cajoling at first and then threatening. Two days later, I got on a plane to California and vowed never to be trapped again; the next time I settled down, I would have a space that was truly my own.

I didn't expect anything to come easily after my escape, but the second the veil lifted the pain in my shoulders went away and I started listening to my own music again. Writing returned, too, and then going on walks, and visiting friends without feeling guilty. It was a recovery, a bringing back of limbs long atrophied, a renewal of confidence, friendship, and connection. Leaving was like waking up from a long nightmare. A year has slipped by and the memories are hazy. I don't recall most of my day-to-day life with him, but I remember the tension. Sometimes I find myself thrown back into the past during those dizzy moments between wakefulness and sleep, failing to remember that the danger isn't real anymore.

This year is my life inside-out; sometimes it feels as if the ugliness that built up inside our old apartment has seeped out into the rest of the world. I am no longer the only one who feels trapped. Even now, I am sometimes shocked to find myself alive. And the silence of the world during the pandemic, the repetition of the days, seems to confirm this unreal feeling. For some, this legal confinement is actively dangerous; sheltering in place can be done only when the shelter is there. Law enforcement officials across the country have reported an increase in domestic abuse calls since the start of quarantine, and domestic violence shelters are struggling to accommodate victims without inadvertently allowing the virus to spread.[7] A WHO report specifically notes that "violence against women tends to increase during every type of emergency, including epidemics."[8]

My story is nothing new: there are hundreds of such tales all over the internet, occupying the liminal space between personal and universal. All echo the sentiments of being trapped, but by forces within the home as opposed to without.

In my new life, I take our new dog for walks in the morning and we are quiet and peaceful, with the feeling of being very small and very alive. We walk through the canyon near my home while listening to the frogs and peacocks. California feels like all the warm summers I dreamt of last year. Even as I feel personally safe for the first time in months, I still worry for my family and friends every day. I wear my face mask while walking, thinking that I was lucky to experience domestic violence and COVID-19 in that sequence; I cannot imagine the lives of those who are dealing with both right now.

The healing comes in small steps, in simply sitting and feeling that I have a room of my own, in not jumping a mile when someone leans over my shoulder. Sometimes I catch myself crying when my current boyfriend is kind to me: every word of praise or reassuring touch is something I will never again take for granted. Some days the pain of the world seems so omnipresent, so natural, that it's easy to slip into thinking I deserve to suffer too. But there is no such thing as deserving

---

[7] Tolan, Casey. "Some cities see jumps in domestic violence during the pandemic," CNN, April 4, 2020, https://www.cnn.com/2020/04/04/us/domestic-violence-coronavirus-calls-cases- increase -invs/in dex.html

[8] World Health Organization. "COVID-19 and violence against women What the health sector/system can do," WHO, April 2020, https://apps.who.int/iris/bitstream/handle/10665/ 331699/WHO-SRH-20.04-eng.pdf

something, or, if there is, then we all deserve to have peace. With the light coming through the kitchen windows in soft golden lines, the frogs croaking in the creek over the chorus of the birds, the splendor of sunrise walks, the comfort of soft clothes and warm coffee, with every morning it gets easier to feel grateful for being alive.

❧

Syd Shaw studied poetry and journalism at Northwestern University. She has previously been published in *Helicon Literary Magazine, Snapdragon Journal* and *The London Reader.* Her passions include witchcraft, 80s pop music, and long distance running. She lives in California.

Learning to Be Alone in Social Isolation

Alissa Hirshfeld

At the end of January, I was preparing to fly home from a Doctors Without Borders trip to Cambodia, where I'd been doing trauma counseling, when I heard news reports of this strange new virus. I had traveled to Cambodia to distract myself from the sudden end of my marriage eight months prior, when my husband blindsided me by leaving me for another woman, after twenty-two years together. As a professional caretaker, I tended to deal with difficulties in my own life by helping others. Going to the Far East was a novel adventure. After hearing our patients' stories of intergenerational trauma, I wandered through wet markets, giving dollars to beautiful children who displayed their pet tarantulas proudly. Splayed frogs and roasting locusts simmered on barbecue grills. At dinner with my new international group of friends, a bright green praying mantis alighted on the straw in my iced coffee. Afterwards, I waded in the China Sea under a bright, hazy orange sunset. Throughout the trip, I was transfixed by the large golden Buddhas displayed in city squares. At the great Angkor Wat temple, I sat to meditate, but was overwhelmed with thoughts of my soon-to-be ex-husband, which I quickly pushed away.

At that time, no one understood the gravity of the new coronavirus. I asked some of my doctor friends if I should wear a mask on the plane ride home. Opinions were mixed. But walking through the airport, at least half the Asian travelers wore face coverings—an ominous sign of things to come. The airline announced they'd be randomly checking boarding passengers for signs of illness. When I was seated next to a man coughing, I anxiously demanded to be reseated.

Back home in Northern California, we were all still naïve and optimistic about this strange "flu." It seemed a distant threat. Soon, however, we started to hear about rising death counts in Italy and then in parts of California. The first inkling of our new normal came in early March, when the guy I was seeing wanted to have a party. I had started dating in a time frame that my professional self would've advised clients was "too soon." But since my ex had jumped into a new relationship and bypassed any grief process, why should *I* be left with the messy work of grief? I'd already done the bulk of the heavy lifting within the marriage. Of course, for me, as a grief counselor, this question was deeply ironic. But I was eager for fun. While I'd felt invisible as a fifty-something married woman, as soon as I was single men seemed to come out of the woodwork. Even if a man would just be gravy to my already full life, I was curious to discover my sexuality anew, more confidently in my fifties than in my twenties.

My guy friend's well-informed buddy, who was closely following the COVID-19 news about community spread, suggested it might be unwise to have a gathering, and so it was canceled. This would be the first of many cancellations, large and small: a lecture series I'd organized; a book tour; my daughter's final semester of high school; dance performances; and perhaps most painfully, her graduation ceremony.

Soon we went into lockdown. I'm ashamed to say that I was selfishly focused on my own ravaged heart. My guy was technically a senior citizen. As such, he was part of a vulnerable population. I decided, out of an abundance of caution, to maintain social distance. Not quite six feet, but no touching and certainly no more making out. He agreed with the arrangement. I missed our time cooking and cuddling together—a situation that had provided a soft landing from the domesticity I missed with my ex. Over the weeks of seeing each other less frequently—only for walks, with the awkward tension of no physical contact—this decreased intimacy resulted in the loss of what I'd hoped would develop into a true romance.

Like how the tongue can't avoid fiddling with the empty space when a tooth falls out, I felt the void of a partner like a fundamental part of me missing. The absence was a constant presence. I stared bereft at the new magenta lingerie I'd bought in the Taipei airport. I tried to watch sexy Netflix shows, but found myself drawn to shows about death, grief, and the Holocaust. Petting my cats for physical contact just didn't cut it. I read with interest that in the progressive Netherlands, single folks were advised to find a "seksbuddy." I went on Zoloft, hoping it would squash my libido as well as elevate my mood. I jealously followed friends' Facebook posts about their creative family pastimes, like dressing in flapper costumes to watch *Funny Girl*. Meanwhile, I tried to grab precious time with my teenage daughter when she wasn't isolating in her room, doing homework, snapchatting friends, and watching TV reruns.

Day blended into interminable day, as I did telehealth counseling from my couch, struggling to feel the connection I usually felt with my clients in my office. I considered myself a first responder in the mental health pandemic that resulted from the virus and was grateful to be working. And yet I felt empty, as did the encouraging words I mouthed to clients. I deal with crises, usually, by becoming engaged. After the 2016 election, I counseled my traumatized clients, blogged, made calls, and marched with Indivisible, organized a town hall, and wrote and edited a book. After the 2017 wildfires that devastated the Sonoma County community, I leapt into crisis counseling for local businesses, led meditations, taught self-care techniques in the community, and organized a forum for processing and healing. But the pandemic flattened me. I stared out my dirty window at my new hummingbird feeder, wondering why no birds came.

The awareness of others' pain pulled me lower as my guilt increased. Tens of thousands of New Yorkers were dying. Families detained at the Mexican border were suffering, separated. Latinos in my community were getting infected at four times the rate of whites. But I reminded myself of what I often tell my clients—that suffering is suffering and need not be compared. I didn't stitch masks or volunteer at our local food bank, both things I considered. All I could do was get through the days of counseling the folks for whom I was responsible—through their increased anxiety, panic, and depression—and make sure my daughter was coping. I was in bed by ten, often tossing and turning. While friends posted funny memes about gaining weight, I lost my appetite.

Desperate to feel better and regain a mind-set to support others, I listened to psychologists and spiritual leaders lecture about how this crisis was an opportunity to engage in deep soul searching. It was time for this therapist to "heal thyself." My pain wasn't the same as that of losing a loved one to COVID-19. But losing a partner of twenty-two years overnight was traumatic nonetheless. I needed to face that reality in order for healing to begin. I found my unprocessed grief banging at the doors of my consciousness. My feminist self encountered the child-like part of myself that had been brainwashed by fairy tales and romcoms to believe that happy endings always involve a man. I talked to my own therapist and administered trauma-processing techniques on myself. I journaled, art journaled, and cried. And cried some more.

I revved up my meditation practice. I was reminded by my Buddhist teachers that impermanence is inevitable, as is suffering, but that mindfulness can lead to equanimity. When I focused on the here and now—the butterfly alighting on the lilac bush next to the creek near my condo, swaying in my hammock and counting my breaths, laughing with my daughter while playing a board game, making blueberry scones—I felt better. My beloved yoga teacher started leading Zoom classes from Hawaii, and her flows calmed my body and mind. I picked up my guitar for the first time in years and let the whimsical lyrics of Cat Stevens, Jim Croce, and Phil Ochs replace my endlessly looping sad thoughts. As I reached out to nurturing friends past and present, I began to feel less alone.

Among all the images and stories of death that surround me, I am slowly grieving my old life. As society enters a new COVID-19 reality, negotiating what life will look like in this new terrain, I am figuring out what my new single, soon-to-be empty-nest life will look like. And I am reminded that grief is simply love with nowhere to land. And lord knows, this world desperately needs more love.

꩜

Alissa Hirshfeld is a psychotherapist and writer. She is the co-editor of *Fury: Women's Lived Experiences During the Trump Era*, as well as the author of a novel, *Living Waters: From Harvard Halls to Sacred Falls*, and a memoir, *This Whole Wide World is Just a Narrow Bridge*. Her academic articles have appeared in several psychological journals.

Lost Woman

Angel King Wilson

The first week of quarantine, I smoke a blunt every day, nap three times per day, discover new genres of porn, and cook recipes I find on YouTube. The amount of time that I am spending at home gives me a newfound sense of curiosity.

The second week, my manager calls to check on me, and within five minutes of our conversation, I am sobbing on the phone. I sit on the carpeted floor of my bedroom with my back against the wall. I hold the phone to my ear and pace myself so that I can articulate words.

"I'm fine. I don't even know why I'm crying," I lie.

She says to me, "Angel, sometimes we have to be each other's pillows. The tears will come when we feel safe."

I cry because she is the first person to sense the imbalance in my personality. Before her call, I thought I was absolutely content. I am stocked up on groceries, tissue, soap, and I am still being compensated for both of my jobs. Yet my mental health is in jeopardy.

Another week passes and I have now grown bored with the stimulation of porn and weed, so I quit. If the time length of the quarantine is uncertain, I know I cannot spend my days sleeping and masturbating. The withdrawals from weed include crying every morning, even if I find myself wiping away a few tears before getting out of bed. I wail in the shower for the first time in my life. It is therapeutic, but I wonder where this pain had been hiding.

I knew it was always there. Over the past three years, I had been to three therapists, but I would cancel treatment after two or three sessions. One was overly talkative, the other seemed distracted with her own thoughts, and the last one kept asking, "Are you sure you don't want to try meds?"

These days and weeks of forced alone-time in my one bedroom apartment is forcing me to face myself. The business of life no longer consumes my thoughts: getting dressed for work, preparing lesson plans for college freshmen and for an after school program, complaining about coworkers, and buying or cooking dinner. It is only me and I am my own enemy.

The week before the quarantine, I became single after my partner ended our on-again/off-again five-year relationship. His decision left me perplexed because I thought I was practically perfect. Deep down, I knew I had my faults, but pride had stunted my growth. Usually, I would have persisted with my stubbornness, but time and sobriety made me want to understand the reasons for my hardened heart.

I began watching YouTube videos on "divine feminine energy" in an attempt to heal the part of me that embodied my stoic and egotistic personality, and in a desire to feel womanly. One video per day—heal your feminine energy, how to speak feminine, femininity in the workplace, use feminine energy to attract a man, and so on.

I have entered a world that was never taught to me, a world that doesn't require me to be the strong Black woman who suffers from self-doubt, low self-esteem, and anger. It is the opposite of the ideals I learned in our feminist-driven culture.

At a young age I learned that success and independence were topnotch goals for Black women. In third grade I knew every word to the Destiny's Child song, "Independent Woman." My friends and I sang along, and the lyrics made us want to grow up to become ladies who were liberated, self-sufficient, and confident. The women in my family and in my small church lived by this code of independence—take care of yourself and work hard; and most importantly, they always taught me, a woman does not need a man for anything. This code influenced my belief that independence would bring me material possessions that, in turn, would lead to everlasting happiness. Yet, I have learned that this life is more exhausting than it is rewarding. A new curiosity, during quarantine, has dared me to peer into a life that was outside of what I learned it meant to be a *real* woman. I found myself wrestling with the question—what does it mean to be a real woman? Is it to be a wife and homemaker who can cook, take care of, and educate her children? Or is it independently paying bills, affording a luxurious lifestyle, and obtaining multiple academic degrees?

Because many people are legally confined to their homes, I question if our society has minimized the significance of the feminine and traditional family values. I wonder if my unhappiness, unsuccessful relationships, and exhaustion stem from a lack of femininity? I find myself desperate for answers to these questions.

So, in the eighth week of quarantine, I pay three hundred fifty dollars to enroll in an online class titled, "School of Affluence." The program focuses on fostering personal elegance, grace, and class. The purchase takes five seconds and I wonder, still, if I am *really* serious about an inner transformation. The class presents sixty-six videos, seven workbooks, an e-book titled, *How to be Classy*, and access to a Facebook group of women who share the same desire to become a more elegant version of themselves.

In one week, I have finished chapter one of the e-book, and I have watched the first module of four videos. I feel as if I am growing like a butterfly, slowly and frighteningly forcing my way out of a cocoon. I am shedding an old skin and learning to create my own definition of womanhood. I will not attribute this growth to the "School of Affluence," but to the current quarantine.

Every day I am more curious and I continue to evolve. I am unlearning the ideal that a woman is required to fit a mold. It is more important that I learn to become my own woman and define the type of woman that is true to me, whether feminine, masculine, or aspects of both. I am healing the part of me that had accepted conceit and rigidity as normal behavior. I am also embracing the part of me that desires to be gentle and vulnerable.

I wonder who I will be next week.

❧

Angel King Wilson is an author, activist, and educator from Baltimore, MD. She is an English Adjunct Professor at Baltimore City Community College and the Lead Creative Writing teacher Greenmount West Community Center. Angel's work has appeared in the *Baltimore Sun* and *The Real News Network*. She published her first book, *Am I Doing This Right?* in May 2019.

F.E.A.R.

Bianca Sabogal

One night in March 2020

It's three a.m. in my dark, quiet apartment. I awake to a piercing pain in my abdomen. Alone, frightened, and confused, I head toward my bathroom, trying to avoid waking my sleeping fiancé, Ryan. My thoughts race as I sit on the toilet, pain searing through me. The scattered patterns of pink and red flowers on the shower curtain I bought at the Dollar Tree have a fuzzy, blurry look to them now. I try my best to bring them back into focus, but I can't. I feel my body overheating. Fear and panic spreads its tentacles from my mind down to my toes. Giving up on the toilet, I splash cold water on my face. A pale, physically stressed woman gazes back at me in the mirror. Seconds later, I wake to a crashing sound. I'm flat on the floor. Fainted.

Ryan's voice calls out. "Are you okay? What was that noise?"

Ryan and I are raising my son, now thirteen, and it's a joyful experience for both of us. We are eager to expand the family and have already faced one pregnancy loss, so each jab in my side fills me with dread. But I'm not pregnant, I remind myself. What else can it be? Embarrassed, I reply, "Yes, babe, I'm okay."

I tell myself that if I don't speak *it* into existence, whatever *it* is will disappear. I head into my war of fear vs. denial. I suit up in my emotional camouflage, ready for mental warfare. I bury myself within the dunes; my kevlar helmet is securely fastened; weapon in hand, I brace myself for the unknown, waiting for me on the other side.

I'm a daddy's girl, and Pop was a Marine. I've always admired the way he marched through life, head high and eyes forward, prepared to brave the toughest conditions, both physically and emotionally. Being a first-generation Colombian-American citizen, his childhood wasn't easy. My five-foot-tall, Spanish-speaking grandmother raised five children on her own in a two-bedroom apartment in Westchester, New York. Hard circumstances formed the foundation on which my family built their lives. My dad looked up to my grandmother through the same lens I see him through. She was a soldier too.

My pop has been a mail carrier for thirty-five years, starting from the time he was honorably discharged from the Marines. Shortly after coming home, he married my mother and they got pregnant with me. Later in life, I found out my father has a degree in accounting but chose to remain an employee at the post office to provide and care for our family. Growing up, I watched his every move. Mornings he would come into my room to wake me up for school, always dressed in his pale blue collared shirt, tucked into his pressed navy blue pants, with the long black stripe down the side. It was his uniform for life. He is a man of few words, keeping his deepest feelings to himself.

"Don't let it get to you," was his response to my teenage conflicts and adversities. He would say this with love and conviction. Telling me to believe him and trust him. I wanted to, but I never seemed capable. I developed a distorted understanding of what it meant to cope, telling myself "it" (life, stress, anxiety, or fear) wasn't getting to me. Though on the contrary, "it" was making me uncomfortable, crippling me at times.

I have been in recovery, free from relying on drugs to face painful circumstances, for over five years now. I've been taught that dishonesty and denial keep us sick, and that pain shared is pain lessened. I know that there are two options in response to fear: Face everything and recover, or fuck everything and run. In this case, I choose to run—to the living room couch. I hope if I don't acknowledge the exact nature of my physical pain, it might go away. "Don't let it get to you, Bianca."

I recline on my plush couch and take a minute to breathe. I close my eyes and pray. "Please, God, whatever is happening inside of my body, let me be okay. I'm scared. Thank you for the level of relief you have given me for this moment. Amen." Eyes open, I find a seed of faith but still feel fear. Maybe fear is always there, but sometimes it stays to the side?

My dog, Lolo, reigns in the living room in the late-night hours. I find comfort in stroking the top of her soft little head. I tell her that mommy is in pain, but that I'll be okay. The look in her eyes gives me enough love to fall asleep, fertilizing the seed of faith that I am holding on to.

My "fuck everything and run" mind-set does me no good. The

morning arrives, and the pain has not abated. Thoughts of an ectopic pregnancy rent space in my mind. I recently experienced my best friend's fight for her life after having an ectopic pregnancy. I vividly remember the phone call, hearing her panicked voice. She was taken by ambulance to the emergency room, after fainting in her shower with excruciating pain. I am comparing my situation with hers with growing concern.

Ryan drives me to the emergency room, where we encounter a nurse, blocking the doorway with a mask, clipboard, and pen in hand. "Do you have a fever? Have you been in contact with anyone with COVID-19? Have you traveled outside of the country within the last fourteen days?"

I understand the effect that this virus is having on our hospitals, the staff, and society. I understand that New York's numbers are high and this woman has a job to do, instructions to follow. But my usual uber-polite self has no patience left, just fear and pain.

"No, no, and no. Lady, I'm in pain. I believe it's an ectopic pregnancy and I don't want to die, so please let me through."

I regret my attitude once I am escorted to a bed behind a curtain, where I wait for care. After my years of working as a CNA and going through fieldwork semesters for Occupational Therapy, the hospital setting is an easy one for me to navigate. I know the routine, the waiting, the vitals, how to be still and listen to other patrons in pain and discomfort.

Hours later, Ryan and I leave the hospital with stunning news. I might be carrying a "viable pregnancy." My pain is due to a hemorrhagic cyst in my right ovary, about the size of the baseball displayed on the windowsill in Isaiah's room from a game he won. Should we be happy or scared? Or both?

My recent previous pregnancy ended in five weeks. I will never forget the feelings of sadness we experienced when Ryan and I noticed that there was no more flutter of a heartbeat on the sonogram screen. The ultrasound tech shot us a quick "Good luck" and fled the room, leaving us in shock. My pregnancy with Isaiah, thirteen years ago, was far from a walk in the park. I was seventeen, beginning my senior year in an alternative school, and heavily into drugs when I found out I was pregnant. My life was upside down and a slice of hell at one point. It can still be hard now, but I'm clean, with a newly obtained degree, and we just furnished our first apartment with furniture and succulents.

About four months into my pregnancy with Isaiah, I got the phone call from the doctor telling me something was wrong. My sonogram showed I had a weak cervix, and it was already dilated half a centimeter. I had completely detoxed by then. For the remaining months of my pregnancy I was instructed to lie in a reclined position in my room at the Westchester Medical Center. My responsibility was to keep Isaiah in my belly for as long as I could. Flushed with feelings of loneliness and fear, but determined to protect my child, I followed orders and entertained myself with replays of *Law & Order* and *Charmed*. I was a scared little girl in that hospital gown.

Now, juggling my painful cyst and "possibly" viable pregnancy, back to the couch I go. For the next few weeks I return to the dreaded, somewhat worrisome medical arena for further testing and monitoring. I survive lack of sleep, discomfort, and, yes, emotional warfare. Ryan and I pray vigilantly. We pray for a healthy pregnancy, for acceptance of the outcome, for comfort. We pray for God's will. We keep praying.

The pandemic, and most importantly the shelter-in-place, allow me to retreat and put myself on bed rest. My projections about this pregnancy frighten me. My only success at bringing a pregnancy to term has been behind a curtain in a hospital bed. I'm fearful of repeating this experience, only this time I won't have any visitors. I'll be alone, in a mask. The hospital isn't a place of safety anymore; it's a place of uncertainty and the home to a vicious virus, disabling its victims at a rapid rate. On top of that, I am a member of the "at risk" population, part of the "compromised immune system" club for another underlying condition. I feel like a stubborn child, stomping my feet at God, telling him I don't want to spend my pregnancy in a hospital. I don't want to catch this deadly virus. I need a healthy body and a fighting chance to introduce our new baby into this world. Too many people are dying alone. I don't want to be a number added to the count.

I'm not there yet. Today I am out of work due to New York State lockdown guidelines, which means I have all the time in the world to be good to Bianca, and her body. I rest, eat, pray, and make my recovery meetings via a virtual platform. The meetings restore me to sanity. I feel secure, seeing familiar faces in the small Zoom boxes on the screen as the meeting begins. I wave to them as if they're all looking at me. A banner with twelve steps and traditions hangs on a wall, behind a stranger turned friend. I process feelings and slowly strip away my emotional camouflage. Piece by piece, I remove my layers. I am Facing Everything And Recovering.

It is now late May, and we are turning the corner to begin my fourteenth week of a healthy pregnancy. I'm sitting at my dining room table, with my legs elevated on the chair across from me, a posture full of relaxation and peace. The sun beams through my living room window, spreading love and light onto the same couch where I cried in fear three months ago. What was once my battleground has returned to be a part of my sanctuary, my safe place, a place of deep prayer and gratitude. My lovely Lolo is fast asleep there, without the worry that I witnessed in her hazel eyes that night. In the months that have passed we have grieved as a country and as a family for loved ones; we have watched the numbers rise, the world shut down. And still our child grows.

My spirit is lifted by the sound of birds chirping outside, and the thought of the beautiful days ahead. I look down to see the protruding bump coming from my abdomen. I am no longer in pain. I am in love.

I come back full circle, to Pop's words: "Don't let it get to you." The meaning has changed for me. Though I may not march through the darkest of times gracefully, as I imagine he does, I don't stop marching. I don't let "it" defeat me. Not fear, not pain, and definitely not a pandemic.

ॐ

Bianca Sabogal is a Colombian American woman residing in Warwick, New York, with her fiancé Ryan, and son Isaiah. Bianca has an A.A.S. in Occupational Therapy and is an active member of the recovery community. Ryan and Bianca have over five years clean and are expecting their first child.

Breathe Easy and Other Stories of Healing

Breathe Easy

Pia Wood

I find myself again in the hospital. The same hospital where I gave birth to both my daughters, where I was once admitted for two days for a blood transfusion related to severe loss of blood at menopause. The hospital I had been rushed to three days prior because I could barely lift my head to breathe; the hospital where I am diagnosed with Covid-19 and pneumonia; the hospital where I remained on the Covid-19 ward for three days, before moving to a general ward. Here I am with patients with positive health markers, who are on the mend from Covid-19. My nurse enters the room, passing the patient lying in a bed closest to the door. He is dressed in standard green scrubs with the top of his white undershirt peeking from the V-neck top. He wears an aqua-blue bonnet over his hair, light blue latex gloves cover his hands, and a white mask covers his mouth and nose.

He cheerily says hello, his eyes smiling at me. He identifies himself as my nurse, but more importantly he emphatically insists that I call him Joe. Although he is wearing a mask, his smile genuinely shines from his eyes. Joe lifts the window shade so that I can get some natural light and apologizes that my view from the bed is another NYC building. "So, how are you doing?" he asks.

"Okay," I answer weakly. Then he says the most startling thing. Something I didn't even realize my soul has been longing to hear.

"How is your spirit?"

Tears come to my eyes and fall down my unmasked face. Nurse Joe takes my hand and gently squeezes it as if I am a good and trusted friend. With tender eyes he tells me everything will be okay. Joe walks to my chart board posted on the wall and grabs the black marker. He writes on the white board:

Today: March 23
Nurse Joe (two hearts and a peace sign are drawn):
Plan for the Day: Breathe Easy

That plan gets me through the next few days, till discharge.

Of course, being home is not the same as being well.

The first food that I cook for myself, once I can actually stand up, is a pot of Cream of Wheat cereal. I place the pot on the burner of the stove, turn the flame to a medium setting, then rest at my table for a few minutes, waiting to hear the water bubbling. I pour the Cream of Wheat cereal into the pot without measuring how much is poured, grab my wooden spoon and stir as the cereal is absorbed into the water. I watch the mixture thicken and become creamy quickly. I pour the steaming cereal into a bowl. *I am taking care of myself.* I forgo a splash of milk, a dab of butter, or a dash of vanilla extract. Just a spoonful of honey stirred in. It is simply delicious. My stomach thanks me. I smile because of what I have just accomplished. I polish off the bowl of cereal. A first in some time.

I don't have an appetite yet but I know I must feed myself. Nourish my body. Nourish my soul. Nourish my heart. Meals are delivered to my door by concerned and loving neighbors. One neighbor brings her Greek lentil soup with kale. I said I liked it, but in truth I couldn't taste the spices, only her love. My brother drops off some General Tso's chicken from the restaurant I like, but I can't taste the sweet or the spicy flavors.

My daughters, one in North Carolina and the other in London, order me food via their apps like Grubhub. But when the food is delivered there is no hunger to feed, no appetite to fill. My mind thinks about being pregnant, when for six months, my body was one giant appetite. I remember Easter Sundays when I would revel in chocolate bunnies, after forty days of Lent.

A week after my Cream of Wheat, the extraordinary occurs. I can smell steak and onions. I had prepared the dish the night before. I reheat it for my dinner and it smells like childhood. It smells like a familiar friend. Once I taste the gravy and the slippery, spicy onions on my tongue with the soft grains of rice mixed in my mouth, I become elated-happy. Not only that, "I put my foot in it," as they say in the African American community, when your food tastes so good, so off the chain—so dope you don't need any other compliment. I rush through the meal thinking my taste buds may disappear again, and yet I manage to savor every bite. I am back in the saddle.

All of the meals after that, still in self-quarantine, are simple dishes that remind me of childhood. They are healthy meals prepared with my own hands. I cook each meal out of self-love, new love, and old love. Cooking becomes my therapy.

At a time of uncertainty each meal takes me to a place of certainty during this healing period. Each of these meals reminds me of childhood, of a time when my family ate together and ate simple meals. Besides simple, they were small. No extra portions. We broke bread together to laugh or complain or give thanks for another day lived. Food after this pandemic, and our appreciation of it, should be viewed this way—with deep gratitude.

Tonight is the day before Easter, 2020. I plan on making a lemon roast chicken, some collard greens, and potato salad. Yeah, I am about to put my foot in it. There will be one serving. No seconds. And small portions. Comfort food. Soul food. Heart Food. I sit back with this menu in mind and breathe easy.

❧

Pia Wood resides in Brooklyn, New York. She is an attorney. She is the proud mother of two daughters and the proud grandmother of two granddaughters. Pia describes herself as a Gullah-Abanaki to pay tribute to both her mother's southern cultural roots and her father's Native American cultural roots.

Cold Front

Nikki Kallio

My parents are homesteading again in retirement, and one day in April 2020, they are in the yard cutting apart fallen trees and clearing out branches. It's the mess left by several storms, including a tornado that swept through our community the previous summer, two days before my surgery for ovarian cancer.

Those literal and figurative twisters had left us shaken and without power, forcing improvisation around food and water and emotion within a compact ball of time. A bubble of chaos pressing from every direction: a car breakdown on the same day as the tornado; my father collapsing from seized back muscles while waiting in the hospital; my mother floating between my recovery room and his emergency-room bed, ferrying us separately—in my car—the hour and a half drive between home and hospital.

The six rounds of chemo treatment that followed led into the new year and left us collectively weary, and we awaited spring—a time of recovery, renewal, and new beginnings.

I walk out to our mailboxes and retrieve a package from theirs, junk mail from mine, wondering whether I should have worn gloves. My parents' ages and my condition make us all high risk for COVID-19. I set the mail on the sun-washed stone walkway that leads to their house and sit, running a hand over my hair, growing now so that people's eyes assess me: *Does she have cancer or is she just butch?* My baldness had seemed to offer license for people to strike up a conversation about cancer, about a relative's cancer, alternative treatment options I might want to try, advice on my septic system, what my staging and prognosis was, and how I felt.

I'm youngish, so often one of the first questions is whether I have a gene mutation that gives me a propensity toward cancer. It's an intrusive question designed to provide relief to the questioner. I tell them the truth—that most people who develop cancer have no such gene mutation. It's not what they want to hear, but I can only manage my own feelings right now.

༄

A few days after a follow-up appointment in April—at a different hospital, an hour's drive from my home—I grab a paper towel, then grab the gas pump. It's one of those first days of spring in the upper Midwest when a jacket isn't strictly necessary, but it's sitting on the passenger seat next to the hand sanitizer. I've worn gloves at this gas station before, but a nurse at the oncologist's office told me I'm just cross-contaminating everything. I'm not sure what to believe. I feel exposed and vulnerable. Things seem off-kilter, familiar and also not at all. I check to make sure the pump is working right because the price doesn't seem to be spinning up like usual, and I realize the gas is just that cheap right now.

The outdoor Muzak at the gas station plays the 1980s Glenn Frey song "The Heat is On."

I think about the 1980s-themed party I had planned for the weekend to celebrate a milestone birthday, not to mention surviving cancer, twice.

Are you still having your party? friends texted. *Maybe later.* A trip to New York. *Canceled.* A friend's wedding, *postponed.* During my master of fine arts program, I had written a manuscript, somewhat presciently, about a seventeen-year-old protagonist who had survived a personal disaster and was now living amid a global one. So my mind strays to what high school kids must be missing these days—the devastation of losing long-awaited rite-of-passage events—graduations, proms, end-of-year parties. *Nope.*

In the grand scheme, they're not-so-big things, but they are bell-wethers of greater change, the ripple currents of worldwide suffering.

I finish paying. I touch the keypad with my middle finger and then reach for my hand sanitizer.

༄

In Jim Crace's futuristic disaster novel *The Pesthouse*, a protagonist's shaved head marks her as having a plague, causing people to shun her, sometimes violently. My baldness had the opposite effect. I told my friend about the woman on the beach who stopped to ask me why I had no hair.

"You must have to deal with so many indignities in addition to your illness," my friend said.

It's true, because even with hats and wigs, it's tough to keep my ordeal private. On the flip side, it's caused people to be kinder, in some cases, perhaps like the old days, when people wore black armbands while mourning. If we all had some way of showing what difficulties we're suffering, would we be nicer to each other?

This friend and I talked about this while overlooking the Florida beach where we'd come for a quick getaway, just before the national emergency.

"What do you think about all this?" my friend asks.

"I'm probably not as worried as I should be," I say. I've had to navigate periods of low immunity for the past four months. I've had to ask friends and family to get their flu shot, if they wanted to visit me. I've had to wear masks and gloves while traveling or shopping. Old hat.

We talk about alternative things I can say the next time people ask about my hair. We have fun with this, imagining people's reactions to explanations involving parasites or impulsivity.

For real, I have a friend who shaved her head after Justice Kavanaugh was appointed to the Supreme Court.

Because something had to give.

I set my parents' mail down on the stone walkway and sit next to it. I recall it's the same place where I'd collapsed, weeping, after fussy preparation and self-imposed delays for a trip to the post office made me conclude that I was afraid to go. Since the stay-at-home shutdown, I'd been combating anxiety that manifested in fears of recurrence. I kept turning my mind to the evidence: a clear scan, great blood tests. My medical team wanted to remove my chemotherapy port. That procedure in itself caused anxiety—it involved a trip to the hospital, for one thing, and for another, no one could accompany me. It seemed nonessential, but it was a minor procedure that needed one nurse practitioner and very little equipment. They didn't even put me under for it, involving an incision near my clavicle and some cutting away of tissue. The idea of it had terrified me to the point of tears.

Once, I'd had a stereotactic biopsy where the lidocaine didn't take. Without the benefit of proper numbing, I had a hollow needle shot into my breast.

That had happened during the first cancer, seven years earlier. Perhaps the saving grace was that if I hadn't had breast cancer, we wouldn't have been watching for ovarian. "You're so brave," people tell me, and I feel like a fraud. "You're an inspiration," people say, and I feel like a magical fucking unicorn.

Anxiety is not rational, but it is natural. I'd just been through a trauma, and now, like the protagonist in my creative thesis, I was also thrown into a worldwide ordeal. In a virtual doctor's visit, I connected to my primary care physician through tinny, delayed video. I got a prescription. I meditated. I kept telling myself that my body had anxiety inside it, but no cancer. I focused on what can heal me: healthy foods; hikes in a nearby state park; quiet time resting with my cat, Rocket, a sociable lynx-point Siamese, a miniature mountain lion. Eventually the tenacious feeling began to let go.

My mother stops clearing branches and wanders over to where I'm sitting on the walkway, and my father follows suit. My mother sits on a higher step, my father on a nearby decorative bale of hay. We are a "quaranteam," but try to distance properly since I'd been to the hospital.

They talk about the president's recent idea about injecting disinfectant into our bodies to kill the coronavirus. We look around as if there's someone to explain.

I had plans to celebrate the end of chemotherapy, including a trip in early March. At that time, at least in the rural Midwest, a global pandemic still felt like a nebulous concept. Businesses were starting to set hand sanitizer out, but that was about it. I caught wind of concern in messages from friends in Seattle and overseas, but I was already taking precautions with travel, so I felt safe leaving on March 9 for a short beach getaway. That day, there were 148 deaths from coronavirus reported in the U.S. I was the only one on the crowded plane wearing a mask.

While my friend and I knew coronavirus was happening, a personal sense of urgency hadn't settled in yet. We remained blissfully disconnected on the beach, but a few nervous text messages started to clue us in to university closures and travel disruptions. As late as Thursday, March 12, my town's local weekly newspaper featured the headline, "COVID-19 risk for exposure still low here." That same day, on our way home from Florida, my friend and I ate dinner together in a crowded airport and departed on different flights for the Midwest, largely unaware that we were returning to a different world. A few more people were wearing masks. "Don't sit on the chairs," a father said to his child. "And don't touch anything." The child said something unintelligible. "Okay, well, sit, but DON'T-TOUCH-ANYTHING."

My flight was delayed and delayed again, so I arrived home on Friday, March 13, the day a national emergency was declared.

My ninety-five-year-old grandmother lives near the airport, so I stopped to visit her that day. Looking back, I shouldn't have done it. My grandma's apartment managers had issued a letter, which sat on her kitchen table, stating that there were to be no visitors if they have been out of state within the past fourteen days. I thought of the spring breakers coughing into tissues that they'd left wadded up in the terminal. I'd already given my grandmother a hug.

I showed her the letter. She made a disparaging sound. She had been a Rosie the Riveter, she raised four boys and made her own clothes. She lost one of her sons to cancer; a granddaughter to a head-on collision. A letter telling her who could visit? No, thank you.

My uncle was there that day too, so we took her shopping for supplies. At the grocery store, signs over the bulk food items told us that we were not to self-serve, that we were to get an employee to fill bags for us. "That's bull-crap," my uncle said. "I just saw that guy rubbing his nose."

We took my grandmother to Walgreens for her prescription. The shelves, we already knew, would have no toilet paper.

On the drive home that day, I listened to the White House press conference declaring a national emergency. PBS NewsHour's Yamiche Alcindor asks the president why he closed the pandemic office in 2018, losing valuable response time. "Well, I just think it's a nasty question," he says.

On the PBS NewsHour, conservative commentator David Brooks appears visibly angry. "I found it an enraging week," he says. "Frankly, this is what happens when you elect a sociopath." Anchor Judy Woodruff entreats us to watch out not only for our own families, but for those who are vulnerable and need us to watch out for them.

Later, my grandma's apartment is locked down because of a corona-virus case. There are rumors about its having been a lady who delivered Easter baskets to everyone, but it wasn't that lady, it was someone else. When I find out my grandma doesn't have any masks, I send her some disposable ones. When the apartment was given the all-clear, she tells me she wore one of the masks to collect a shopping cart from the basement, bring it back to her apartment, and use it to dispose of six weeks' worth of garbage. *Six weeks*. No one had been allowed to visit, so there had been no one to help her take it out, and apparently the apartment had had no plan.

I sometimes dream of tornadoes. Not the one that came through here, but other ones, always different. I dream of them more in times of upheaval, and I read somewhere that the dream symbolism is *change*. I have these dreams now and others that I can't remember. I am manag-ing fatigue in my recovery, so I sleep often.

My cat, Rocket, curls up on my stomach. We're still together when I wake up inside the dream, lying in grass on an island full of wild beasts where I've been sent by an unknown *they*, a game to try to survive. There are wild and hungry animals around. A lioness ambles over to where Rocket and I are lying in the warm grass. She strolls a tight circle around us. Rocket doesn't move.

Be still, he tells me telepathically. *Be still.*

Nikki Kallio's creative work has appeared in *Minerva Rising, Midwestern Gothic* and elsewhere. Brain Mill Press shortlisted her novella manu-script *The Fledgling* in its 2018 Unsolicited Novella Contest, and she is a winner of the Wisconsin People & Ideas Contest. She has an MFA from Goddard College.

ED-19

Camille Beredjick

During the height of the COVID-19 crisis, amid mandatory shelter-in-place orders and New York City's round-the-clock chorus of blaring sirens, I started running. I wore a mask and avoided other people, but the risk that running posed to my health went beyond the virus.

My pre-COVID exercise routine consisted of some cardio and some strength training a few nights a week at the gym. Gyms, of course, were among the first establishments to shut down. Hotbeds of germs and cross-contamination that they are, I didn't really mind.

About two weeks into quarantine, as I was starting to go stir-crazy, I went for a three-mile run along the shady, tree-lined parkway near my apartment. My body wasn't used to running on pavement, or outside the comfortable blanket of air conditioning. Back at my apartment, I had to lie on the floor afterwards and massage my ropey calves back to life before my body could hoist itself into the shower. Three months in, I can run four or five miles and then carry on with my day—no floor time required.

For someone else, running might be a solace during this brain-melting time, something to look forward to after a long day. And I do—to an extent. More salient, unfortunately, is the menacing whisper in my head telling me that if I don't run a certain number of days a week, if I don't stick to the schedule, I'll end up "letting myself go" (whatever that means). When I grab a Rice Krispie Treat from the cabinet after dinner, my eyes drift to the nutrition facts on the back, calculating how long it will take to "run it off." In mere weeks, a healthy outdoor activity transformed into yet another obsessive ritual. That's how mental illness works: it sneaks up on you when you're vulnerable, twisting your pleasures and sacred spaces into coves of fear and shame.

I haven't considered myself anorexic in years, but recovering from an eating disorder is less like a light switch and more like a dimmer. The line between recovery and relapse loops, twists, and fades; "how

I'm doing" varies a lot from day to day. Before the pandemic broke out and ushered us all indoors, I ate well, worked out a couple of times a week, and went to the office in clothes that made me feel confident and strong. I managed.

But COVID-19 rattled my recovery routine, taking away my carefully curated coping mechanisms. Instead, I look directly at my mental illness—through a blurry front-facing laptop camera—for several hours of every day. When the workday is over, I can't scroll through Facebook without glimpsing memes about the "Quarantine 15" or hot takes about Adele's weight loss. Socially isolating in my apartment has given me a lot more quality time with my wife, but it's also stripped me of the opportunity to practice being better in public, something that's crucial to recovering from any mental illness. I feel as if I've taken a dozen steps backward.

Before the pandemic I was in year five of recovering from an eating disorder. I thought constantly about what my body looked like and what others thought of it, but I could quiet the critical voices in my head enough to eat, move, and live how I wanted.

In the midst of the pandemic, I'm not sure what recovery means anymore.

As early as April, experts predicted that mental illness would be the "next wave" of the COVID-19 crisis.[9] Indeed, mental illness is creeping up in new waves for people who have never experienced it before, and for those of us already afflicted, it's worsening. The Substance Abuse and Mental Health Services Administration's Disaster Distress Helpline experienced a staggering 891 percent increase in calls in March 2020, compared to the same month of the previous year.[10] Mental Health America saw higher screenings for clinical anxiety that February and March. Eating disorder charities have seen spikes in outreach, too.[11]

Reading these stats as the pandemic unfolded reminded me of the last crisis whiplash we faced: the days and weeks after the 2016 election, when hotline calls to LGBTQ advocacy groups like The Trevor Project[12]

[9] https://www.cbc.ca/news/canada/british-columbia/months-isolation-mental-health-covid-1.5521649

[10] https://abcnews.go.com/Politics/calls-us-helpline-jump-891-white-house-warned/story?id=70010113

[11] https://www.theguardian.com/society/2020/may/17/like-losing-control-fears-eating-disorders-on-rise-amid-lockdown

[12] https://www.thetrevorproject.org/trvr_press/crisis-contacts-from-youth-to-

and Trans Lifeline surged.[13] There are many reasons for heightened emotional and mental distress right now: worrying about ourselves and our loved ones getting sick, mandatory social isolation away from our support circles, stress about the economic impact of the virus, and the unending barrage of pessimistic news coverage, to name a few. It's no wonder incidences of mental illness are high across the globe.[14]

But talking about mental illness remains stigmatized in too many communities and circles, keeping us from seeking the support we need even in normal, non-pandemic circumstances. So many of us are barely hanging on, but we're terrified to talk about it, cognizant of how much worse things could be. Even I feel silly complaining; my mental health is in terrible shape, but I have a job, a decently sized apartment, a loving wife. Every week I tell my therapist on the phone that I can't believe I'm preoccupied with my eating disorder when so many people are experiencing this pandemic in deadlier ways than I am. There's a voice in the back of my head telling me not to say anything at all, to crumple my issues into a tiny ball nobody can see.

I've always felt safest when I take up less space; I think a lot of women do. That feeling plagued me when I was still closeted and couldn't bear to tell anyone I was queer—at my first job as an assistant trying to prove herself to the men in charge; and most certainly at the height of my anorexia. Shrinking into the background is a precautionary measure; danger can't find me if it can't see me.

That's what's so risky about dealing with a pandemic while having a mental illness: Keeping away from others is life-saving and life-threatening at the same time. When my anorexia was at its most insidious, isolation allowed me to fall deeper and deeper into the disease until I couldn't pull myself out. I ate all my meals alone, and nobody noticed when they got smaller and smaller. I exercised alone for two hours a day, with nobody there to tell me it was time to stop. For people living through eating disorders, this kind of isolation makes it impossibly easy to fall back into old, dangerous habits, with no one the wiser. Staying apart is necessary right now in order to keep ourselves and our communities healthy, but it has severe consequences.

I'm incredibly lucky to share a home with my wife, a supportive

the-trevor-project-surge-immediately-following-the-election/

[13] https://www.out.com/news-opinion/2016/11/10/trans-hotline-receives-record-number-calls-after-trumps-election

[14] https://www.cnn.com/2020/05/14/health/un-coronavirus-mental-health/index.html

partner in my recovery who reassures me that I'm not going through this alone. But sometimes on my runs outside, I still feel like that twenty-two-year-old version of me staying late at the gym, flying on a treadmill for hours at a time, surviving off bananas and dry lettuce. Shrinking and shrinking. Exposed and invisible all at the same time. As we crawl through this pandemic, my heart is heavy for the millions like me who are finding themselves alone again, months or years into their own recovery. I'm devastated and I'm angry that something out of our control has set so many of us back.

Transitioning to virtual recovery need not be impossible. Therapists can take phone appointments; medication can be delivered to our doorsteps. But what we are missing is the safety net of public social accountability, the power of entering public spaces armed with our coping mechanisms and our toolkits and taking on the world, one step at a time. You can't practice eating at the office lunch table in quarantine. You can't work on your social anxiety by striking up a conversation at a party, or tackle your claustrophobia by meditating on your morning subway commute. Coping with mental illness requires a carefully considered routine, cues to follow, and tactics to employ—and right now, we can't employ them.

Women in particular are privy to fears and anxieties related to how we're perceived by the world. From the time we're born, we're conditioned to distort ourselves in order to accommodate those around us and encouraged to take up less space so that those nearby might not be rendered uncomfortable by our wholeness. It takes a lifetime to unlearn these habits and patterns, and it requires constant reinforcement.

At the height of my anorexia, I didn't look like the wispy, rail-thin figure we've come to associate as the marker of an eating disorder. You wouldn't have known anything was wrong unless you'd asked. When we emerge from this socially distant world, my loved ones will have no idea how I fared, apart from cursory updates over Zoom calls and quick check-in texts. Our current circumstances are the perfect pressure cooker for keeping mental illnesses to ourselves instead of getting the help we need.

I'm scared of what it will be like to emerge into the light again—to be seen by those who have only looked at me through a camera lens for months. How long will it take to adjust to the hustle of a morning subway commute squished into dozens of sweaty New Yorkers; to the feeling of eating a to-go salad at my desk in front of my coworkers; to the exhaustion of having to perform for ten hours a day? I'm so excited to see my loved ones again, but terrified they will notice changes in my body that even I haven't caught. I can't wait for this to be over, and I'm scared I won't be able to handle it.

I think about how my community of women with mental illnesses is coping—especially queer women, women of color, and others living on multiple margins—and how we'll all adjust to the other side when the time comes. But during COVID-19 and its aftermath, smallness will not save us. Taking up space will: not necessarily in public places, not just yet, but in how we see ourselves, how we value ourselves. Those of us who are well enough to advocate for justice in health care—including accessible and affordable mental health care—must not pass up the opportunity to demand it.

As I write this, the end of the pandemic is not yet in sight. Neither is my own recovery, my sense of calm, or my belief that I'm going to be "back to normal" anytime soon. If COVID-19 has made one thing clear, it's that we all deserve to be well, and to modify our lives in order to uphold and savor that wellness. I've spent years trying to believe that I'm worthy of recovering; that I can take up as much space as I need in order to heal. When we reach the other side of this, I hope that's part of my new normal, too.

❧

Camille Beredjick is a writer and nonprofit marketing manager living in New York City. Her essays on LGBTQ issues, mental illness, and relationships have been published in *BuzzFeed*, *Narratively*, *Autostraddle*, the *Daily Dot*, *Mic* and elsewhere.

Birthright to Breathe

Melba Nicholson Sullivan, PhD

Saturday, February 29, 2020

I don't feel well. After spending a workweek in Paris, I'm experiencing sharp pain and tingling in my chest and left arm. I say nothing to no one. These can be heart attack signs, but I know from my training can also be our bodies' stress response. The pain I feel could just be me being tired, jet-lagged, and/or my body expressing and releasing work-related anxiety, anger, and sadness, and/or my limited upper-body strength intersecting with my luggage. Chest and nasal congestion also signal possible allergies. Trying to find a doctor and use American insurance would induce more stress and is not how I want to spend my one free day in Paris.

My symptoms will subside when I get home. I'll rest, take my Flonase, follow my grandmother's hot toddy recipe, and prioritize my self-care plan.

But for now, I'm taking a bike ride at Versailles.

I enjoy this last day, and the always colorful subway rides back to my hotel. I enjoy discussing French protest rap with the driver who takes me to my flight home: New York City.

When I arrive home I learn that the Louvre staff, in the face of the emerging Covid-19 scare, have been standing up for their right to breathe—and forced a temporary closure of the museum.

Sunday, March 1, 2020

I felt feverish on the flight and it hurt to breathe, so when I arrive home I keep a safe distance from my son.

What transpires over the next several weeks can best be understood in the context of a combination of familial, community, and sociopolitical dynamics, which contribute to my lifelong tendency of letting my symptoms intensify before seeking professional attention. Growing up, my Southern Black elders did everything they could to avoid doctors. They had natural remedies and remembered the Tuskegee syphilis experiment (1932-1972) when U.S. healthcare workers withheld treatment from 400 Black men and watched most take their last breath. The government allowed these deaths in order to study the disease.

In my home, my own parents initially responded with, "Are you sure you're really sick?" before visits to the pediatrician. As an adult, my Black women friends and I share strategies to navigate health disparities and implicit bias in U.S. healthcare—disparities that contribute to Black women dying preventable deaths, especially during childbirth, at a far greater rate than the general population.

On my own, I prefer the dignity and agency that self-care brings. Today, however, I feel bad enough to play roulette with the healthcare system. A primary care practice is open—on a Sunday no less! An echocardiogram and routine physical ensue. The doctor does not mention or offer a coronavirus test.

The test results confirm I did not have a heart attack. My swollen glands and inflamed (but not sore) throat are most likely from a bug I picked up from a dirty tray table on my outbound flight to Paris. The doctor prescribes antibacterial wipes to clean future trays, Alka-Seltzer Severe Cold Remedy, and rest. Before I can finish asking the question, she interrupts, "No. Don't go to work. Rest." I explain, "I'm an entrepreneur, and it's only one client." She approves, "as long as you don't touch them." As she exits, I ask, "Is it COVID-19?"

"Maybe."

I don't want to privilege her "maybe" as a diagnosis. She said it in response to a topic I introduced as she was leaving and I'd rather have an unremarkable virus, so I don't push further.

Monday, March 2, 2020

I rest and go to work. I take a subway from Brooklyn into Manhattan and walk down sidewalks full of New Yorkers and tourists, before entering my office across from the Empire State Building.

I close my client session with an Aikido practice that requires the palms of our hands to touch. Afterwards we pump hand sanitizer.

She told me not to touch! But I don't have a fever. Fuck! I'm overreacting, it's no big deal, just a bit of jet lag and some dirty tray. Get over yourself!

A crowded subway carries me home. I go straight to bed.

Wednesday, March 4, 2020

After drinking Alka-Seltzer for two days, I feel much better. I choose to keep dinner plans with a West Coast colleague. We enjoy sharing professional dilemmas that people of the global majority (people of color) uniquely understand. The micro/macro-aggressions we navigate with descendants of American enslavers: those who inherited white skin privilege, those who have internalized all the *isms* and actively/passively perpetuate it against those who share their own oppressed/resilient identities; those who believe they are "woke" and judge how woke others are, yet don't see how their us/them, hierarchical, comparative thinking perpetuates "that which (they) seek to destroy"[15]; those who don't see color and aren't "racist" so they practice a peculiar covert violence; those tired folk who work individually, not collectively.

Friday, March 6, 2020

I resume school drop-off because my husband, Jamal, goes to work early. I'm uncomfortable going inside. A friend says "Yes!" to pick-up.

Monday, March 9, 2020

After a client session, I'm too tired to ride the subway home. A car delivers me to our front door, and I crash on the other side.

Tuesday, March 10, 2020

"I recently returned from Paris and was diagnosed with a bug last week," I tell the allergist. I mention coronavirus. They stare at me, blink as though horns adorn my head, and offer only silence.

"I don't have asthma, but you're prescribing me an inhaler?"

"Yes. You failed the breath test."

The doctors make no connection between my problematic breathing and coronavirus.

Thursday, March 12, 2020

I'm back in the allergist's waiting room seated amongst chronically ill people, oblivious to the connection between my potential COVID-19 symptoms and their vulnerability. Every person I encounter, including those in doctors' offices, also seems oblivious. My allergist informs me that the food allergies I was diagnosed with years ago were false positives. "Testing," he says, "is not foolproof."

Our son brings home a school packet and a request for all students to stay home for the time being, if they can.

---

[15] Rep. Barbara Lee's floor statement in opposition to the Authorization for Use of Military Force joint resolution on September 14, 2001.

Friday, March 13, 2020

Some of my Black family and friends believe this is a white people's poor hygiene disease, a function of 5G cell towers, the U.S. government repeating a Tuskegee-like experiment, or major corporations finding a way to generate future profits.

I go to BJ's Wholesale Club. Empty rows exist where toilet paper and paper towels used to be. Rubbing alcohol? No. Hand sanitizer? No. Lysol? Oh Hell Naw! No need to worry, it turns out. Naturally, I find all these items at the neighborhood bodegas that have sustained us when we were not welcome in other businesses.

Monday, March 16, 2020

Our son's private school's distance learning begins. (Meanwhile, Mayor de Blasio keeps public schools open.) He goes from ten hours of professional instruction to a thirty-minute meeting and second-grade self-study. Our son's education and my switch to video conferencing sessions with clients significantly shift my lifestyle. Jamal transfers his animation courses online, even though some of his students have only limited access to computers. Technology is not a birthright. I feel both guilt and gratitude for our son being in private school. The difference in resources seems inhumane.

Monday, March 30, 2020

I pass Brooklyn Hospital en route to Trader Joe's. Police are directing traffic as workers remove bodies from an eighteen-wheel freezer truck. I catch my short breath, telling my colleague on the phone what I'm witnessing. She reminds me of the compassion practice from our mindfulness training. Songs from my gospel heritage move through my mind. I realize my work is just beginning; the grief and trauma will not be quarantined.

Thursday, April 2, 2020

I guide our son through assignments, then tag in Jamal. After my midday nap, I return upstairs; out of breath before the top step. Coughing.

I learn that my Howard University classmate, Sean Boynes, PharmD, has died of Covid-19.

Friday, April 3, 2020

I'm hanging out with my book club, a multigenerational collective of Black women. Tonight's collection of short stories triggers my memories of growing up in educated and affluent African American communities where I needed to navigate the day-to-day realities of a community that was predominantly white and Jewish. More recent experiences of the intersection and impact of racism and sexism in my professional life also arise. Most importantly, the book club and memories support me in tapping into the collective and individual wisdom and resilience that are always available to support my thriving, no matter the circumstances. Club members share how they are managing the intensifying rates of illness and death COVID introduces to the communities they lead.

Saturday, April 4, 2020

After a family bike ride with face masks, I use the inhaler for the first time in the month that I've had it.

I share in our family Zoom call. My sister juggles teaching her elementary class, managing remote learning for two children, and caring for our elderly parents who live nearby. My parents plead with Jamal and me to leave New York.

Later, I catch up with my Sisterfriends during a Zoom Happy Hour. This group includes old and new friends. It's the kind of friends where we don't really know what each of us does for a living because our relationship is built on how we live our lives. We laugh and let each other know *I hear you, I look forward to seeing you.* This group is giving me LIFE! They are not having my nonchalant update about my health: *shortness of breath, fatigue, history of chills and swollen glands, recent Paris trip, coughing, living in New York City symptoms.* Their inquiry connects disjointed pieces of my experience forgotten in day-to-day adjustments to our new lifestyle. They command me to schedule a doctor's appointment and use my inhaler as one of my two-drink minimums.

Monday, April 6, 2020

Telehealth-only means my doctor *listens* to my cough and otherwise relies on my symptom descriptions. "Yeah, you've got it." When I ask what "it" is she responds, "COVID-19. You're a New Yorker. All New Yorkers have it." She instructs me not to bother getting tested because there's a 40% false-negative rate and it wouldn't change my treatment. I tell her I've been using an inhaler. "Sure. Whatever helps," she says glibly.

I ask if I should self-isolate. She says there's no need for that either because I've already been canoodling so it's too late. If I want to go see my parents, she says I need to wait until I've been symptom free for a week and once there I'll need to quarantine for another week, then wear a mask.

When I get off the phone, I tell Jamal all the doctor said, but he has different ideas. "If we both get sick, we're screwed, so you're going to quarantine yourself." I stay in our basement bedroom.

Wednesday, April 8, 2020
New York Times headline: *Most New York Coronavirus Cases Came from Europe, Genomes Show: Travelers seeded multiple cases starting as early as Mid-February.*

Friday, April 10, 2020
While on a call with a business consultant, the pain of losing loved ones without the physical connection and support of community is made real and surreal. He expresses surprise at how much we are able to accomplish, given that in the past week both of his parents, residing in a nursing home, died. He and his brother were at their gravesite alone because the laws only allow up to three people. I offer human connection and compassion and also my opinion: "That shit's fucked up."

Saturday, April 11, 2020
I'm now in my sixth week of what the doctor said is a two-to-six-week thing. My symptoms are mild and seem to be resolving. The hardest parts of this is not being ill; it is not being able to support others—Jamal and our son, freaking out my parents, and, of course, losing friends.

Sunday, April 12, 2020 (Easter Sunday)
My son and I have a regular reading time where he sits at the top of the basement stairs and listens to me read from the bottom. I've always tried to make Easter special for him. It's the first year I can't. Jamal does his best and FaceTimes me as he sets up the egg hunt in our apartment.

Thursday, April 16, 2020
I attend Sean's virtual funeral. It's my first. The pastor, another Howard classmate, leads the service on the church's private platform. Virtual

hugs, memories, and condolences stream throughout the service, facilitating a sense of community among more than 500 people. The service reflects Sean's forty-six years of breathing. Afterwards, I eat the lunch placed at the top of the steps for me and reminisce with my college bestie by phone. The experience feels full, including catching up with someone because we attended the funeral "together."

Friday, April 17, 2020
When he struggled to breathe, three NYC hospitals turned away our friend, Jonathan Ademola Adewumi. The fourth admitted him and put him on a respirator. Today he died.

Saturday, April 18, 2020
I reunite with my family!

Thursday, April 23, 2020
I'm struggling to breathe again so I call my doctor. Her colleague Face-Times me and notices that my previous telehealth visit and COVID diagnosis are not in my record. He believes I'm overusing the inhaler and prescribes a steroid to help me breathe. He, too, tells me not to get tested.

Friday, April 24, 2020
"I walked around the corner and got a test," says my white, asymptomatic Manhattan colleague. My friend and I in Brooklyn and Queens are still not being offered tests. In our boroughs, people are overrepresented in death and infection rates. My book-club friend encourages me to ignore doctors' orders. In a covert information-sharing operation, I lie about the recency of my symptoms in order to get a COVID test. The NY public health official schedules me and my family for tests.

Sunday, May 24, 2020
I don't feel well. I'm experiencing sharp pain in my chest and tingling in my left arm. I've said nothing to my doctors. The pain intensifies when I move my arm, so we choose a Manhattan ER. I share my history with the white New York attending physician. She tells me to use my inhaler and is sending me home. Unsure whether my race and gender are contributing to this dismissal, I request a chest X-ray before I leave. My chest X-rays are clear; due to limited supply and questionable validity,

no antibody test is given; COVID and heart attack tests are negative, as they were the first time. The traveling nurse, a woman of color who's been listening to me, summarizes, "You probably had COVID and it's not active anymore. I see lots of patients like you." When I press the attending, she responds, "It's allergy season."

Contexts, privileges, and biases shape our individual and collective opportunities, choice-by-choice, breath-by-breath. If I had known or believed I had COVID, I would've quarantined when I returned from Paris. "We (doctors) are working with the information we have at the time. If a hospital has traveling nurses it means they're overwhelmed," a happy-hour friend/ER surgeon, shared. Stressed systems, coupled with doctors' discomfort with not knowing, constrain our ability to learn and evolve. The inquiring minds of Jamal, family, friends, and I honored my life enough to connect the dots. My staying alive required my dependency on this village, self-advocacy, and a healthy mistrust of systems that value some lives over others. They withhold resources and fail to recognize our shared humanity until we die like Sean Boynes, Jonathan Adewumi, George Floyd, Breonna Taylor....

Our breath uniquely expresses Life. COVID-19 invites us to stand for our birthright.

ॐ

Melba J. Nicholson Sullivan, PhD, is an Executive Coach, People, Culture, and Systems Consultant, and licensed clinical-community psychologist with more than twenty-five years of leadership experience. Currently, she consults with human-rights organizations globally, serves as faculty for the United States Citizenship and Immigration Service (USCIS), Refugee, Asylum, and International Operations (RAIO), and practices as a therapist independently.

A Day Not to Remember

Susan Quigley

"One of the keys to happiness is a bad memory."

— Rita Mae Brown

"So, we're at the *hospital*?"

"Yes, the hospital."

"Why?"

"Because something happened."

"What happened?"

"You were teaching yoga on Zoom and you couldn't remember how you got there."

"Why would I teach yoga on *Zoom*?!"

"Because there is a pandemic. Coronavirus."

"What's coronavirus?"

"It's a virus making people sick. Just try to rest."

This was the enthralling conversation that my husband and I covered repeatedly for several hours on that fateful Sunday at the end of March 2020, just after COVID-19 led to the shelter-in-place order in our county. Repeatedly, as in every ninety seconds. When my brain would reset, and my mind returned to blank.

I remember none of the following events: thirty minutes into teaching an online yoga class, I told students that I was experiencing low blood sugar and gently asked them to rest in child's pose. I repeated this a few minutes later. Then I said it again. And again.

As "luck" would have it, I recorded the class, and could—if I had the courage—witness these repetitive instructions, as well as my looking up, confused, and asking the group, "Am I teaching *yoga*? It's lovely to see you all but I have no idea how you got here!" Again. And again...I do think it was prescient that I chose child's pose, a position of safety and surrender. One student recalled the sweetness of resting luxuriously in her favorite hip-opening pose, until my repetitiveness caused her to worry.

Finally a friend asked if my husband was at home. He was not. She reached him on his phone and told him something was off with me, and he had my son, who was in the house, bring me some juice while he hurried back.

Students tell me they jumped into action, triaging me over Zoom, asking me to stick out my tongue and raise my arms, quizzing me on my children's names and my birthdate. One student called her brother, an ER doctor, who insisted I needed to go to the hospital ASAP. My husband returned and rushed me—in his "cool as a cucumber" manner—to the ER. Nervous hospital staff immediately took my temperature and gave me anti-stroke medication. They reluctantly allowed my husband to enter with me "due to my condition" and rapidly arranged an MRI, CAT scan, and EKG.

I have no recollection of any of this. I don't remember anything past nine a.m. that day—don't remember eating breakfast, setting up for yoga, starting the class, nothing. From that morning until about nine that evening is almost completely wiped from my memory.

In terms of Covid-19 and whether it could have been the catalyst for this strange incident, I had experienced a very brief fever, cough, and chest constriction a few days prior, but it had passed quickly. I was suspicious, but I have a strong immune system, so I shrugged it off.

Though my yoga students feared I'd experienced a stroke, or an outright mental breakdown, a clever ER doc quickly assessed, once stroke was ruled out, that *Transient Global Amnesia* (TGA) was the likely culprit. Yes, I'd been struck with it in front of about twenty folks on Zoom. The doctor warned my poor husband that my incessant repetitive questioning would happen every ninety seconds, as my brain was not making memories and resetting each time. My husband tells me that at one point he actually asked me, "Are you just fucking with me?" My poor memory is a long-standing joke with my current family and family of origin. They know not to start any question to me with "Remember when….?" I can't blame him for asking.

In the meantime, my sixteen-year-old son and eleven-year-old daughter were huddled at home wondering if their poor mom had gone off the deep end. Due to shelter-in-place restrictions, no one could come to the house to comfort and reassure them. Electronics and junk food provided necessary distractions, until the evening when their auntie bucked the rules and came over to be with them.

From what I understand from my research, TGA usually strikes only once and doctors don't know why. Men are more likely to be affected than women, and some research has found that people who suffer from migraines (which I do) are six times more likely to have an episode of TGA. Doctors don't believe there is any long-term damage, but patients often lose several hours of memory—sometimes memories that form prior to onset and often for several hours after.

In the late afternoon, the docs decided to admit me because my memory was not returning as quickly as they'd hoped. I do vaguely remember being wheeled into the room, with an elderly woman in the next bed. This is concerning, in retrospect, given my previous fever and cough and the fact that they did not test me for COVID-19. About eight p.m., when my wits and memory were starting to return, I recall a nurse coming in to check my IV. She stood so close to me, without a mask, that I could feel a drop of spittle fall on my hand. I remember looking at her incredulously and asking, "Why aren't you wearing a mask?"

I was discharged late that night, although my memory was not yet fully intact. The neurologist really didn't want me in the hospital unnecessarily, due to the COVID risks. I slept through the entire next day, with a sort of migraine hangover, leading me to believe that one was the likely trigger for this episode.

Besides the uber-bizarre "lightning only strikes once" nature of this event, the hardest part for me was the embarrassment of "losing my mind" in front of twenty (lovely, supportive, compassionate) students. My ego definitely took time to recover.

I failed to mention, and often avoid in subsequent conversations, that one of the suspected causes of TGA is *acute emotional distress, as might be provoked by bad news, conflict, or overwork.* As a therapist, a yoga instructor, and someone who preaches self-care, I shuddered at the idea of being perceived as an emotional wreck, a stress case, *unhinged.* Never mind that we were two weeks into the worst pandemic in modern history, that both my husband and I are essential workers, and that my sixteen-year-old works at a grocery store. Never mind that I was trying to transition to telehealth to support my therapy clients who were struggling with depression and anxiety in the face of the epidemic, while homeschooling my eleven-year-old daughter with learning challenges. Forget that I was deep in a delicate negotiation with her Catholic school whose idea of a "fun project" was to assign the students to create a bloody diorama of a bleeding Jesus in one of the "stations of the cross." During a pandemic. Yes, really. Throw in sparring regularly with my sixteen-year-old about the actual meaning of "shelter-in-place" and intermittently with my husband, whose idea was closer to my son's than mine.

None of that could *possibly* have led me to lose my shit in front of twenty people...could it? I concede that it is likely a world-class migraine put me over the edge and checked me out. And sure, the stress of a pandemic might have invited that migraine into the existing chaos.

But on the other hand, who would not want to forget all of this crap? Living through a pandemic is like living under a magnifying glass under the blazing sun—something is bound to catch fire. In this case, it may well have been my brain.

I chose to teach yoga on Zoom to longtime students (at no charge) because I *could*. Because we were all craving connection, and I thought it would be a fun and sweet way to support others during this challenging time. But the other thing about a magnifying glass is that it enlarges and clarifies things that you might miss with your non-pandemic eyes. What I've been forced to see and to reconcile during this pandemic are my own needs, my capacity, and my limitations. As I often tell my students, the *real* yoga is often learned off the mat.

This clarity has been my silver lining, curated through all of the conversations, arguments, negotiations, reconciliations, and soul searching that has occurred both before and after that fateful forgotten day. It's still a work in progress. I didn't quit teaching Zoom yoga, but I did cut back to every other week, so that I'd have some weekends where I was responsible for *nothing*. I said a resounding *no* to my daughter's bloody diorama assignment. I even took my daughter out of Zoom classes, as they created too much anxiety for her and too much stress in our home. My husband has stepped up to be the "bad cop" more often and my sixteen-year-old has mostly come to terms with the sacrifices we all must make during this time.

The most precious part of that fateful day is captured in a video my daughter created for me, with her voice coming from the face of a "talking dog" (a much better use of her time than a diorama.) She says, in her cute dog/eleven-year-old voice, "I love you to the moon and back, Mama, and even though you won't remember this day, remember that." And *that* I will never, *ever* forget.

அ

Susan Quigley is a lover of dance, water, sunshine, yoga, and music. She enjoys many roles in her life, most important among them "mom" to an eleven- and sixteen-year-old. Lucky for her, she also enjoys roles she is paid for, including psychotherapist, yoga teacher, and leadership development consultant...and maybe writer.

Bananas and Other Stories about Life with Children

Poetry in the Time of Coronavirus

Anndee Hochman

On Monday, two days before the World Health Organization declares COVID-19 a pandemic, the principal waits outside her K-5 public elementary school, smiling beatifically and greeting students with hugs. I get one, too; I've known her for almost two decades, ever since I started visiting this New Jersey school each spring as a writer-in-residence.

When I ask about coronavirus, she is insouciant. "We're not closing. There are no cases in the county. The kids need to be here."

And here they are: three classes of squirrelly second graders standing in lopsided circles. For the next five days I tell them, you're going to look at the world through your "poet's eye."

We try it. *Rain is not rain*, one writes. *It is a bear banging on the window.* The sun is a copper penny, a soccer ball rolling onto the moon, a bowl of chips. I walk around, peeking over shoulders, keeping my distance from the sneezing girl in the flower-sprigged jumpsuit, willing myself not to touch my face.

And then I stop, because someone has written, *The stars are not stars. They are the dogs of dawn getting led to the good parts of your heart.*

How long can a virus live on a piece of paper? I ask permission from the writer—a shy, brown-haired boy—then I lift the sheet from his desk and read that line to the entire class.

By Wednesday, the principal has stopped hugging. She starts each morning with a "mindful moment" on the public address system, urging everyone to "settle your body and close your eyes." I dash to the bathroom during the Pledge of Allegiance, but I pause, for real, during the mindful moment. I feel my heart rate slow from its the-top-of-the-news-hour canter. I stand in the conference room, eyes closed, and wait for the chime.

Back in the classroom, the kids add line breaks, goof with metaphors, and go shopping on "Alliteration Avenue," where you can buy slithery snakes and cold cucumbers, but never pinto beans.

What is the taste of yellow? What is the feeling of green? What sounds live inside you? What's going on with the girl who eats her school-provided French toast nuggets in the classroom, then sinks her head onto her folded arms? On Tuesday, the teacher gestures for me to leave the child alone. But the next day, after breakfast and a brisk antiseptic swabbing of her desk, she writes, *Inside me is my grandma humming her favorite song.*

While driving to school I listen obsessively to public radio, the new vocabulary of disease: aerosolized transmission. Abundance of caution. Social distancing. High-touch. Even the generic name for COVID-19, "novel coronavirus," has a lyrical ring. A bug with kingly aspirations. Little germ with an outsized ego. I could make a found poem from the e-mails that ping into my box five times a day:

Out of concern
wash your hands
for the continued health and safety
for at least twenty seconds
of our audiences, artists, and staff,
wet, lather, rub, rinse, dry
we will be suspending
sneeze into your sleeve
all public programming
stay home if you are unwell
for thirty-one days.
Do not panic.
We will keep you
informed.

Each morning, a new restriction: the barista at Starbucks can no longer touch my personal mug. Theaters and museums close, and my nineteen-year-old daughter will finish her first year of college from the couch. What will these next months look like? How will we stay connected? My partner shows me a video from Italy, an entire country on quarantine. A narrow, crooked street. People singing out their windows.

The second graders tug me back to this moment, this place. There is a girl whose every poem includes the words *oof-oof-oof.* Another who writes, *Blue is the sound of hand sanitizer.* They follow me around the room, holding their writing out like alms.

On day three, I lose ten minutes of teaching time while the kids wash hands before lunch: they lather up at the single classroom sink, then form a new line to rinse and dry. Some mold the antibacterial foam into cotton-candy peaks.

On day four, they write about what scares them. Twenty students, and not a whisper about coronavirus. They are frightened of one-eyed monsters and Voldemort, of trees and porcupines, of going into the ocean. Four say they are scared of the dark. One writes, *I'm afraid of losing my friends family and teachers.* Maybe that is about coronavirus after all.

I learn there will be no day five. The district calls an emergency in-service session so teachers can prepare for online learning. For some of the children at this school, staying home means no free breakfast or lunch, no access to the nurse. What about the kids whose homes lack WiFi, or laptops, or adults whose jobs allow them to work remotely?

Will there still be mindful moments? How will they learn, so far apart—these kids whose "ahas" come at close range: me kneeling by a desk, questioning and coaxing, our faces bent over a penciled sheet of paper.

We have ten more minutes. I gather them into one final circle and recite a poem by Naomi Shihab Nye that ends, "There is a place to stand/where you can see so many lights/you forget you are one of them." What I hope, I tell the kids, is that you won't forget. That you will stay awake in the world, notice everything, then write it down. Words are not a cure—for coronavirus or anything else. But they can be a balm; they are connective tissue, especially at a time when we can't touch.

They wiggle, they poke each other, and the girl in the jumpsuit sneezes, forgetting once again to use her sleeve. What will they remember from this week? What will I never forget? The dogs of dawn. The child whose grandmother hums inside her. The one who wrote, "I remember when it was summer for the first time for me."

As I leave the room, I pump out a glug of hand sanitizer. It sounds blue.

❧

Anndee Hochman is a journalist, essayist, storyteller and teacher in Philadelphia. She is the author of *Anatomies: A Novella and Stories* and an essay collection, *Everyday Acts & Small Subversions: Women Reinventing Family, Community and Home.* Her column, *The Parent Trip,* runs weekly in *The Philadelphia Inquirer.*

Bananas

Ashley Espinoza

There's a pandemic. No one in your rural town has coronavirus so far. You check your phone too often.

Your daughter points outside to her swing set. You tell her it's too cold. A March snowstorm is supposed to hit by the weekend. You consider bundling her up just for a little bit, but you know the backyard is filled with dog poop that hasn't been cleaned up since October.

You decide to take a drive. You buckle your daughter in her car seat. You bring your mom along for the ride. The three of you drive around and your daughter notices the small man-made lake, lights reflecting on the water. She gets excited and says, "Water! Look, Mommy, water." You tell her to look at the pretty lights. She's two, and this genuinely delights her.

You tell your mom about a jolt of pain that goes from the bottom of your chin all the way down your neck. You ask if she gets that too. Her eyes look downward, she doesn't want to say it, but she confesses, she gets the jolt of pain too. You ask her if she thinks it's from clenching from anxiety. She says she doesn't know. You ask if she thinks you should both consider anxiety medication. She says she's been avoiding anxiety medication her whole life.

You take your mom home, and when you get to your own house the dogs are barking. They are always barking and howling at the train. "Pepper, Pyxis," your daughter calls to them. They look almost identical: short legs, black fur. "Chihuahua-Wiener dogs," you answer, when asked what kind of dogs they are. You don't want to pet the dogs but your daughter has called them. You pet them. It's past bedtime, and you're tired and need her to go to bed, but she asks for a banana. She takes a few bites and runs around the living room. She eats half the banana before setting it on the table. You leave it there, even though you know you shouldn't. You should put it in the kitchen, or perhaps the fridge so she can finish it tomorrow. Otherwise you'll find it days later and throw it away, wishing she had eaten the whole thing. It's on the table as you carry her to her room.

You get her ready for bed. First you help her brush her teeth. You direct her to spit out the toothpaste. She swallows some. You wonder how much toothpaste she's swallowed in her short life. You put on her zip-up fleece pajamas and wonder if this is the last time she'll get to wear them. After the snowstorm, spring will arrive. She says, "Mommy, sit down." She wants you to sit in the rocking chair until she falls asleep, needing your presence. Sometimes you oblige, sometimes you leave and let her cry, sometimes you leave and she doesn't cry. You tell her you'll be right back, you need to get your book. Sometimes she lets you sit in the rocking chair and read in peace, sometimes she asks you to read aloud to her.

Back in the living room, you notice the banana is missing from the table. You're outraged. With all your anger-strength you move the couch. You know that's where the dog Pepper will be, eating the banana. It won't be the other dog, Pyxis, because she's not fast enough to get to the banana. You crawl behind the couch. The peel is there, the banana is already eaten. You stay there on your knees and the tears fall. It's all too much for you. Your daughter needing you, the dog eating the banana, the world in chaos. You're exhausted from the clenching you have done all day. Your neck hurts from staring at your phone. You just want a hug, but there is no one to hug you.

You sob a little and it happens again—a jolt of pain zaps you from the bottom of your chin all the way down your neck. This has happened three other times in the course of the day. You think back to the conversation about anxiety medication. You mom said she has been avoiding it all her life. You too have been avoiding it all your life.

The thought of that makes you sink lower. You move the banana peel so you can lie down behind the couch, in order to cry in a small, safe space. Your finger gets a little sticky from the banana, but you don't care. The other dog finds you, tries to get you to pet her. She wags her tail. She's happy.

You wonder why your daughter isn't crying for you yet. Maybe it's because you're behind the couch and she can't see you. You consider staying there for as long as possible.

You take a little peek, and she's there in the doorway looking at you. You dart behind the couch again. A minute passes and you decide this is ridiculous; you get up, banana peel in hand, and you run to the trash can so your daughter doesn't see you. If she sees you, she'll beg you to come to her room and lie down with her. You want to be alone. To be free from being a mother for just a little while.

You consider taking some Advil to calm down all the anxiety-induced clenching you've done all day, but you don't have very many. What if later you get sick and get a fever and there is no more Advil? What if you can't get to the store? You lie down in your bed alone and try to fall asleep. You wonder when someone will hold you.

☙

Ashley Espinoza is a MFA candidate in creative nonfiction at the University of Nebraska-Omaha. She has published an essay in *The Magic of Memoir* and is currently writing a memoir.

Relativity

Finding The Courage To Be Kind

EK Bayer

I've long wished my kids could have science in the forest and PE on a bike, with a whole lot more agency and freedom in their education than they get through San Francisco Unified School District. When the lockdown hit, despite feeling a communal sense of doom, a small part of me was excited by the opportunity to try out my dreams of homeschooling.

Ironically, just days before the end of the world as we knew it, I wrote this note:

"To my son, who woke up on the wrong side of the bed this morning—

You are not the first person to yell in anguish, 'I HATE MONDAYS!' and you won't be the last. Swearing at me, slamming doors, and kicking things did not make Monday go away. School waited, as always. Your frustration darkened the morning for me, Maddy, and your brother. Your storm was just a little scary. Good storms always are. I told you to suck it up. Truthfully, though, your anguish mirrors mine. With every fiber of my being, I hate having to drag myself out of bed when my body wants to sleep more, to ignore the hard deadline of a school bell. But I pick my bones up while it is still dark...."

I didn't finish the note. I was never going to give it to him, just add it to the other notes I've collected for my boys as they grow. They are twins, Luka and Dylan, in different third-grade classes at the same school. They get along well, like unruly puppies. Maddy is what they call their other mom, my wife, as in, daddy-with-an-*M*.

We helplessly watched the news as Covid19 spread and finally hit California in early March. All large events were already canceled. The tragedies unfolding in Washington State and New York foretold our own lockdown. School shutdowns were inevitable. Thursday night, March

12, the announcement came. Friday the 13th, Dylan and Luka had an unremarkable school day, and our imposed foray into home-schooling began the following Monday. To me it was a massive, temporary shift in scheduling and responsibility. To them, it was a sudden loss without comprehension, like when a beloved pet dies and you can still feel them, hear their noises, and smell their smell. It didn't seem real. However, we were all pretty happy about not having to make the school bell, which rings for us at 7:50. I confidently created a daily routine for my boys similar to school, but with electives like art, cooking, or a scooter ride and ending with a five minute meditation. I even tried on a teacher name, "Ms. M.," for Ms. Mom, to help transition into school time.

As lovely as it was, my schedule was received like carrots on Halloween. Luka shoved his fingers in his ears and made noise when I tried to start our school day. Dylan tried to pay attention, but was swayed by his brother's shenanigans, easily distracted. Every time I got either kid on task, his twin would pounce on him. Nobody could focus. It was chaos. Before the first day was finished, I stormed out, yelling, "I'm done! You broke me!"

How I longed for the toddler days when my plans were always met with enthusiasm. On day two, I tried and failed to get them to write about their experience. I launched Math Games, and got their attention long enough for them to realize I didn't yet know how to play any math games. Luka said miserably, "Mr. R. is a better teacher than you!" Obviously. Later, in a moment of calm, I asked him how. Unlike me, he explained, Mr. R. made a promise to never yell. What a profound promise, I realized only then.

I tried to keep my cool like Mr. R., strove to be a homeschooling supermom. Three days in, I let my students tape cardboard all over their room for a giant marble race and called it science. They were actually busy long enough for me to catch up on email. But if I launched actual math, writing, or spelling, I was met with fights and tears, apathy or abject refusals. Luka, especially, rejected all things school. At first I reacted as if he had a bad attitude or laziness and tried to rally and cajole him through. I pushed from morning to night trying to get him to work. By day four, I was exhausted. It suddenly hit me that he was in a classic denial stage of grief. He was going through a major loss. Maddy and I had discussed the chance that school might not re-open this year, and I'm sure he overheard. He missed his teacher and his school. He missed his friends and the safety of a well-established daily routine. What better way to deny this was all happening than to reject all things homeschool? Once I said this out loud, finally understanding, he had himself a good cry. He was a different child after that, though homeschooling still galled him. I had to realize my sons did not want homeschooling, they wanted their life back. I let go of my dreams. I missed my life before lockdown, too. Responsibilities and routines that I had put off to make room for homeschooling began to loom.

After what would have been our spring break, the saints who call themselves my sons' teachers finally launched a full daily schedule through Google Classroom, and Maddy set each twin up with his own workstation using an old laptop and older desktop. Both boys tuned in to their teachers with relief and gazed with longing at their classmates on Zoom. For Luka, Mr. R.'s good morning message became a daily elixir, his video lessons a calming balm. The real Ms. M. invited her students to a Zoom talent show, and Dylan spent a week perfecting a Lego masterpiece to share as his talent. I listened in as the real Ms. M.'s voice, while remaining utterly gentle, conveyed an excitement that kept students engaged while it inspired creative thinking. How does she do that? How does Mr. R. stay so calm?

Online school was pretty straightforward. Lessons were posted. Students clicked on links, watched videos, followed instructions. Luka actually woke up early to jump into assignments from Mr. R., but he demanded the freedom to do his schoolwork on his own schedule. This was fine with me. I figured Dylan would follow suit. If school-work was finished by three-thirty, they could have an hour (or two) of a video game, a treat that, pre-pandemic, was reserved for weekends. I am nothing if not flexible.

Maddy and I blindly clung to the idea life would go back to normal, and that our boys wouldn't need their own new computers for a few years yet. We could have borrowed Chromebooks from school, but decided to leave those for families who didn't have old computers lying around. I did not realize that for online school, I'd been drafted as an admin for two manic bosses with no computer skills and no tolerance for old technology. Or, maybe I was the one with no tolerance. Math alone required inserting diagrams using a program that hadn't been updated since 1992. It took me three times as long to print and upload worksheets as it took my boss-babies to do them, which the bosses took as valid reasons to launch wrestling matches or Lego projects. I set up their teachers' lessons on screen, then left the room for one of the myriad other tasks on my plate. As if under a magic spell, their ability to focus followed me. Luka used his freedom to procrastinate, distracting and antagonizing his twin. Dylan floundered like a fish out of water, which was exactly what he was. Did we really expect them to sit by themselves in front of a computer navigating this new world all alone? Our days grew discombobulated: the boys interrupted my work, which interrupted housework, which interrupted their work, which was waylaid by technical glitches, and I raced between everything like a squirrel lost in a maze, hiding nuts and losing them. Both boys completely melted down with the stress of finishing their schoolwork in time for video games.

I called a friend to compare. Her two girls were fairly independent with their schoolwork. She said she got out for a run every day, and that really helped. How dreamy! I added running to my to-do list. If I went while the kids were awake, the house might not be standing when I got back. Yes, Maddy worked from home. No, she was not available to wrangle marauding children. By taking responsibility for the kids and their days, I enabled Maddy to stay focused on a career that was intense and unpredictable. We were too old and too *lesbian* to ever take her job for granted.

Crankiness consumed me, and it spread. Between school, online reading, movie nights, and video games, it sank in that my boys were now addicted to the screens I'd been so careful to keep at bay until now. And I was beholden to the discordant technology required for them to work. Maddy called my issues "user error," and I snapped back that I had not signed up for a master class in outdated technology. After another frustrating day, as the video-game deadline loomed, I tried and failed to scroll through a YouTube lesson that kept glitching. If I could just get the gist of the assignment, I could walk my son through it, but the deadline ticked by. Dylan broke down. Through real tears he cried, "Mama, I liked your schedule better!"

An unresolved question from my school days hit me fresh. Isn't there enough suffering in this world without contrived deadlines? What does a student under duress actually learn? Then again, my parents' beliefs were strong: people become good, responsible citizens when they finish their schoolwork. How else will the work get done?

I attempted to impose a tighter schedule for Dylan's online school, working around strange new late bedtimes and even later mornings. I was already lost in a maze of short timeframes and conflicting demands, as frazzled as when the boys were three, only without any breaks or the elixir of their undying adoration. Trying to support two different sets of assigned schoolwork on two different schedules for two cranky inmates with different needs, while doing everything else required to get through a day, turned my life into an Escher painting, where you run up a flight of stairs toward a child's cry only to find yourself at the bottom of the same stairs holding a dripping paintbrush. Maddy couldn't relate, making my new reality even more surreal. One evening, I rushed into the kitchen to start dinner late, leaving some important task to do so, making mental notes about all the balls in the air that still needed to be caught, and found food left out and the kitchen sink full of soapy dishes. It was like finding my desk rearranged. I had no memory of getting interrupted while washing those dishes. The disorder brought me to tears, my brain snapping and fizzing with a million short circuits, and I had to admit defeat. I was miserable. So were my kids. Where was the joy?

The next day, the kids and I went for a bike ride. We had a socially distant visit with a friend who had broken her arm, and brought muffins to Mr. R., in part to verify he was still real. Relationships were the glue to get us through this, and the one with my kids was no exception. We had a great day, but failure gnawed at me. Who am I, if I can't get my kids to do their schoolwork? A new, inner voice answered. I am my kids' support, their shelter, the one interested in what inspires them, not in forcing them to suffer through work too disconnected from its source to carry meaning. I am Mama.

Their schoolwork was still there to do and I was still there to help, but it no longer took precedence over my mental health or theirs. They did not get it all done, and I had to accept that. There were more important lessons to learn, like how to be kind through a pandemic. Others were wrangling with more kids or in circumstances much more dire, so I thought I had no excuse but to keep it all together and get everything done. That line of thinking had never actually worked for me; it's amazing how it persisted. Teaching kindness included giving myself a break. The truth was that the extra time with my kids was a chance to slow down and listen to them. I had to quiet my inner manic squirrel and tap into the love that connects us. If I could do that, maybe I could teach my kids to do that, too.

There were only a few days left of third grade. Dylan woke up at eight and started playing a math app while I was out for a morning walk. Luka slept until almost nine. Instead of schoolwork, I told them they could choose alternative tasks: come up with two challenging goals, then accomplish them. Dylan challenged himself to finish his math and social studies online assignments. Luka challenged himself to write a card to his grandparents and build a solar oven. I got other things done while they worked, and Maddy ordered pizza for dinner. My kids and I were on the same peaceful page, an entirely different scenario than a week earlier. Nobody appreciates a pandemic, least of all me. However, I did appreciate being homeschooled in finding the courage to be kind.

When her twin boys started school, EK Bayer was excited to devote her extra time to writing. It turns out, as parents know, there is precious little extra time. When the kids are asleep, she chronicles the joy and heartbreak of raising twins in San Francisco as an old, stay-at-home, lesbian mom.

Remotely Yours

Lori Jakiela

Dear Student,

I promise I will get to the essays you sent me as soon as possible. I am working from home. Thank you for your patience as we all adjust to our new normal.

I am working from home and my husband is working from home and my children are schooling from home.

Schooling from home is different from home-schooling because homeschooling is a planned and chosen thing. I believe homeschooling has a schedule. I'm pretty sure said schedule does not include six meal breaks and snack breaks and extra time for Tik Tok-ing and collapsing in the hallway to shout, "I so hangry. Why you no feed me?"

Right now, as I am about to work on the essays you sent me—thank you for these!—my husband is sitting across from me at our home office, also known as our dining room table, blasting Faster Pussycat from his computer.

If you haven't listened to Faster Pussycat, the metal magazine Sleaze Roxx gives the band its Super Sleaze rating. Super Sleaze gives extra points to the band members for extending their teenage hormones into midlife. Super Sleaze gives double points to Faster Pussycat for making it out of the 80s alive.

My husband loves hair metal. Right now, he's wearing the same hair-metal T-shirt he's worn for the past who-knows-how-many days.

I'm not judging.

I haven't showered for two days, maybe three, and I haven't worn a bra in weeks. My hair is yanked into a messy bun that looks like a rabid groundhog gnawing on my head.

You probably didn't need to know about the bra.

I apologize.

That was unprofessional of me.

Today when the UPS guy delivered my case of subscription-service wine, he took one look to make sure I was twenty-one and therefore allowed by the great state of Pennsylvania to legally imbibe subscription-service wine.

The UPS guy made a squinchy face. He gave the box a shove with his foot and backed away fast.

I like to think he was social distancing. I like to think he had many deliveries and miles to go before he slept.

I sniffed my pits just in case.

Then I asked my husband to sniff me.

These are things people who love each other and who've been married a long time do.

Also, one symptom of COVID-19 is loss of smell.

Trust me. We're fine.

My husband's favorite day-shirt is swag from a Kiss cover band called Mr. Speed. Kiss cover bands were big in our neighborhood before the pandemic. My husband and my brother-in-law Dan loved to go see these bands at a place called The Lamp.

Remember theaters?

Remember concerts?

Kiss cover bands always sold out at The Lamp, even though the beers were warm and served in plastic cups. Warm beer in plastic cups belong at frat parties.

Imagine frat parties—all those people crammed together, keg-standing in a basement, slam dancing to 80s hair metal, someone puking on someone else's shoes, forever and ever amen.

Was that even a thing?

Last I checked, Mr. Speed, the best Kiss cover band in the history of Kiss cover bands, was clocking quarantine making Kiss collages to post on the band's website.

Collages are fun! Once, at a campus retreat, our college president made us make collages. We cut pictures out of fashion magazines. We cut letters from *The Chronicle of Higher Education*.

Where do you see yourself in five years? In ten?

In five years, I saw myself as a best-selling novelist. I look nothing like Stephen King, but I glued his face to my collage anyway.

In ten years, I saw myself as a best-selling novelist. I have never read *Fifty Shades of Grey* or a single Harry Potter book.

At night, when I am supposed to be working on your essays—which I am sure are brilliant—or writing a book that will not be a bestseller, and my husband is supposed to be writing a book that may be a best-seller, I change into black leopard-print fuzzy pajamas.

Black leopard-print fuzzy pajamas sound sexy, but are meant for comfort, which means baggy-crotched.

When I change into my pajamas, my husband changes into his bright orange T-shirt, the one he bought for five dollars at Shop 'n' Save this past Thanksgiving.

The T-shirt says Gobble 'til You Wobble.

Thanksgiving was in November, whatever.

Remember: Time = construct.

The Gobble T-shirt is soft and comfortable. Before he hangs up his Mr. Speed shirt, my husband sniffs it and passes it to me to sniff. We both deem it good for another day's wear, at least.

Rock on, Mr. Speed.

I am working at home.

Did I mention that?

Also, Faster Pussycat is not a bad band, but the speaker on my husband's computer statics a lot and even though there is a nice Bluetooth speaker within reach, my husband prefers to let the static ride.

Static is the sound of my brain on quarantine. Or it's the sound of the bacon I keep cooking for breakfast. Every day it's bacon and bacon and bacon, since my husband and kids and I are home and so what if breakfast is now at three p.m.?

Physicist Carlo Rovelli says time is an illusion.

Ancient Egyptians invented time, or at least the hourglass.

Cyndi Lauper's song "Time After Time" was big at my college homecoming dance. I wore a polka-dot minidress and drank grain punch from a hollowed-out pineapple and puked in the bathroom.

Cyndi Lauper used to babysit my friend Joe from Queens years back. Joe became a cop, then a criminal, then a life coach and security guard, which is kind of like a mall cop.

Have you seen *Paul Blart: Mall Cop 2*?

Watch it. You have time.

Einstein said time is a burrito, folding in on itself.

Cyndi Lauper is sixty-six now and her hair is still pink fluff.

The Egyptian's hourglass became a clock, which became a watch that takes a licking and keeps on ticking.

Magritte said a pipe is not a pipe and a clock is the wind.

Dali melted all the clocks.

We are all Dali now.

My dear student, I would be finishing your essays right now, which would normally take me an hour tops, but now my husband is reading Metal Sludge stories aloud.

Did you know the band Ratt just did a Geico commercial?

Did you know Sebastian Bach, who according to Metal Sludge's Penis Chart is about average, didn't shower much—even before quarantine—and is now selling Kiss collectibles on eBay?

Many years ago, I dated a guy who looked so much like Sebastian Bach people would stop us on the street in New York. The guy I dated had good hygiene, but he wasn't into Kiss. He was into muscle cars. Meth maybe, though he had great teeth and beautiful hands. He was a painter and a musician and his hair smelled like toasted marshmallows.

My aunt Peggy, maybe eighty back then, fell in love with him because she thought he was cute—that golden marshmallow hair and all. He'd kiss her to make her happy and she'd giggle like a schoolgirl.

My aunt Peggy has been dead for years.

My parents have been dead for years.

Some days, I'm grateful they're not alive because if they were alive, what then?

Is that selfish?

I wonder if my old boyfriend is still alive.

I hope he is. I hope he's happy.

I hope everyone I've ever loved or hated or been ambivalent about on this earth is well and loved and loved.

"Greetings and Salutations, a Man in Quarantine Says Upon Seeing Other Humans," a recent headline from the *Onion* read.

Greeting and salutations to you.

Just as I was about to begin working on your essays—which I should have finished, no excuses—my daughter Phelan sat down next to me. Right now, she's examining the breakfast sandwich I made her—scrambled egg, the aforementioned bacon, American cheese on a sweet roll—like she's about to taste-test poison for Henry the Eighth.

Phelan likes scrambled eggs, crispy bacon, American cheese, and sweet rolls.

"But not all together!" she says and tries not to cry.

I hope she won't cry.

I will her not to cry.

When she cries, my daughter calls it "draining the bathtub." It takes a while.

Phelan puts the sandwich closer to what may or may not be her good eye.

She's due for an eye doctor's appointment.

She's due for the dentist, the orthodontist, her annual physical.

Locklin, her brother, is due for all this, too. Plus, his wisdom teeth need to come out.

I need to remind myself to remind myself of this.

And now, as I was about to turn my full attention to your excellent work, Locklin sat down too. He sighs. He sighs again. He sighs and puts his head on the table. He bonks his head on the table, just once, until I have to ask what's wrong.

He's furious because today is April 20—you know, 420—and he's out of weed.

He's in college, a legal adult, and he has a medical card, but it doesn't kick back in until tomorrow and all his friends are on Tik Tok, partying on and so.

"This is not good," he says, and I say, "What's not good?" and he waves his arms every which way to show me the world.

Did I mention our pet rabbit Waxy may have either ear mites or ear wax? Waxy is named Waxy not because of ear wax but because she came from Waxahachee, Texas. She's a rescue bunny.

"Waxy is a dumb name," Locklin said, so I added Kardashian to Waxy's birth name because Waxy's backside could break the bunny internet.

Also, as an adoptee, I am against changing people's or animal's birth names. It seems traumatic.

"We should call her Snoop," Locklin says, for Snoop Dogg.

Waxy Kardashian Newman is a girl.

Waxy Kardashian Newman is a rabbit.

I met Snoop Dogg once when I lived in New York. We were in a tiny bar in the East Village, red carpet on the walls, red vinyl bar stools. Snoop bought me a shot, something sweet, peach schnapps, maybe.

Snoop Dogg killed people, probably, but he's nice. He's friends with

Martha Stewart, who he calls "10-Toes-Down" because Martha Stewart is no snitch.

When my son is alone with Waxy, he calls her Snoop anyway. I hear him. He says, "Yo, Dogg." He says, "What up, Dog?" He says, "I feel you, bro."

I feel you, my dear student.

I feel everyone now.

I really am sorry about how long it's taking me to get to the essays you sent.

Phelan tries to swallow a tiny bite of her sandwich and her eyes roll to the ceiling like she's waiting for a lightning bolt to save her.

Locklin drops his head to the table and stays there.

Phelan would like to know what's for dinner.

My husband would like to know what's for dinner.

Locklin would like to know what's for dinner.

Locklin would like me to learn how to make carrot bacon because he's seen carrot bacon on YouTube and thinks he'd like to start a diet centered around carrot bacon.

Waxy the rabbit is jiggling her ears a lot, like antennae trying to tune in aliens, but her appetite is fine. She likes carrots just the way they are. We have canned baby carrots. We have baby carrots in the freezer. There are dandelions all over our lawn.

"I can't go on," Samuel Beckett said. "I'll go on."

My husband swears rabbit hair is everywhere, so I vacuum and vacuum, to keep the peace, to keep things nice, to keep us steady.

I'm trying.

I am.

I promise I will have your essays to you as soon as possible. Just as soon as my internet goes back up. Just as soon as I take a nap.

My internet keeps saying "unstable."

"You're on earth," Samuel Beckett said. "There's no cure for that."

How are you, my lovely human?

How's your internet? Is it strong? Is it stable?

Once I'm stable, I will get to work on the essays you sent me, first thing. I promise.

Thank you for your patience.

Be well.

Yours always,

LJ

❧

Lori Jakiela is the author of several books, most recently *Belief is its Own Kind of Truth, Maybe* (re-released by Autumn House Press in 2019), a memoir that received the William Saroyan Prize for International Literature from Stanford University. Her work has been published in the *New York Times* (Modern Love), the *Washington Post*, Vol. 1 Brooklyn, the *Pittsburgh Post-Gazette*, *Pittsburgh Magazine* and more.

Play With Me

This is a love story that begins on Friday, March 13. A rather ominous day to start a love story, but then these are dark days. The coronavirus is mushrooming. Hour by hour infection and death rates climb. There is talk of hospitals becoming overwhelmed, states shutting down; lockdown orders are imminent, and we have not even begun to see the devastation and the life changes this pandemic will bring.

These past nights, the only way I can sleep is if I take a Lorazepam. I have not had to do this since the miscarriage, when panic attacks ravaged me relentlessly. I am exhausted, but I cannot shut my mind off.

This morning, anxiety looms like a Dickensian ghost signaling death. Alone in the raw gloom before my son wakes, I cower before the news, feeling old and childlike at the same time. I picture Scrooge on his knees before Death, trembling at the sight of his own gravestone—

What must I do to wipe my name from that stone? Spare me! What must I do?

Then—"Mommy!"

Down the hall, my three-year-old son, Julian, waits in his doorway, wearing fleece footed pajamas with a felt applique bear face smiling from his chest. His tawny hair stretches in all directions and his eyes glisten, puffy with sleep.

"Good morning, I say. "I'm so happy to see you."

"Good morning," he says. "Look! The rain is dancing on the roof!" My precocious boy leans against the windowsill of the long, hall window, pointing to the water streaming from a faulty gutter on the third floor and splashing on the porch's roof below. The splashing stream bounces wildly.

Delighted, Julian jumps and giggles. "It looks like fireworks, Mama!"

A smile blossoms from deep inside. If I still had a womb, I would say that's where my smiles for him begin—where he once listened to my heart. I think of how life begets life. Joy begets joy.

"It looks like fireworks," I repeat softly. "Yes, it does."

My active, healthy boy stills for a moment, his eyes glowing with delight. He is all heart. All moment and life. Kneeling beside him at the windowsill, I place my arm around him while he rests his cheek against mine. Together, we watch the water dance on the roof.

Later, anxiety-fueled adrenaline spurs my daily cleaning frenzy. My body feels wired. There must be something I can control. Some germ I can eliminate. So I mop the floor. Every floor. Scrub every bathroom, wash every article of clothing, bedding, towels; scrub the pantry shelf, disinfect the coffee maker, the mixer, the refrigerator, the toaster, phones, laptops, door knobs, handles, backs of chairs, countertops.

"Oh no! Mommy, Travis had an accident."

I rush down the hall and watch my dog shit on the floor. The entire length of the house. He just walks and shits. The house reeks.

"No!" All of my anxiety-fueled, pseudo-energy drains in futility. He doesn't mean it, poor thing. He's old. He doesn't even feel it. Travis is a fifteen-year-old black lab, the grandpa of the house, and he is always patient with Julian. For the past year, he's been having accidents. He gets confused and sometimes can't make it to the back door.

Grumbling, I put the dog out and clean the floor. With a treat, I bring the dog back inside and tell him that I know he doesn't mean to do it. Still, the frequency of these accidents is frustrating when I am trying to kill germs. This is my battle against the reaper. And he shits on my mission.

"Did you clean up all the poop, Mommy?"

I suddenly feel ridiculous.

When my husband, Theo, returns from work, he strips in the laundry room, puts everything in the wash, and showers before he even says hello. He manages environmental health and safety and works nearly seven days a week now. He creates strategies to limit risk, to send people for testing and quarantine, and to keep workers safe and healthy. I have never seen him so stressed.

With the virus spreading, I fear he may get exposed, though he reassures me (and himself) that he is taking every precaution. At home, at night, on weekends, his phone is constantly ringing and buzzing with calls, texts, and emails, invading even the intimate haven of our marriage bed. This continues for weeks with no end in sight.

One night I come downstairs for a cup of chamomile tea, and I see him at the counter with his head in his hands. The only other time I'd seen him like this was after his father died, when he carried the world on his shoulders. I know he wishes he could talk with his dad now.

"Can you take a day off to rest?"

"No, not until this thing is over."

"But we don't know how long this will go on."

"Exactly," he says.

"How about shutting off your phone for an hour? Just an hour to rest your mind."

"I can't! Even if I could, my mind doesn't shut off." He tells me that even when he sleeps, he has COVID dreams. "I can't escape it."

"I wish they would shut down for just two weeks, or let you work from home."

"We need to be grateful that I'm still working."

But how long can he go on like this? What will the long-term effects be on his physical and mental health?

What must I do to wipe our name from that stone? What must I do?

"Make funny faces in the mirror!"

Every time Julian and I walk up the stairs, he gives my hand a little tug and we stop to stick out our tongues or scrunch our noses at ourselves in the wall mirror. He laughs every time. Whatever else is happening, we have his moment. A pause in the climb.

Gifted with a sunny disposition, Julian appears happy with uninterrupted "mommy-time" for weeks at a time. I think, if only I can continue to shelter him from this virus and my anxiety—the fear-reaper that has become my life's companion.

We make flower pot bunnies, paper plate suns, drums out of oatmeal containers, paper butterflies. We paint boxes, trace our hands, tell stories, string beads, and read every book he owns twice over. We have spontaneous dance parties, sing loudly and mimic farting sounds to make each other laugh. I now have a favorite hot wheels car that Julian calls mine. It is white with purple rims and a purple crown painted on the hood. We bake cookies, decorate for Easter.

Then, one day I catch him staring forlornly at the neighbor kids playing outside. Since we moved next door, this family—with the kindest children I've ever met—have accepted little Julian as "one of the crew," introducing my only child to a world of sibling laughter and teasing that he would not otherwise experience. I think of how he might have had two older siblings, and I realize with a pang, that my miscarriages are his loss, too.

When we go outside they wave, but my neighbor and I remind the children we must keep our distance because of the bad germs. My heart hurts. Still Julian doesn't cry; he just looks at them as if they are very far away. As if next door is now another world.

I try to distract him, scooting him to the backyard where we blow bubbles together and play tag. But I feel a poor substitute for the carefree children with their language of laughter. I can only enter his world so far, for I am his mother, the one who must keep him clean and fed and safe. I am the one who weathers his frustrations, his big emotions. I am the one who teaches him to regulate himself, just as I battle to regulate myself when anxiety gets a hold of my mind.

"No one wants to play with me. No one at all," Julian says in my arms that night. There is a deep sadness in his little voice that should not come from a child. In the dim, bedtime room, the haunting look in his eyes resembles the dark bottoms of ancient wells. I recognize that look as one of loss. My son is grieving his village.

The coronavirus has ripped his world from him. Grandparents that used to visit weekly, he hasn't seen in months; his library program, now gone from his life. There are no more soccer practices or trips to the YMCA. We have not even ventured to a grocery store, since everything is now delivered. And he can only watch from a distance while the neighborhood children play.

"Everyone wants to play with you. Everyone misses you! But right now, they can't play with you because of the bad germs. Soon we can be together again."

I hold him close, feeling guilty that I cannot fill this need. Nor can I give him a sibling to play with in this strange time. What kind of later impact will this time have on him?

"You can tell me your feelings," I prod gently. "It's okay to have feelings."

"I can't talk! I can't talk about it!" He shakes his head vehemently.

As spring finally blooms with sunnier and slightly milder days, word comes with increasing frequency of a quarantined friend who has been exposed, a first-responder; an infected relative on a ventilator, fighting to live; family in nursing homes, infected; a friend of my grandfather's, dead.

I can't talk about it. I can't talk.

We must wear masks in public now, Theo tells us one night at the dinner table. Even Julian's imaginary friends wear masks. He describes them to us during supper.

When I cover my son's mouth and nose for the first time, I shudder inwardly, though I know wearing masks is for the good. Still, it feels like a silencing of innocence; a childhood held captive. He wears it without resistance, but his muffled voice wavers when he speaks and there is a strange look in his eyes. He wants to be a big boy; he is still my baby.

I can't talk about it. I can't talk.

I have stopped reading the news so often. Stopped going on Facebook. Am I forgetting or forgotten? I miss small talk; miss my friends at the YMCA where I taught PiYO. Over rainbow-colored yoga mats, the other moms and I would talk about the challenges and the humor of mom-life. I miss baking biscotti and tricolore with my neighbor, trading family stories and recipes as the kids darted in the kitchen for treats; our long front-porch discussions about books while we watched the children play.

It has been so long since I have had a conversation with a friend that there are times I wonder if I even can. When my brother wants to Zoom one evening and have a virtual drink together, I simply can't. I just can't talk.

I am mentally exhausted. Some days I feel like I am sinking. Failing. Never enough. Then, Julian looks up at me with eyes bright as sunshine and his soft little hands reaching up.

"Play with me? Let's dance!"

There is no music on, but I take his hands and we spin in the kitchen and wiggle our hips.

What must I do to wipe our name from that stone?

Only this. Play. The reaper cannot touch this moment. Fear has no place here.

❧

Maria Ostrowki's nonfiction has appeared in *34th Parallel*, *The Book Smuggler's Den*, and in *Letting Go: An Anthology of Attempts*. Her (unpublished) novel, *Yet From Those Flames No Light* was a 2019 finalist for The Daphne du Maurier Award.

Azalea

Victoria Livingstone

I cross the living room of our two-bedroom apartment. My six-month-old daughter is in my arms. She is old enough now to be curious about the world beyond her immediate field of vision, so I walk her over to the window. Our apartment is on the top floor and our window gives us a good view of the street for several blocks west. The town is quiet, as it has been for months. Of the few people who walk by, about half are wearing masks. My daughter straightens her neck and leans forward to get a better view. She puts a chubby hand flat against the glass and then gets distracted by the lock on the window, to which she shifts her focus.

My partner and I are both teaching online—we are fortunate enough to still have our jobs. Some of my students have been sick. At least three have lost family members. Another wrote to me saying he couldn't concentrate because his grandmother was in the hospital with symptoms of COVID-19. My husband, who works for a college in the Bronx, has lost three colleagues to the virus.

I went back to work before the pandemic, when my daughter was exactly three months old. My partner dropped her off at daycare and then cried in the car. I was okay until I got to work and one of my colleagues asked how I was doing. She passed me a box of tissues. The baby was too young and sleepy to be upset that we were handing her off to strangers, but for me the separation was hard. Between classes and meetings, and on zero sleep, I used my breaks to go to the lactation room, a converted supply closet that was meant to serve all nursing mothers at the university. When I pumped, I could hear administrators chatting in the hallway. In March, when it became clear that COVID-19 would not be contained, classes went online. It meant I could be home with my daughter.

As the campus shut down, several countries closed their borders and some of my international students were separated from family.

One was quarantined in Hong Kong for two weeks then stuck in the airport for another week because, on the last day of his quarantine, Vietnam stopped letting people return. Another Asian student was able to go to an aunt's house in New Jersey, where he convened with ten other people. In New York, he told me, his family became the target of racist attacks. Unable to go home, a Tunisian student went to Queens to stay with a friend, who then got sick. My student left her medications outside the bedroom door. In the meantime, her grandmother died in Tunisia.

We named our daughter Azalea in part for the resiliency of the flower that grows in many parts of the world. At the beginning of this strange and stressful period of self-isolation, I lamented that her exploration of the world would be limited. I have moved dozens of times, lived in five different countries, and traveled extensively. In the last couple months, we have only left the apartment for morning walks around the neighborhood.

We recently introduced Azalea to solid foods. She gives us a huge smile. She now has two little bottom teeth and bangs on the highchair in excited anticipation. She examines a strawberry, turns it around and strokes it before bringing it to her mouth. She inspects everything: the strap on her diaper bag, which is leaning against the couch, the edges of our carpet, which she tries to pull off the floor, and the round metal logo on our dishwasher.

Azalea came to us after a period of grief, after years of failed fertility treatments. "What are the chances I could get pregnant without more medical intervention?" I asked the doctor after three unsuccessful rounds of IVF. We had hit our limit with insurance and couldn't afford more treatment without going into debt. "Unlikely," she responded. I was forty-one. Every month felt like a missed opportunity, and with every menstrual cycle I felt my would-be child slipping away from me. The doctor had told me that at my age every month mattered. I think now of all the people whose fertility treatments are on hold. While others may feel that quarantine has blurred the days and weeks and months, how acutely they must feel the passage of time.

Grief is not organized. When we experience one loss, it's tangled up with those that have come before. My mother died of pancreatic cancer when I was in my late twenties. Although she had been sick for months, I was not prepared for her parting. When she took her last breath, I felt that the earth had been ripped out from beneath me. "There is a real energetic bond that is broken when a person loses her mother," a therapist later told me. I was holding my mother's hand when she died. I was with my siblings and a family friend, who turned away unwanted visitors.

One of the women in my—now virtual—new moms group lost her mother to COVID last month as the disease took hold in nursing homes. Her mother had been a "brittle diabetic" whom she had cared for over the course of years, she told me. She could not be with her when she died. Her family could not hold a funeral. I tried to offer my empathy via Zoom before the meeting ended and the screen reverted to the static display of the desktop.

When our last round of IVF failed, a familiar force surged up and tightened my chest. It's a strange feeling to grieve for someone who has not yet existed and may never come into the world. I did not allow myself to feel it at first. I started a new job and booked a trip to Taiwan to visit a friend. I decided to focus on work and travel for a while.

Then I got pregnant. Despite my age, my pregnancy was perfect, easy, free of complications. So was my labor, but my daughter—apparently hungry from the beginning—inhaled something in the birth canal. We had one blissful hour of bonding before the doctors determined that she had fluid in her lungs and took her to the NICU. On the first night, the nurse told us not to touch the baby for fear of stimulating her and aggravating her respiratory distress. We could only see her at certain intervals. The rest of the time, I sobbed in my hospital room.

She is thriving now, but everything else feels uncertain. It's not clear if my campus will reopen in the fall and, if it does, we don't know what we'll do for childcare. I worry about the stability of my job in the wake of severe budget cuts. We can't visit friends or family, can't take Azalea to the playground to try the swings for the first time, and certainly can't travel. I miss the in-person communion I might have had with other new parents and wish my daughter could see her cousins and surviving grandparents—the kind of contact I never had growing up in an immigrant family. I worry that this period of isolation will affect her development, though she won't remember the pandemic and may never know that she was the force that sustained me.

Azalea recently figured out how to propel herself forward. She army crawls toward the cables of our floor lamps, toward the plastic liner of the garbage can, toward a plant in a small ceramic pot that she manages to tip over. When I'm not pulling her away from peril, she helps me see the detail in everything: the grain of the wood of our dresser, the subtle pattern on our cheap grey couch, the satisfying sound and vibrations you get if you bang your hand against the base of the oven. She does not distinguish between the banal and the beautiful.

It is morning and there is a patch of sunshine on the hardwood floor. Azalea rushes over to it—as much as a little person can rush when she can't lift her bottom off the floor—and runs her hands across the floor to see if sunlight has any texture. When quarantine makes the world seem small, she shows me that it is still vast.

ॐ

Victoria Livingstone's poetry, translations (from Spanish and Brazilian Portuguese), academic essays, and journalistic pieces have appeared in *The Café Review, Metamorphoses, Hispanófila, Asymptote, Truthdig,* and elsewhere. Awards include a Fulbright grant (Brazil). She teaches at New Jersey Institute of Technology. You can find more of her writing at https://victorialivingstone.net/freelance-writing/

Tomorrow or Today and Other Stories of Reflection

Tomorrow or Today

Dawn Marlan

I wake up slowly. I drink my coffee in the hot tub. Before the shelter-in-place order, I rushed through my morning routine, a shot of espresso consumed standing, a frantic search for parking at the university, the half-walk-half-jog to the office. Now time has stretched, and I notice things again. The apple trees in bloom. The scent of Daphne. The shadows on the stone walk. The elastic quality of time itself.

I remember things, too, like the time my mother warned me not to rely on a man for my income.

Most days around noon, everyone emerges for breakfast, some with sleep in their eyes, stretching and groggy, others awake for hours and positively starving. Someone will scramble eggs, toast corn tortillas, scoop out the avocado. We will eat outside. I don't have city-envy anymore. I am content to live here, in this sprawling mod ranch house in Oregon.

I am holed up with four others who have the luxury of working from home: my husband; my daughter, who is finishing her semester of college online; my son, a recent post-college graduate, working on a script; and his girlfriend, a graduate student trying to get through finals.

I feel grateful and guilty about this luxury. I remember, though, that luxury is not just something, it is also the absence of something. Like pain.

On Sundays I will wake up early. My daughter and I will head to the living room, which is now a dance/yoga studio. We will log into *Dance Church* and crank up the music and somehow it won't be a sad simulation of something that was once joyful; it will really be joyful.

At some point today, I will FaceTime with each of my parents. We'll talk about what we are cooking or what show we are streaming, or what old pictures we are finding. My father will mention the will he prepared; my mother, the precautions she's taking.

We'll hang up and I'll regret forgetting to ask them for an old story. This is where we are. Needing to preserve fruits and stories.

In the afternoon our house will be full of people sprawled every-where—on the deck, in the dining room, cocooned away in a bedroom, reading, writing, moving. Then, someone will want to replenish the tequila, the bourbon, the floral-scented Calisaya. I will hand them spray bottles of disinfectant and say, *please don't get close to anyone, please spray the credit card after you use it.*

At home again, I will scroll through Instagram and Facebook and the News. I will rage at the country I no longer recognize, where the so-called Justice Department exonerates a man who has pleaded guilty—twice. I will bury this feeling, lingering over friends' posts where I'll catch glimpses of their children, their cats, their queries, their homemade bread, the ten albums that have most inspired them. I will exit the platforms where I am overwhelmed by indignation and anxiety and hope, where I love people and despise them in equal measure. I will leave my phone in the other room to get away from it all.

I will try to work. I will be distracted by whispers of revenue short-falls, consolidations, and possible closings. The university administration will fear students dropping out because online education will not be worth the money. Or it will be, but they won't yet know it. They will forget that there are no jobs, no travel, nothing to do but stretch the mind and stretch the body.

I will get the message that we writers and teachers are increasingly irrelevant, a terrible irony in a moment that tests our collective capacity to occupy ourselves with a sense of meaning, purpose, and pleasure. And whether they acknowledge it or no, the public will immerse itself in novels and poems, movies and TV series. We will want full absorption.

I will remember that we are failing to turn to the doctors and scientists to solve the problems with too many syllables, like ep-i-de-mi-ol-o-gy. We will call it something easier to say, like fake news. So it should come as no surprise when we forget the social function of dreamers.

The university administration tells us that students want "career-leg-ible" educations, they will say, business-speak for business jobs. They will deceive the students into believing that those are the *only* jobs that exist. They won't set the writers on the task of re-imagining, only the fat-cats. So, no wonder.

There will be "non-renewals" in Romance Languages. Loss will creep closer. I will remember that there's another year on my contract.

I will hope it protects me. I will know that this possible protection is only temporary.

I will prepare dinner for my friend's family, because my friend is in the hospital. I will deliver it to their doorstep, text them, and wave from afar.

I will focus on today. On online shopping the glitchy system, on curbside pickup, and disinfecting routines. It will take hours to fill the sink with soapy water and scrub the oranges and bananas, to hand-wipe the bags of pasta. I will not know whether all this is necessary.

We will minimize exposure by shopping just once a week. I will learn to use the freezer. I will make mistakes. I will defrost flank steak in the microwave, submerge it in marinade, and pack it in Tupperware, and only when the steak is sizzling on the grill the next day will I realize that I've messed up—the steak itself is probably contaminated. I will not want to risk it. It will land in the garbage and I will know that this waste—of food, of life—is the ultimate luxury.

Just because I can't see something doesn't mean it isn't real.

It will soon be dark and we will eat together and I will be quietly bursting with gratitude as I soak in the sight of my family, because it has not always been so easy and so smooth. There were big things to work through, rifts to heal, and this time together will be a gift. The best possible. A godsend.

After dinner, the twenty-somethings will bake something. Chocolate chip cookies, fudge brownies, honey cake with fried bananas. I will still be connected to the world enough to worry a little that my pants are getting tight, but I won't miss out on this. I will wear big loose dresses if I have to.

When it is dark, we will sit outside drinking wine, watching the flames flicker in the fire pit.

I'll remember the time when my grandmother was already dying of pancreatic cancer, but we didn't know it yet. All we knew was that she was suddenly thinner. It was Thanksgiving and we were at my aunt's house in New Jersey and my grandparents stood in the kitchen, their hands clasped together. In front of all of us they sang, "These are the Best of Times." Ten months later she was gone. They knew it was the last Thanksgiving, and yet they sang without holding back, sang with their whole hearts in it.

I'll wonder if these are also the best of times.

I will walk my Shadow, breathing heavily on the path, for now still with us. I will want to take his picture. My beautiful old-man puppy.

I'll remember that there wasn't always this much quiet. There were obligatory social gatherings, time spent getting to and fro, parking, schlepping, navigating airport chaos and lines and turbulence and all kinds of things I don't miss at all. When there was a real economy, there wasn't time to ask, *What do I care about?*

I will feel an aching longing for the rest of my family. They are my soul. I will push back the thought that I might not see them again in the flesh. It will be hard to catch my breath.

I will think about my grown children. How they should be moving forward. How they are champing at the bit. How they manage to be remarkably patient under the circumstances.

I will remind myself that what is a gift for me can't last without hurting them, that I would give it back to them if I could.

Tomorrow I will go for a run and will find that my body registers the sight of another human as a threat. When I see someone, my heart will race madly. I will visualize the air stream they leave behind just by breathing, new news I can't evaluate.

Tomorrow my son and his girlfriend will pack up and go back to California.

Tomorrow I will wake up in the middle of the night because of vivid dreams and I will suddenly realize what I've always known—that I am utterly dependent.

I failed to follow my mother's advice.

I will realize that if my husband were to fall to this virus, I will have no health insurance. I will not be able to protect my children.

The university is clever that way. Professors make careers both "calling out" exploitation and actively participating in it. And because their institutional power is naturalized, some of my truly lovely colleagues will shake their heads with a resigned tsk-tsk at The System, which reaffirms their sense of their own value. Which is also true and real.

Usually they don't spend much worry-time on the fact that they make twice or thrice the money for the same work as other employees, disproportionately women like me, with the same degrees from the same institutions. We are all just so used to the fact that some of us work for chump change and lunch money. Even I forget.

Because of my husband's job at the same university, I have the luxury of forgetting—until the faculty meeting where they will be busy advocating for some constituency or other, never mine, and my face will redden, and I'll hope they won't notice, even though I want them to remember that women like me have been in their midst for fifteen or twenty years, laboring invisibly like housewives.

I will usually forget all this by soaking in the pleasure of the work, the pleasure of having something painfully beautiful to offer bright-eyed students, like the passage in Virginia Woolf's *Orlando* describing literature as something "wild as the wind, hot as fire, swift as lightning; something errant, incalculable, abrupt...something useless, sudden, violent; something that costs a life."

I will remember these pleasures and wonder why I can't read in this deafening quiet.

I will wonder if these pleasures will cost a life.

I will remember the time several years ago when I woke every hour on the hour drenched in sweat from a terrible case of pneumonia. I will remember the sheer effort of breathing, how I could feel my lungs, how gingerly I walked from my bedroom to the kitchen for a bowl of broth. How weak I was. It's a state that, once experienced, one can't forget.

It is possible to fall ill suddenly. It is possible to die.

My husband is older than I am.

Tomorrow I will wake more acutely aware that this virus could take everything and everyone as swift as lightning. I will remember that the strength I enjoy in the world—by virtue of the family I was born into, the one I married into, even the degree I "earned"—all accidents, all chance—could disappear in an instant.

I will make myself remember the people to whom this has already come to pass.

I will remember that chance and chance alone distinguishes us. I will be forced to admit that I fear losing what others never had, the good fortune that keeps my sink full of eggplants and oranges, bobbing in soapy water.

I will not blame anyone for thinking, "Ah yes, now it is happening to you. Now you notice."

The great equalizer. Except not. Because statistically speaking, I am still likelier to survive.

I will try to master myself. I will try to be as brave as those who feel this all the time.

I will not want to worry my family. I will not want to bring anyone down.

Tomorrow or maybe today, I will run on the country roads past the bright blue pickup truck, past the wild turkeys, roosters, and alpacas, past the trailhead where people will be chatting across the road. I will remind myself that it's probably all right. I will keep running up the long windy hill and around the bend, descending until the pavement stretches flat under the hot sun, past the meadow where I used to take the dog, crawling up that last hill, breathing heavily. I will feel the shape of my lungs. And then I will be home again. I will think, *I made it.* For the first time in ages my muscles will ache and my skin will glisten.

Tomorrow or today, we will talk about our family project. Someone will choose a song. Those who play instruments will play, others will choreograph. Someone will splice it together and it will be Zoom Art, tiny little squares of sound and movement collaged together. Most of my work is so solitary that this idea will make me ridiculously happy. Punch-drunk happy.

Tomorrow or today, I will go to bed knowing that I could wake up in the morning to news that will rend my world apart.

But today is a gift. Today my kids are still here. Today I am one of the lucky ones.

Dawn Marlan teaches Comparative Literature at the University of Oregon. She has published literary nonfiction as well as essays and reviews on literature, art, film, and politics in scholarly journals, literary magazines, book anthologies, newspapers, and art exhibition catalogues. She is currently at work on a novel about virtual intimacy.

Bahala Na

Ella deCastro Baron

How to escape the cultural call to become a nurse:

1. When Mama insists you study nursing because it is "the path that makes most sense, and your sister and everyone else are making a good living serving the Lord this way," shrug and say *okay* and add it to your other college applications.
2. Lie, and say that you didn't get into the nursing program that your sister and cousins attended. (Because you didn't send in your application; because you want to go to a public college and figure out your "thing.")
3. Apologize to Mama for lying. Absorb her disheartened, "Bahala na!"

The Filipinx phrase *Bahala na* is one we understand to mean, "It is in God's hands," like the song "Que Sera Sera." What will be, will be.

When Mama sighs, it is fatalistic, as is her Christian religion. "The scriptures predict these are the End Times!" she says. "But oh Lord God, we pray you are merciful. Bahala na."

I challenged myself this week—how many family members could I name who are nurses in the United States? *Go!* Within several minutes, I had fifteen names from both of my parents' sides, thirteen of them women, Filipinx Americans. My sister is one. My aunt's family alone has nine nurses in the California Bay Area!

These are the people who have visited me during my different hospital stays, who called with healing advice for broken bones and recovery from three C-section childbirths. An inherited skin disease debilitates me for years at a time and these family members keep me in their minds. They alert me to the latest medicines and procedures and holistic healing treatments. I am who I am because of their "whole person" care.

These are the loved ones I worry about losing to this pandemic.

My sister, Elise, finished an accelerated nursing program near Napa,

California, to become a registered nurse at twenty years old. Our family beamed as she was haloed with the white winged cap. In the early nineties, Elise walked across the graduation stage into her very adult Sunset District apartment in San Francisco and into a new career. She made a legit salary, drove a sporty white Nissan coupe, and took her first assignment on the AIDS floor, which had, Elise said, a "100 percent mortality rate." As the first treatments were still under development, all of the patients on her floor died. Her essential role was to try to ease their inevitable passing.

As we shelter in place, I shift my city college teaching into online distance learning. I search for articles on the pandemic to update critical thinking material for my students. Among graphs of COVID-19 cases and casualties, I see iterations of the same question—"Why are there so many Filipino nurses in the United States?" This question forms headlines in major publications such as the *New York Times, Los Angeles Times,* the *Atlantic.* Almost every article and interview has been tethered to one book: *Empire of Care: Nursing and Migration in Filipino American History,* by Catherine Ceniza Choy, ethnic studies professor at UC Berkeley.

Choy asked the same question as she grew up, also surrounded by Filipinx nurses at family gatherings and in hospitals. (Incidentally, Choy is the same age as my sister, and she now teaches at my alma mater, years after I left.) Choy's work is striking because it:

...challenges celebratory narratives regarding professional migrants' mobility by analyzing the scapegoating of Filipino nurses during difficult political times, the absence of professional solidarity between Filipino and American nurses, and the exploitation of foreign-trained nurses through temporary work visas. She shows how the culture of American imperialism persists today, continuing to shape the reception of Filipino nurses in the United States.[16]

I'd like to say that my deft avoidance of my mother's advice three decades ago was a brave refusal to submit to the colonial manipulation of nurses as disposable labor. None of this crossed my mind until now, but I don't doubt the far-reaching tentacles of settler colonialism.

Once the United States liberated the Philippine archipelago in 1898—over 7,600 islands in Southeast Asia—from hundreds of years of Spanish colonialism, they replaced the imperialist tradition with America's version, replete with Christianizing Manifest Destiny.

---

[16] from Duke Press, book description for *Empire of Care: Nursing and Migration in Filipino American History,* (dukeupress.edu/empire-of-care)

Americans descended on the islands with their Western-style, English-speaking school systems. Among this earnest push to "civilize" the developing nation of barefoot islanders who ate with their hands (as my parents and relatives had done in their homes) the American educators set up Westernized nursing programs.

Even after the Philippines gained independence from the United States in 1948, the U.S. created programs to recruit foreign professionals, nurses included. This system helped to funnel Filipinx nurses into the U.S. to fill a need after World War II. The Immigration and Nationality Act of 1965 facilitated a bigger influx of laborers from around the world into America. The corrupt leadership of former Philippine president Marcos also conspired to send Filipinx workers overseas in the 1970s, partly to boost a failing Philippine economy, a move that has led to billions in remittances. This imperial mindset exploits Filipinx laborers with long hours and lower pay than American-born workers. Yet Filipinx people continue to choose overseas nursing because they can make up to fifteen times the pay than at home.

Since the 1960s, over 150,000 Filipinx nurses have immigrated to the United States. Add to this the second- and third-generation American born, like my sister. Internationally trained nurses in America today are *still* predominately of Philippine descent (including one out of five nurses in New York and California). Filipinx nurses were heavily recruited during the AIDS epidemic in the 1980s and 1990s and now, again, during the coronavirus pandemic.

If you conduct a Google search for top exports from the Philippines, items like *semiconductors* and *coconut oil* wink from the computer screen. But what about the 2.3 million Overseas Filipino Workers (OFWs) who constitute a force of human labor, a quarter of whom are caregivers?

I imagine my sister on the AIDS floor in the early 1990s, a five-foot-one angel of mercy, with black bobbed hair, attentive almond eyes, smiling full lips, and an unshakable disposition. I remember when she was pricked by a needle as she helped a patient. There was no reliable treatment for AIDS at that time, and the makeshift protocols seemed hollow. The hospital gave her immunity-boosting vitamins and tested her for HIV every six months until she transferred to a different hospital.

"Remember telling me that?" I ask her now, when my sister calls on the phone to check in.

"Oh, you remember?" She's surprised. How could I have forgotten the implicit lament that my sister might die doing her job?

"I started looking into why there are so many Filipinx nurses in America," I tell her. "Did you know that it came about because of American colonization of the Philippines?"

"Oh, really?" I can imagine Elise's dark eyes widening.

Why are we still surprised about how the legacy of colonization influences our choices today?

"Yes," I say. "It's upsetting. In addition to the general lack of PPE for healthcare workers, there's a historical reason for why you and our cousins are more at risk."

I blister with concern and frustration for my sister and cousins. I don't want to accept the fatalistic *Bahala na*. When the Bay Area committed to flattening the curve, all nurses in my sister's county hospital started cross-training, learning to work in ancillary isolation tents. Elise is assisting the ICU nurses with COVID patients. Since she is not herself entering the sealed spaces to treat patients, my sister is given only one pleated surgical mask for her entire shift. I mailed her several hand-sewn masks to wear over her issued ones, but she is not allowed to wear it and is offered no explanation for the reason why.

When her shift is over, she is told to toss the pleated mask into a re-cycling bin that is, I would guess, disinfected, to be used again by some-one else. Elise has been repeatedly exposed to patients who later tested positive for COVID-19 but (so far) she is negative. Filipinx-American nurses are again placed at high levels of risk: AIDS **and** COVID-19, with the same meager protection protocols in place.

Buzzwords like *immunocompromised* and *co-morbidity* puncture our family line. Like many Filipinx Americans, my sister has hypertension and asthma. At fifty, she is a breast cancer survivor. If she contracts the virus… My chronically sick body swells, itches, and bleeds whenever it cannot metabolize prolonged stress, and I wonder if the pre-existing condition my sister and I both carry is a colonial mentality? A notion that, no matter what we do or say, we are never American enough, never counted as full citizens. (2020 is a census year after all.)

Instead of recognizing our willing and dedicated labor, those of Filipinx descent are coughed on, yelled at, spat on, forbidden service, even stabbed, because we—the monolithic Asian—"brought the Chi-nese virus" to the United States. Over 1,700 incidents of anti-Asian discrimination have been reported across forty-five states within the first two months of the shelter in place.

Are shame and guilt co-morbidities of being *other-ed*? Do Filipinx have high blood pressure as a result of our hearts trying to stay intact while caring for our *kababayan*, our countrymen? As we strive to de-colonize our own inherited impulses, can we build immunity against imperial pathogens? Are we fated to recite a beleaguered psalm of "Bahala na"?

The word *Bahala* is thought to relate to the Philippine god of cre-ation, Bathala. When Mama invokes it, she surrenders everything to God's will. But *bahala* is also a Tagalog word meaning "a care or a burden."

When nurses show up for their shifts, they promise to carry all of us who are ill as far as they can. They are committed to alleviating the suffering of others at devastating risk to themselves, and yet they are denied adequate protection, respect, and dignity. And I am helpless to protect them. Perhaps by sharing our history, I can help carry the weight. Perhaps I can provide a sense of comfort, a form of justice. Who could have told me that one day I'd be holding my sister and many cousins in my open hands, praying surrender, "Bahala na," as I exhale?

Mama calls me *anak*, or child, as I share my fear of losing our family. "Yes, we say, Bahala na," she tells me. "But always, we do it with a heart of *bayanihan*."

I struggle to place the word. "Is that the word for when people work together?" I ask.

"Think of a nipa hut," she says. "You know—a thatched house built on stilts in order to stay dry during seasonal flooding. They're called *bahay kubo*," Mama continues. "And when waters rise too high, when conditions become untenable, neighbors gather together with bamboo poles to lift a family's home, their *bahay*, to a new place. Pilipinos always work together to reach a common goal, for a common good. *Bayanihan*. It is how we have always been."

In an interview for *Berkeley News*, Professor Choy offers a deep, cleansing breath, dare I say, of hope: "We often think about the Phil-ippines…as a colonial possession, as an extension of U.S. ideology… But what we ought to think about is how the United States is also an extension of the Philippines." In other words, "while training Filipinos in American nursing began as a way to spread American culture to the

Philippines, it has also brought Filipino culture to the U.S."[17] I think of the Filipinx charge nurse in Hollywood, California, Celia Lardizabal Marcos, who rushed in to try and save a COVID patient who went into cardiac arrest. Three days later, she reported symptoms of the virus. Two days after she was admitted, she died in the same hospital. Celia Lardizabal Marcos had worn the same paper surgical mask that my sister now wears on her shifts. I think of my family across America, committed to caring, committed to lifting this yoked burden of *Bahala na* and *bayanihan* across their strained shoulders, with extended hands, hearts broken but still pumping.

༼

Ella deCastro Baron is a second generation Filipinx American professor in San Diego, California. Her work has appeared in *The Rumpus*, *Last Exit, Fiction International*, and more. Ella's memoir, *Itchy Brown Girl Seeks Employment*, is a candid, ironic curriculum vitae of her ethnic upbringing, inherited faith, and chronic illness.

[17] from *Berkeley News* podcast, "Why are there so many Filipino Nurses in the U.S.?" (news.berkeley.edu/2019/05/28/filipino-nurses-in-the-us-podcast/)

COVID-19, Lupus, and Me

Meghan Beaudry

As a teacher, I spent the week of spring break in 2020 watching my dogs play in the dog park, sipping bubble tea with friends, and digging into the stack of novels near my nightstand. Then COVID-19 hit. After the initial switch to Skype lessons, Zoom meetings, and online assignments, little about my routine changed. Because of the chronic illness I'd lived with for eleven years, I was prepared for the COVID-19 outbreak before it ever happened.

Masks, Lysol wipes, and a gallon of hand sanitizer from last flu season already sat stacked in my bathroom cabinet. While others scrambled for groceries, I already had several weeks' worth of healthy meals in my freezer, which I cooked ahead of time every month due to unpredictable bouts of chronic fatigue, which can make daily cooking difficult. And while friends on social media panicked over their sudden loss of income, I had a rainy day fund set away, knowing my disease sometimes makes me too sick to work.

I've always been a planner—the type of person who scribbles out a five-year plan in a notebook, then tries to accomplish it in three; the type of person who never runs out of milk, oatmeal, or toilet paper. I thought all of this planning would keep me safe and healthy through the pandemic. What had chronic illness prepared me for if not how to deal with quarantine? But all it took was one news article for me to realize that the fortress I'd built around myself was nothing but a straw house.

At the end of March, a woman with my disease (lupus) was refused a refill of her life-saving medication because it was suddenly in high demand. Since the COVID-19 outbreak, chloroquine, a medication taken by the majority of lupus patients, has been touted by the president and others as an experimental treatment for COVID-19. There is scant evidence that the medicine actually helps coronavirus patients, and in many cases, it may make their health worse. Despite the fact that this medicine is critical for this woman's survival, she was denied her prescription in the form of a letter from her insurance company. "Thank you for your sacrifice," it read.

Sadly, I wasn't surprised to read this. People living with chronic health conditions are used to having their lives undervalued by the able-bodied. It's okay to sacrifice us, as long as "real" people aren't inconvenienced.

It's an attitude that has been writ large during the COVID pandemic. Consider, for example, how at the beginning of the crisis, people comforted themselves that they were safe from coronavirus because "only the elderly and those with underlying health issues" would be affected. There are over one billion people in the world with chronic health issues. Are our lives worth less because we've suffered more?

Historically, the American government and health insurance companies have demonstrated that they are all too willing to sacrifice the most vulnerable among us. Consider the Virginia Sterilization Act of 1924, the opposition against the Americans with Disabilities Act, or the attempted repeal of the Affordable Care Act and its coverage for those with pre-existing conditions. America has developed a clear set of instructions for discriminating against the chronically ill: distinguish disabled Americans from "regular" Americans. Blame the sick for their poor health. Then claim that sacrificing the sick is for the greater good.

This recipe for the marginalization of the chronically ill and disabled has thrived during the pandemic. Yes, we need to stop the spread of this horrible virus. But do we need to trample the chronically ill to do it? How is a life lost to COVID-19 any different than a life lost to lupus?

As a chronically ill woman, I read the news on COVID-19 and access to hydroxychloroquine with diminishing hope. My disease is severe, attacking internal organs like my brain and central nervous system. I have survived brain inflammation twice. The second time, I was bedridden for eight months and in a wheelchair for a year. I'd lost my ability to walk, to form sentences, and to remember entire years of my life. For nearly a year I lay in bed, missing my students, my plan for recovery taped to the headboard of my bed. I forced myself to write a paragraph each day, to have conversations with my caretakers, and to swallow the pills that would save my life despite their painful side effects. I'd like to think that my determination and wise decision-making saved my life.

But in reality, what has truly saved my life is access to health care, and more specifically, my medication.

Even with the handful of pills I still take each night, including hydroxychloroquine, I don't live a normal life. I sleep ten to twelve hours each night and wake up tired. I can't work full-time or in the mornings, when the fatigue is at its worst. I keep a daily record of symptoms to try to prevent myself from tumbling back into the abyss of brain inflammation. Medication doesn't give the sickest among us a normal life. It gives us life. Period.

I try not to take the restriction of medication I need personally. Rationally, I don't believe that lawmakers in Washington or insurance CEOs are plotting my death. More likely, they probably don't see people like me at all. When you never experience chronic health issues, it's easy to look past them. It's easy to forget that every morning there are people who struggle to get out of bed, who have to rest after showering...who walk the tightrope of staying healthy every day.

When Americans think of the chronically ill, I hope they picture me. A woman who loves to read novels while snuggling with her dogs and drinking Rose Lychee bubble tea. A teacher who worries about her students and can't wait until she sees them again. Someone who plans and dreams, even with the odds stacked against her.

And someone who values her own life, every bit as much as they value theirs.

ॐ

Meghan Beaudry began writing as part of her rehabilitation from a brain trauma in 2014. Her work has been published in *Hippocampus*, *Ravishly*, *Folks at Pillpack*, *Al Jazeera*, and the *Bacopa Literary Review*. She was nominated for a Pushcart Prize in 2017. In 2019, she was selected as a finalist in the Pen 2 Paper Creative Writing Contest.

A No Stay-at-Home Order State: Living with Underlying Conditions during COVID-19

Karen Rollins

Every morning on my drive to work, I cross the road that leads to my grandmother's house. Often, I take a moment at the red light to think of her and my favorite aunt, who shared her home. Both are gone now, but the memories live on. I think especially of the mornings I spent with them as a young girl while my mother worked. The sound of my grandmother's cautious footsteps across her creaky hardwood floor, the hot and humid Arkansas mornings when we kept the windows open and a box fan running to help keep us dry. My grandmother's hymnal hums led a choir of chirping birds, distant trains whistled, and my aunt called out greetings from the front porch to familiar faces passing by. Later she would come back inside and prepare my breakfast, filling a white melamine bowl with cornflakes, spoonfuls of sugar, and a mixture of evaporated milk and water. I didn't know it at the time, but she combined the latter two because we couldn't afford whole milk.

One of my clearest memories took place in the mid-1970s, when I was nine years old. Nestled in the sofa, my aunt and I watched an old black-and-white thriller. In a melodramatic and clichéd scene, a beautiful blonde raised her limp wrist to her forehead, screamed hysterically, and then fainted. As the screen faded to black and a commercial began, my aunt nudged her shoulder against mine. "That's not what we would do," she said. "Me and you would have kicked that monster where it hurts and went about our business."

Forty-five years later, I've become accustomed to facing real-life monsters that threaten an early end to my life or at least to interfere with its quality. From the moment I wake up, I start gathering or putting away weapons that fight against those monsters: diabetes, asthma, glaucoma, sleep apnea, and high blood pressure. Once I throw eczema cream and antacids into a spacious travel tote I pass off as a purse, I'm about my business.

Nothing about my health on paper signals that I'm a productive person, but my breadth of living shows otherwise. I've never been without a job, and for the last seventeen years I have worked as a "non-essential" civil servant, in a department I love. My personnel records show fewer sick days, per year, than some of our healthier Millennials. In addition, I have fulfilled lifelong dreams like vacationing in Europe and buying a house. I volunteer, donate, and support various causes because a better world means a lot to me.

Before the Arkansas Department of Health's website took down the information about which underlying conditions were most correlated to dying with COVID-19, diabetes and hypertension topped the list. That meant I was high-risk, so I began the many ministrations to protect myself—frequent handwashing, social distancing, sanitizing, and masks. I work in a call-center environment where three shifts of workers cover the lines twenty-four hours a day, seven days a week. Two-thirds of our employees are within the age group now testing highest for COVID-19 in our state. We've got all of the recommended PPE suggested for our type of environment on site—finally—but I'm the only one who wears a mask. I wear one because throughout the day I hear coughs, sniffles, and sneezes. I know these don't have to be indicators of COVID-19 and I know we've been told standard masks don't protect us from others, but it's not always possible to convince myself otherwise. Even though I've got my own office, we share a small break area and bathroom that we tend to enter into one behind the other. I meet with delivery drivers, maintenance crews, pest control technicians, mat rental employees, bottled water providers, and our equipment technicians, among others, who come into our building on a regular basis. Few of them wear masks, and in the state of Arkansas, no one, including the governor, will make wearing one a requirement.

My elderly mother lives with me and depends on me. I'm childless (by choice) and spouseless, and I have no close family members living nearby. My mother is a widow with no grandchildren of her own. Her husband of forty-four years, my beloved stepfather, died six years ago, and her only other child, my brother, is deceased.

Like many mothers and daughters, we had rough moments where it was questionable whether we would ever speak to each other again.

I was independent and always wanted to learn by trial and error, and her ways were more conforming. If I had to choose a theme song for our relationship during those early years, "Don't Rain on My Parade" would be it. Later I resented her relayed disappointment in me for not pursuing a family and the life of a homemaker. I would argue that it was difficult for those ideas to transpire because during my formative years, in states like Utah and Wyoming, I stood out like a bloomed cactus tree on an icy, snow-covered hill. I spoke differently, I looked different, and I was different. Boys were not lining up to take me to prom, so I turned my focus to other things, like books, music, friends, and my dreams.

After years of butting heads, it seemed unlikely that we would be roommates someday, but here we are. We've buried judgment and guilt-trips and uncovered newfound acceptance and forgiveness. From church events to casino weekends, we are a perfect match. We consider ourselves footloose and fancy free, but without each other we would spend birthdays and holidays alone. She's given me the opportunity to honor her, and it blesses me in return. Recently, we've added the sweetest little boy to our family: a brown four-year-old Chihuahua/Terrier mix whose white paws look like little boots, adopted from a nearby shelter. The additional joy he has brought has been immeasurable. He keeps my mother company, so she no longer spends her days alone while I'm at work. And when I come home I'm greeted by his love and affection, ending my day on a beautiful note. Losing one of us to COVID-19 would be devastating to the other. To lose both of us would mean the end of our immediate family, and leave no one left to care for our handsome pup.

The most logical way to better protect myself and my mother would be to shelter in place, at least until the curve flattens. But my employer requires a doctor's statement recommending that I work from home, and my doctor will not provide a statement without a stay-at-home directive from the government. So, high risk or not, I'm off to work each day, knowing that it could be the day my weakened immune system is introduced to COVID-19 or that I bring the virus home to my mother. If it were just my life at stake, I would feel less hopeless.

Though essential businesses and most government offices in Arkansas remain open, others like restaurants, salons, tattoo parlors, movie theaters, and casinos, among others, were ordered to close, or operate via delivery and pick-up. Closed businesses provide me a sense of relief by preventing at least some of the spread. But as of early May, many of the closed businesses have already started to reopen, even though the number of active cases and deaths continue to rise in the state. Reopening too soon may cause an extensive amount of sickness and loss of life, but it's a chance our governor is willing to take for the sake of the state economy. And reopening is one part of the federal guidelines to which the governor subscribes.

Our governor, Asa Hutchinson, is one of the handful of Republican leaders who have never issued a stay-at-home order. Anyone who has listened to his press conferences over the past few weeks understands that saving Arkansas' economy is priority number one. In answer to criticism that Arkansas has put profits over lives, his health secretary, Dr. Nate Smith, responded that Arkansas has been saving both the economy and lives. But I feel the scale certainly tips more heavily on the side of profits.

The State seems to pick and choose what part of the federal guidelines for COVID-19 it will follow. The first sentence of the Federal Phase 1—Guidelines for Opening Up America Again—reads "ALL VULNERABLE INDIVIDUALS should continue to shelter in place." So, I sent an email to the Arkansas Department of Health asking when Arkansas ever recommended that their vulnerable citizens shelter in place. The response I received read: ...*there has certainly been a historical disconnect between our President and the States. In recent times, many things have been said on TV from our Presidential office that are not necessarily in the purview of that office's jurisdiction. We would highly recommend that you look over our website, and additionally watch our state Governor's daily updates on YouTube to gain a more relevant update on the State's happenings.* Of course, nothing on those websites or YouTube videos speaks to employers about protecting the older and vulnerable workforce. Eventually, we will know: is it more important for a healthy economy that it must save the sick and dying people, or for healthy people to save a sick and dying economy?

I recently read a tweet from someone who was anxious to have his "freedom" back. He lived in a state with stay-at-home orders and wrote that "the country could not commit suicide for the sake of high-risk people." I'm sure this is what the governor of Arkansas has been saying in a more strategic but kinder way. It's funny that some compare staying at home to committing suicide, while others, like those with underlying conditions, compare going out to committing suicide—especially since the virus is still active.

These battles freshen the memories of my grandmother and aunt's health struggles. A doctor's poor care resulted in my grandmother's losing her eyesight to glaucoma when she was in her early sixties. After a lifetime of cleaning houses, she was deprived of living her golden years with vision. My aunt came into contact with acid as a toddler and as a result her mouth and jaw were left twisted and scarred. She endured a lifetime of stares and whispers behind her back. They faced their obstacles with grace, sometimes fierceness, but never with apology for their limitations. Both have been guiding lights as I've faced my own health challenges. And even though I feel scared, challenged, and powerless during this COVID-19 crisis, I'm inspired by their courageousness.

My wish for high-risk Arkansans, and Americans, is to be valued, even when the message from their doctors, employers, and state government indicates they are not. In some cases, the message is that it's their fault for having diseases that make it more difficult for them to survive COVID-19. A pandemic is not the time for illness-shaming. Diseases should not be ranked according to how much sympathy they yield. If federal guidelines and national medical experts explicitly state that those at high risk should shelter in place, states should follow suit with clear and concise directives for physicians and employers. If a high-risk employee has requested to work from home, the human resources department should grant the request, not a supervisor, who may have biases. If a high-risk employee has unused sick and vacation leave, they should be allowed to use it during this crisis, without a doctor's statement and without judgment. Better yet, allow them paid leave if they have no cumulative leave time to use.

Our COVID-19 crisis leaders in Arkansas proudly recite our state's lower case numbers and deaths. Imagine how much more impressive it would be to announce we've had fewer or no deaths because we sheltered in place early on.

My final wish is that employers would stop viewing their high-risk employees as adversaries. According to the American Diabetes Association's website, the number of reports of discrimination involving employers and their actions during COVID-19 has tripled the Association's normal caseload. These employees are the same dedicated employees they were before this unprecedented pandemic event, and they will be the same after this is all over. Have your employees' backs. Those who are most likely to lose their battle to COVID-19 need a fighting chance to further protect themselves and their families. I ask for our government and employers to replace hindrances with humanity.

In the meantime, I hope to handle this pandemic like the monsters of the past—kick it where it hurts and go about my business.

❧

Karen Rollins currently lives in the metropolitan Little Rock, Arkansas area. For pleasure, she enjoys writing, road trips, and attending book festivals. Her writing has appeared in the online journal, *The Write Launch*, and she is working on a memoir about her childhood in Utah.

Starry Night and Other Stories Around the Table

Pandemic Quiz

Best Practices for Quarantining with Your Young Adult Children

Eswen Allison Hart

1. Your adult children moved back home and immediately fell into old habits, including not picking up after themselves, not helping with the dishes, never cleaning a toilet, and playing loud music late at night. You:

   a) Order noise-canceling headphones (low-budget option: earplugs) and wear them every night after 9 p.m.; ask everyone to pitch in; and remind them to put things back where they belong.

   b) Do everything yourself, despite being quietly resentful, because it's easier than nagging them, which isn't effective anyway. Tell yourself that it's a worthwhile trade-off for being together.

   c) Create a colorful chore chart so everyone can see what needs to be done and take turns; create incentives for compliance.

   d) Put up with it, then lose your shit and yell at everyone, which makes *you* the asshole.

2. Anxiety often keeps you awake, so you refill your old Xanax prescription; everyone else is feeling anxious, too. You:

   a) Encourage everyone to brainstorm creative ways to manage anxiety, including yoga, meditation, long walks, painting, baking, and warm baths.

   b) Stockpile mood-altering substances: dark chocolate, Sumatran coffee, your current house red, and cheap vodka.

   c) Hide the Xanax in your wardrobe because you don't want your children to think you use drugs and you absolutely don't want *them* to use drugs. Especially not your Xanax; you have a limited supply.

   d) When your children are chatting about how weed really takes the edge off, admit to having Xanax but tell everyone you hardly ever use it.

3. After several years of believing you have completed the work of processing sibling rivalries and resentment, your adult children resume constant bickering with one another. You:

a) Volunteer to mediate, helping them to communicate more effectively with one another. (Note: you should *never* do this.)

b) Lose patience with them, ask them how old they are, and tell them they're making everyone else miserable.

c) Take sides with one of them; usually it's the youngest, who the older two claim is your favorite anyway.

d) Say nothing, keep knitting.

4. One of your children is hypervigilant and insists that all Amazon packages and groceries stay overnight in the garage before coming into the house; she also monitors everyone's handwashing and mask wearing. You:

a) Support her wholeheartedly and encourage everyone to see how her totally justifiable caution protects the family.

b) Reassure her that she is not wrong to be careful but remind her that everything is better in moderation—food, alcohol, weed, pandemic precautions. Family time.

c) Point out that contamination is just as likely to come from handling the items *inside* the boxes.

d) Agree to her rules and, when she isn't looking, smuggle in packages and groceries.

5. You've now been in isolation together for over two months. Your children are asking whether they can have a friend over or go camping together. You:

a) Validate their feelings but ask them to continue only virtual visits until the governor eases restrictions on social distancing, based on advice from the CDC and other reputable sources.

b) Give your permission for a friend to come by as long as the friend stays outside, wears a mask, and maintains six feet of social distance; camping together is still out of the question.

c) Invite your own friends to come visit because you miss them.

d) Encourage your children to go camping or to a friend's house or, really, anywhere because it would be worth the exposure to have a day of blessed solitude.

6. Your two oldest children had to leave their college campus and self-isolate in your old house, which is close to campus but 400 miles from where you now live. You:

a) Stay put with your husband and youngest child, because you prefer your new, smaller house, which has all your books and your bed and the blue velvet couch and, most importantly, is *not* on the island where political infighting broke your heart and forced you to leave.

b) Tell your college-age kids you can't possibly join them but insist your husband and son join them. Reassure everyone that you will be fine quarantining alone—after all, it can't possibly last *that* long.

c) Agree for the sake of family unity to relocate for just one month—exactly—and prepare by refilling your Xanax prescription and packing enough yarn to knit continuously for thirty days.

d) Agree to go, taking your various comfort objects, but discover once you are there that it will be all right and, in fact, that you are strangely happy; come to see the pandemic as a serendipitous experience for your family.

Answer Key:

D is the actual answer for all, but that doesn't mean it's always the correct answer.

&

Eswen Allison Hart earned an MFA in Creative Nonfiction from the Vermont College of Fine Arts in 2017. Her previous work has appeared in *The Sun*, *1859: Oregon's Magazine*, *The Cornell Quarterly*, *Three Sheets Northwest*, and the *Journal of Vernacular Architecture*.

A COVID-19 Ramadan

Talia Basma

The front door opens and my dad walks in, placing the mail on the dining table. I smile and say, "Hello, Baba."

He smiles back, his eyes tired. He asks if I got any exercise today. My smile turns tight. "No."

"Just remember, the gyms aren't going to be opening again anytime soon."

I nod and he leaves the room without any other commentary. It's week four of shelter in place and I still can't decide if I'm grateful to be with my family or wishing I lived alone. Mama has been buried in online work, Baba has been coming and going from his office. Despite the danger, he has no choice but to report to his small office every other day. No matter how much I want to believe that life is on pause—that the world is on pause—it's a lie. Life is still going, still draining out of me.

"Go grab the tomatoes from the other fridge in the garage," Mama tells me in a string of Arabic as she rises from her computer. I wait too long to respond, and she looks up with frustration. "What? You don't know what tomatoes are in Arabic?"

I sigh. "I'm going. I'm going. Give me a minute." I walk to the garage door. The knob is broken so I have to lean against the whole door, push the knob up, and pull. Inside the garage, there are piles of both dirty and clean laundry.

"How many tomatoes do you want?" I shout.

"What?" she asks. I repeat it a little louder.

"One is fine." She pauses. "No, bring two," she says.

I hold them in one hand and close the fridge with the other.

My little brother runs into me as I come out of the garage. "I want iPad," he demands.

"No more iPad, go shower," I tell him.

"No. I don't want to shower."

"Please. Go shower. I have to help Mama make food."

He frowns but concedes. Bless the seven heavens.

I offer Mama the tomatoes, and she nods toward the cutting board. "Cut them into cubes. Rinse them properly first."

I'd prefer to be in the room napping, but instead of arguing, I grab the vegetables and cut. Just as you never forget how to ride a bike, I remember how to slice the lettuce down its spine and then in half. I dice the tomatoes, avocados, radish, and cucumbers, and combine them all in a large bowl. I toss the pita bread into the toaster. From the kitchen fridge I grab the glass jar. It used to have strawberry jam, but no jar goes once-used in this house. For now, it holds the ten lemons I juiced, a third of olive oil, a tablespoon of sumac, and some salt. I give it a vigorous shake and pour the dressing over the rest of the ingredients, just enough to lightly coat everything. Then I mix everything together.

Mama tuts. "You should have waited to put on the dressing."

"Iftar is only ten minutes away," I point out, with admittedly more sass than is necessary.

"Oh dear. Has time really gone by that fast? I still need to do so much," she says.

I separate the salads into smaller bowls—for Mama, my older brother, younger sister, and littlest brother. The rest stays in the larger bowl for Baba. I take the toasted pita out of the toaster and crumble it over the top. I make sure to make Mama's a little extra crunchy. She loves toast. I grab the dates and place two in each bowl for my youngest brothers. He always complains that they look like cockroaches. How very unappetizing.

Done with my part, I walk into my room and scroll on my phone. My feed is full of semi-inspirational Instagrammers telling people to stay home, to find their Zen. The concept of finding my Zen with my family suffocating me surpasses laughable; it is almost infuriating. I throw the phone onto the bed and decide that staring at nothing would be better than reading all that nonsense. Strangers telling me to be positive; random Muslims insisting that the spirit of Ramadan cannot be altered despite the fact that everyone has to maintain the shelter in place. The worst ones are the kids posting verses of duaa and Quran as if they're suddenly learned leaders.

I close my eyes and release a long, slow breath to calm myself. I know I'm unnecessarily irritated. *Alhamdulilah. My life may be stressful, I might not know what I'll be doing three months from now, but I do love my family and I do, overall, love my life.*

As I fall into a rhythm of imagining apologies to all the virtual people I am annoyed with, Baba shouts, "Iftar time!"

I grab a date from my bowl and mutter under my breath. *"Alah huma laka sumtu a-lah rizkikah aftartu. Fata kabal min ni salati wa sauwmi."* And then I bite into the date. I know that if I don't pray now, I'll find myself procrastinating, leaving the prayer until later. I finish the date and head to the bathroom for wudu. When I'm done praying I go into the living room to join the family. Baba is still praying. We all eat, the murmur of my dad's sports channel playing on the TV in the background.

My oldest brother says, "This is a good soup, Mama."

She replies, "It's the nutmeg, I think."

The youngest of us all declares, "Carrot soup is not good."

I roll my eyes. "Just eat it, so you can get big and strong."

He grumbles, "One more bite." He looks to Mama for permission.

She says, "Three more bites and then you eat the salad."

"Okay." He quickly eats his required amount of soup and moves on to his salad. I'm eating salad still, so I have nothing to say about the greatness of the soup. When Baba comes into the living room and takes his seat on the couch, he turns off the television and turns on the duaa. I read the translation, since my Arabic is trash despite my belated efforts to learn it. Some parts go by too fast, so I miss them, but it's fine; a week into Ramadan, I've read it over and over. While I couldn't tell anyone exactly what it's saying, it does heal some wounds.

I fall in and out of touch with Islam. Some days I'm desperate for an escape, not from religion, but from this stagnant reality that I must endure on repeat, daily. Other times I talk to God on my prayer mat. Sometimes those conversations end with cathartic tears, other times with a relaxed sense of self. Ramadan usually heightens a feeling of calm, but having been stuck with family for a month, my sense of relaxation is being sorely tested.

The duaa ends and I go back to my room to watch a show on my laptop. My sister follows closely behind with the same idea, so instead of hearing my show, I'm mostly reading the subtitles. Will there be no peace? I give up and eat dinner. Chicken and rice—nothing original but tasty and filling. Chugging water afterward, I go back to the bedroom with earbuds to watch the show. After a certain point, Netflix asks me if I'm still there. I'm about to click "keep watching" when I notice the time. It's a little past eleven.

I have two options: I can pull an all-nighter and sleep after Fajr, or go to sleep now and set an alarm for suhoor. I'm grumpy when I don't sleep properly, but I want to know how the season of my show ends. Deciding I can watch tomorrow, I close the laptop.

Lying down and snuggling deep under the covers, warmth engulfs me and I'm on the brink of sleep when my bladder lets out a warble. With a huff, I make my way to the bathroom. The light is on in the dining room and I see my mother working late on her computer. I give her a quick kiss before going back to my room. When I'm under the covers again, a sense of calm I haven't felt in a long time descends, and finally lulls me to sleep.

❧

Talia Basma graduated from the University of California, Davis studying English with a concentration in both Creative Writing and Literature. She enjoys writing poetry and fiction influenced by society and personal realities. She has been published in the *Huffington Post* and self-published a small collection of poetry called *Being*.

In a Pandemic, Returning to Ritual

Emma Bruce

People are sick and we are told to stay inside.

I check my inbox and see an email from the dance festival where I have been hired to intern for the summer. They are canceling due to the virus, but I should keep them in mind for career opportunities in the future. When I read this, I realize my tea is cold and I reheat it in the microwave even though that will make it taste bad. I want to cry but can't, so I eat cold lasagna at the kitchen table and stare out the window.

Days before, I canceled my flight to Paris. I was supposed to go with friends in May. We were going to stay out late and get drunk on sangria and have conversations about Wendell Berry under string lights on patios. I was going to go thrift shopping and find a beautiful dress. When people complimented me I would say, *Thank you, I bought it for five euro in Paris.* That part would be better than the dress itself.

Now the summer is empty. I am back in my parents' home in the Texas suburbs where the air is thick with my childhood. I feel as if I have to push my younger self aside to move anywhere. I eat applesauce for the first time in years and think I am regressing.

I am becoming nihilistic, even though this is something for boys who love Hemingway and David Foster Wallace. To keep the feeling at bay, I decide to make a quilt. I dig through my mother's armoire and find scraps of fabric, then iron them and cut them into three-inch squares. I arrange the blocks into a gradient—green to yellow to red to purple. I am almost done piecing the blocks and then I will quilt the layers together. If my hands are busy, I won't be able to think about anything but the next stitch.

My college courses have moved online, and so has my parents' church. My first Sunday home, my father stands in the doorway of my bedroom, tells me I need to get up.

"Church is at eleven," he says, and I nod, burrowing deeper into the gray decorative pillows my mother puts on the bed when I'm not home. I don't dislike church, only that until I left for college I never had a say in being there or not. I leave my bed minutes before the start of the service, brew myself English breakfast in the kitchen, then join my three siblings on the red suede couches of our living room.

My father has connected his computer to the TV and set up a split screen with the liturgy and hymns on one side and the live stream on the other. I sit curled in a ball with my head on a pillow.

My mother does what she can to make the ordinary space holy, lighting tiny candles that she scatters around the room, on the coffee and end tables. Our TV is mounted to the wall, and on the table beneath it she places two pillar candles on little pedestals like the ones that would usually frame the altar.

The service feels at once ordinary and absurd. We sing the same hymns, repeat the creeds that I still have memorized, move through the physical positions—kneeling, sitting, and standing at the appropriate times. But we are in our living room and there are no other parishioners to drown out my father's loud, off-key singing.

Midway through the service I feel nauseous and realize I haven't eaten. I leave the living room and walk to the kitchen where the only convenient thing I can find is a cooked potato in glass Tupperware. I bring it back to the living room where I eat it cold out of the container during the sermon.

"How was the online church?" my friend Carly asks over Zoom. I begin to laugh and so does she.

"Unreal," I say, shaking my head. I tell her about my father's singing, the cold potato.

"So last Sunday was Palm Sunday," I say, "and we didn't have any palms to wave so my mom took the artificial dogwood she keeps in a jug and we just waved that."

I don't tell her that my mother and father and fourteen-year-old brother danced through the kitchen waving the dogwood. Or that my sister Elizabeth and I stood in front of the TV, avoiding eye contact because we knew we'd start laughing.

I am frustrated later that week when my parents mention the Maundy Thursday and Good Friday services. It has been years since I celebrated these holidays. I'd forgotten them so completely that I set up Zoom meetings with friends during the times of the services. I text them saying I can't come—family religious obligations. *I am no longer a free woman*, I type.

Attending church is an unspoken rule and the only excuse my parents will accept is work or sickness. I have never refused to attend a service, and I do not want to learn what would happen if I did.

❧

"What if there were a secular church," I told my friend Ivy years ago, lying on my bed in our shared dorm room.

She smiled, perhaps unsure of what I meant.

"Okay, listen," I said, rolling onto my stomach to face her. "Instead of communion there'd be good food like breakfast tacos and cinnamon rolls. And the sermon would be a really interesting philosophy lecture, like on Sarte or Camus or something. Oh, and we'd sing Dolly Parton and Queen, and ABBA and classics from every genre."

Ivy started laughing. "And we'd get high at some point," she contributed.

"Definitely. That could be part of the communion," I said.

I love inventing this church. It's mostly an exercise in matching, replacing things I don't like with similar things that I do. But on another level, I think I'm trying to reconstruct the sense of focus and togetherness I had in church as a child.

In high school, my friend Marika joked that I would be part of every religion if I could. I have always loved ritual, even when I no longer believe or have never believed in what it represents. There's a part of me that loves to honor things and be reverent. I am constantly projecting narratives onto events I know are random and coincidental.

❧

After the Good Friday service, Elizabeth and I remain in the living room to talk. I arrange my quilt blocks and she sits in a chair watching. We are like this often: I make something with my hands and she keeps me company, telling me when I am doing it wrong.

"I love Good Friday because it's the only church holiday that's really despairing," I say, and she nods. "Christianity is just so happy, everything is redeemed already so no one is really allowed to be in pain for very long." This bothers me because the world is often terrible, and the only thing worse than being in pain is needing to hide it.

"That's why I like Ash Wednesday," she says. She goes to the service on her own, now that she, too, lives away for college. "I do too," I say.

We love Ash Wednesday because of the way the service ends: everyone walks to the front of the sanctuary in rows and the priest marks their foreheads with ashes, says, "You are dust and to dust you will return."

Even now that I no longer believe in God, I would like someone to do this for me, more than once a year. Look me in the eye and say, *One day you will die.*

Sometimes I think that I would have liked religion more if I'd found it on my own, if it hadn't been a requirement when living with my parents. Going into a church without my family feels like a renunciation of the freedom I've waited to gain.

I don't tell my parents I'm not a believer because it would break their hearts. They would literally believe that I am destined to burn for eternity. It's easier, less painful, to go along with the ritual, the endless Sunday mornings, than face their tears, their belief in my damnation. Besides, there are aspects of church that bring me comfort and peace— singing the old folk hymns, repeating liturgy, being blessed.

The Good Friday service at my parents' church is especially grim. Seven speakers share trauma from their lives that they relate to Jesus's last seven words on the cross. There is no room here for the usual optimism. It is the one time at church where people look into the congregation, often in tears, and say they feel abandoned by God, or that they are irrevocably lost.

This year, one of the speakers tries to include redemption in his story. He sits before the camera in a pink button-down, and talks about how his father abused him. They reconciled eventually—his father was dying of Parkinson's in the hospital, and the man baptized him with a Dixie cup.

After this, we sing a hymn and the camera cuts to a beautiful woman in a sage-colored dress. Fighting back tears, she tells the story of her young daughter, who dressed herself one morning in mint green shorts and a coral top and went to the library with her father to pick up the seventh Harry Potter book. At the library, a man assaulted her in the bathroom.

The woman begins to cry visibly. Her daughter is afraid to be alone in public spaces. When a man accused of sexual assault was confirmed to the Supreme Court, her church friends celebrated. She looks into the camera and says, "I don't know who I can even trust with this story."

When she walks off camera, I can hear her heels echoing through the empty sanctuary.

The camera pans to a woman playing Bach mournfully on the cello. I resent the online format because the remoteness is translating on a metaphorical as well as physical level. I want to be in this woman's presence. I want to sit between my siblings in the dimly lit sanctuary.

My parents' church announces that they will be providing communion for Easter. Everything will be done according to our city's and the CDC's guidelines for social distancing. On Monday night my mother bakes the circular communion bread with the cross imprint on the top. They are flatter, crustier than I remember, but they smell just the same. My father drives to the liquor store and comes back with two jugs of Taylor port, and the next evening he takes the unconsecrated elements downtown to church.

"I just drove up and Father Warner was sitting at a table in the parking lot." He is explaining that night, at dinner. "He had a mask on, it looked homemade—had some kind of print on it. And I rolled down my window and we just talked for a little bit and he asked how y'all were doing. And then he just blessed the elements from where he was sitting."

We laugh because it is so silly yet wonderful.

On the way home he stopped at my grandparents' house. They aren't leaving except to play golf and meet in a cul-de-sac with their book club, chairs spaced six feet apart. ("I can't go to the grocery store but I can play golf," my grandmother tells us over Zoom, delighted.)

My father waved to them through the glass door, then left the consecrated port and loaves on their doormat.

When I walk into the kitchen Easter morning, I see the baskets my mother lined up like when we were children, the same crinkly paper at the bottom. Mine is full of mini chocolate eggs, a honeysuckle and rose soap, and a little spray bottle that says Aura Mist. I read the label and learn that it is supposed to purify and protect me. I spray it in front of me and walk through the earthy scents of sandalwood and lavender.

We gather in the living room for the service. My older sister and her daughters drive over to be with us. My mother has lit the candles on our makeshift altar again, but this time a glass of port and a loaf of bread are at the center.

When the live stream begins, we are invited to say *Allelujah* again for the first time since the beginning of Lent. The word feels foreign in my mouth, but no less joyful.

When the sermon begins I lose focus and watch my three-year-old niece playing with a toy ambulance on the rug. I love ritual, but I hate being told exactly how to think about the world, especially by priests. I regain focus only when I hear the priest say "nihilism."

I feel my mother's gaze on me. She knows I spend my time embroidering flowers and listening to philosophy podcasts.

I have heard many versions of this Easter sermon. The priest begins by describing a grim universe where there is no overarching meaning. He uses (often misuses) words like nihilism and determinism, then reminds the congregation that Jesus has risen, and now our lives have a purpose and a goal.

I've always thought nihilism is an easy way to understand the world. Like Christianity, it feels too simple, almost prepackaged. There's little room for nuance, interrogation, the creation of meaning, or sacredness. There are so many ways for someone to understand their life outside this nihilist-Christian binary and I wonder why the priests never pick up on this. It's probably because they only ever preach to people who agree with them. This used to make me angry, but I recognize now that they are creating their own story, their framework for living what they think is a good life. Is that any different from what I do?

When the sermon is over my parents serve each other communion, then serve us.

In high school, as I became agnostic, I felt guilty about receiving this sacrament, a testament of faith that is made concrete, intimate. Because I no longer believed in its meaning, I felt hollow performing the ritual. I wanted to cross my arms over my chest, and refuse the bread and wine like the young children who are not yet confirmed. But my parents would have asked me why, and I knew that I couldn't tell them. Over time, I have given the rite my own significance as I think about the literal meaning of communion—eating with people, serving, being served. I believe in the significance of that.

My mother says, "Body of Christ, bread of heaven broken for you," offering me a piece of the bread. It feels appropriate to be ritually fed by the woman who nursed me and still bakes me muffins with oats and fresh blueberries.

Then the service is over. I hold my niece on my hip and feed her red seedless grapes while the priest tells us to "go in peace to love and serve the Lord. Allelujah. Allelujah. Allelujah."

I am still sad that I will not be able to work the internship I was hired for or spend a week in Paris with friends. Some days I want to cry and not leave my bed in a pathetic kind of protest. Others I get up early, take long showers, do research for an essay at my childhood desk. On these days I am more optimistic. I remind myself that I can work on grad school applications, get tan, and read books.

Going back to church remotely has given me a sense of calm and comfort. It allows me to understand, as I read in Wendell Berry, that there are no unsacred places.

I remember something my mother said as she lit little candles she had scattered around the living room: "The nice thing about this is that it lets us make our living room sacred."

I, too, love to make spaces sacred. I gather things to be happy about—the jade plant in my window, the dark chocolate with sea salt I keep in my desk drawer, the postcard of Georgia O'Keeffe I hang on my wall. These things allow me to be in a place that reflects me.

After Holy Week I feel better. The sun is strong but it is still cool outside, so I sit on the porch and read. The sky is cloudless and there's a slight breeze. My mother's Carolina jasmine is in full bloom and the whole porch smells sweet. Out here it is easy to believe that things are good. For now, I'll let myself.

Emma Bruce is a writer and undergraduate student in the BFA Creative Writing program at Emerson College. Her work has been published in *Concrete Literary Magazine* and *Xecult*.

Starry Night

Heather Diamond

At breakfast my sister says, "I think we should dump that puzzle." We turn toward the fold-out table in our mother's living room. Since the Washington State governor's stay-at-home order two weeks ago, we've assembled little more than the edge pieces. The problem is impressionism. If you step in close to Van Gogh's *The Starry Night*, sky, stars, trees, and village dissolve into color and texture. For us, this means a box-top ideal and one thousand disconnected blue and yellow brushstrokes. "Let's give it one more hour before we give up," I say. "If we don't make any progress, I'll help you trash it."

Only a year apart, my sister and I were a bad fit as kids. I was older but smaller. She was loud, and I hated noise. She was fearless, and I was a crybaby. She and our younger brother liked to jump out from under the basement stairs to make me scream. In our shared room, her closet was too stuffed to close. My side of the shared desk was neat, and the pile on her side was an avalanche waiting for a yodel. She taped a line between our twin beds, the door on her side. When my cats bit off her gerbils' tails and later their heads, I felt little remorse.

Covid-19 and cancer stoke our fear of dying, but you can't catch cancer from droplets launched by an errant sneeze or cough. Cancer patients should avoid sick people, but they need frequent hugs and foot rubs, sympathetic smiles unsheathed from hospital masks, a hand to hold during treatments. To be sick with the former in the time of the latter is to be denied the basic elements of healing and comfort.

Our hour trying to make sense of impressionism stretches into days, but it's slow going. Aside from regular comments like, *you'd think it would be easier to find this,* and occasional hoots when one of us clicks a piece into place, we are silent for long stretches. I've claimed the right-side-up, and I stand where I can survey the whole table. As always, I search for patterns, hold out for the single piece that will unlock the whole. I'm convinced the sky will fall into place if I can just construct the horizon line, the steeple that bisects the sky, the windows that dot the village. Bone-tired from her chemo treatment, my sister sits across from me. She methodically chooses pieces and tries them in every possible configuration. She assembles little constellations inside and outside the border—in twos, threes, and fours. Her constructions are hard to move, and when I ask where they go, she shrugs and says, "I'll leave that to you. You're better at that."

Into our forties she spouted, "It's not fair! You always get the good stuff! You got real doll furniture, and I got plastic. You got Grandma's ring and dishes, and I got nothing." I argued back, tit for tat: "You never went to see Grandma. You got Mom's ring and dishes. You don't have to pay rent." She was right about the doll furniture, but couldn't she see the flip side of my leaving home at eighteen? My more husbands, occupations, college degrees, and addresses came with more trouble, mistakes, and distance. Grown-ups sitting at our mother's kitchen table, we measured and compared our relative worth like kids counting Christmas presents.

Like ovarian cancer, Covid-19 colonizes the body. Once lodged inside, the virus can catapult from lungs to brain to heart. Some cancer cells weep, and a third of women with ovarian cancer develop ascites, an uncomfortable buildup of fluid in the abdomen that acts as a superhighway to convey cancer cells to the abdominal lining and other organs.

My sister has tucked her thinning hair under a scarf, but I still pluck strands from among the puzzle pieces. Chemo has whittled her face and body skeletal, her skin translucent. She's become a stylish waif whose clothes drape the way mine did when I was the thin one. Next to her new lines and angles, I feel smudgy and fragmented. *Enough,* I tell myself. I came home to help, yet here I am, envying the artistry of cancer.

One New Year's Eve my sister and I double-dated at a pier-side restaurant. I was with husband number two, and she was with a boyfriend I don't recall. Just after midnight, her champagne bubbled into a tirade. "Meet my sister," she mocked while strangers at nearby tables turned toward the commotion, "who always uses hundred-dollar words when five-dollar ones would do! She thinks she's smarter than everyone else!" I feigned shock, yet it's quite possible I'd egged her on. Another time she declared, "I'm sick of you and your thousand-dollar words!

Tired of you making me feel dumb." The family know-it-all, I donned an icy smile and mentally noted that my word value had risen. I savored thinking I was the smart one.

Under attack, the body can become its own worst enemy. The immune system of an unwitting Covid-19 host goes into battle mode. The resulting showdown is an all-or-nothing war where the body defends itself so well it dies. Chemo takes the battle in another direction, attacking the cancer cells in the body of a patient and killing off the immune system as well. Flattening the field, not the curve. Patients in chemo are at high risk of infection from everything and everyone, from the common cold to Covid-19.

My sister and I segregate the puzzle pieces by color until we notice that some of the blues are infused with yellow, green, or black. Some have diagonal brushstrokes while others swirl or are dabbed or hatched. The parts refuse to be separated from the whole. "I hate this puzzle," I say. "So do I," she replies. Yet for hours we forget to look up at the water and trees misting beyond the picture windows. For hours, I forget we are marooned on this island and stop taking mental inventories of the refrigerator and plotting my next run for supplies.

In our fifties, my sister told me about a neighbor who took her fishing. "I was excited to have a friend with a boat," she said. "Then we got out on the water, and she wanted to have deep conversations. I hate that! I'm not deep. I just wanted to fish!" *That*, I thought, *sums up the gap between us.* I'm the thinker and dreamer. She's the problem solver and practical doer.

There is no vaccination for Covid-19 or ovarian cancer. Testing for either disease, if you can get it, is inconclusive. Not everyone with Covid-19 gets a fever. Some carriers are asymptomatic. Ovarian cancer has an assortment of symptoms that may or may not be related to the disease, so it is difficult to detect. The five-year survival rate for stage 3 is 39%, but many women are not diagnosed until they reach stage 4. Their chances drop to 17%.

My sister wears her red reading glasses while she turns pieces one way and another. She needs a new prescription, but she has a pile of medical bills to pay out of her social security check. "When you look at the pieces," I ask her, "do you see people?" "Not really," she answers, staying on task with each piece until she succeeds. I notice I hold spaces in mind by repeating defective shapes: *two innies and an outie, thalidomide arms, hammer head, club foot.* As I find a fit for one of her constructions, I realize my ability to see the big picture isn't much good without someone who can fiddle the smaller bits.

In our early sixties, my sister and I commiserated after our father's death. We, who'd once had our smart mouths washed out with soap, who were supposed to grow up to be nice girls, found comfort in irreverent girl humor. "No wonder Mom collects dolls," I say. My sister laughs and says, "I think they're kind of scary." If the dolls were us, I'd be the serious one with glasses and a book. My sister would be the friendly faced one who looks like she is generous and knows how to make kids laugh.

Disease is a lurker, a sneak. The Covid-19 virus hitchhikes on sneezes and hitchhikes on kitchen counters. It leapfrogs through families and communities. Cancer emerges out of nowhere like a magician-less rabbit hopping out of a hat, or it slithers between generations like a snake in deep grass. Women of Ashkenazi Jewish descent are more likely than the general population to carry BRCA1 and BRCA2 gene mutations, markers that sound ovarian and breast cancer alarms. I picture the DNA of our Jewish grandfather notched into the rest of our heritage, a motley assemblage. Stay apart to stay healthy, Covid-19 experts say, but cancer insists that even apart, we—all of us—are the sum of our parts.

Four weeks into *The Starry Night*, and too many fragments of sky litter the tabletop. I fidget and wander and circle back. We check for missing pieces under the table, lament the scatter of blue. As we tinker, we talk about what we will plant when the weather improves, the visit I want my sister to make to see me in Hong Kong when the world returns to normal. My sister says, "I wonder when the new puzzle will arrive." "Not soon enough," I reply. She fits together several more pieces while I rotate stars and wonder if Van Gogh was afraid of the dark, if he painted the night to inject it with light.

❧

When she is not stranded on Whidbey Island in Washington State, Heather Diamond lives in Hong Kong. She has a Ph.D. in American Studies from the University of Hawaii, and her occupations have included bookseller, folklorist, community college English faculty, and museum curator. Her writing has been published in *Memoir Magazine* and *Sky Island Journal*.

The Brisket on the Table

Jennifer Fliss

On the first day of Passover I hear a great *thunk* on my front porch. A big black box dares me to open it. I *want* to leave it in the garage, in what we call mail jail, in attempts to keep any rogue hitchhiking germs from our house. But it's eleven pounds of meat and I know I can't, so I wipe the plastic wrap with disinfectant wipes, rolling my eyes at myself, and also worrying and wondering if I got every crevice.

I have mail-ordered brisket this year because during this lockdown we aren't having a seder. No one is traveling—near or far. But I am determined to provide something for my current in-house family—daughter, husband, and my mother, who is convalescing after a car accident and several months in the hospital.

Ordering this traditional meat online is definitely not something the ancestors would have anticipated, but to my dismay, the local groceries don't have brisket in stock. Not enough Jews in town, I think. Though the butcher tells me that they do have corned beef if I'd want that. *Not the same thing.*

It arrives fully frozen. And it is the size of my tall six-year-old daughter if she curled herself up on her side. Miraculously, I find room in the fridge. I check on it every day. The days of Passover pass. The meat stays frozen.

I have always cooked and baked and been the primary food preparer of our household. I enjoy it. Only now, during this pandemic lockdown, I am more pigeonholed into the role of domestic housewife. My husband is the one with the full-time job: the bigger paycheck and the health insurance tied to it. I work part-time. My extra freelance work can be pushed off and away. I am the one to clean the house, teach my child, cook the food, and caretake for us all: my daughter, husband, my mother, and myself.

In recent years, family and friends convened at a cousin's house for Passover. People came from Florida and California—north and south, and closer, Seattle and its suburbs. We ate matzah, we read the story of Jewish freedom from Egypt, we laughed and sang raucous versions of *Chad Gadya* and *Dayenu*. All this under the homey familiar smell of cooking brisket.

Brisket has been a holiday staple in Ashkenazi families since the 1700s. It was kosher and cheap—perfect for shtetl life. During the 1800s—when much of my family came over to the U.S.—immigrants brought their brisket traditions.

Cooking was my grandmother's love language—one of them, anyway. (Let's call her a love polyglot.) She inscribed her love on index cards, which I still have. Edna's Sweet Yeast Buns, Sylvia's Jello Mold, Leah's Heavenly Lemon Pie. These mostly handwritten index cards were her missives—only just legible, but some contained the block lettering of typewriters.

The one card I am looking at now, for brisket, is slightly discolored with age; mystery sauce stains watercolor over my grandmother's cursive loops like tiny hugs from beyond. Like so many diasporic grandparents, this recipe says things like "add salt" and "rub some mustard on the meat" and "cook until done." Less a how-to and more a reminder of the things she did. For all of us. For me.

The second to last day of Passover, the meat seems thawed enough. I pull out the hunk of it, not easy since I feel many of my muscles have atrophied during these months of lockdown. I cut away the plastic. I stare at the ropy redness, the congealed fat. In foresight or coincidence I recently had my husband sharpen the good knife. I place the shimmery edge of the knife on the meat and it goes in smoothly. I slice the brisket in half and then quarters. I use kitchen shears to trim the fat. I use my shoulder to wipe my face.

I cut the onions and cry, which I never do when I'm wearing my contacts, and I'm wearing my contacts.

I toss small bits of fat to the crows. They are pleased.

I measure the ingredients. I shake and rub and stir. I decide to make it in the oven so I can cook the entire thing in one go. It will take only four hours to cook in an oven, rather than in the slow cooker. But when the timer goes off, it is not yet done. I cook it some more.

When it cools a bit, I slice the meat into manageable strips before putting it in the fridge. The whole process takes time. The next day I easily remove the fat layer that has risen to the top. I remember doing this with my grandmother, desiring to eat some of the fat like it was dough. She tapped my hand with the wooden spoon and smiled, and I still snuck some because she did the same thing with cookie dough and brownie batter. Not equal, I learned. It was gritty but also smooth on my tongue. She never said *I told you so*.

There's a lot. Enough for an entire table of Jews. A seder. A seder we do not have. It is now the last night of Passover. Sure, we ate some matzah over the week, but it's the brisket that we are *doing*. The brisket *is* our Passover this year. This food is our tradition and it will have to suffice. According to Jewish law, it is okay to forgo certain rules if it means we are saving a life. And, we are. In a way. In many ways. We are staying home to keep ourselves and others safe.

My mother—an incredibly picky eater—declares that the brisket is good; she makes sounds of pleasure when she eats. *It is just like grandma's*, she says. My daughter dips a forkful into applesauce, just like I do, just like my mother does. We eat it for a week. It ages well and as I devour the last saucy onions, the cozy sour-sweetness lingers.

I know I have done it. I have brought something familiar and safe into my home during these uncertain times. We didn't read from the Haggadah or hide the afikomen. There weren't sixteen people at our table. There were just the four of us, eating brisket that tasted like it had tasted on so many tables before. We didn't sing *Dayenu*.

And still, like so much these days, it was enough.

❧

Jennifer Fliss (she/her) is a Seattle-based writer whose writing has appeared in *F(r)iction*, *Hobart*, *Rumpus*, the *Washington Post*, and elsewhere, including the *2019 Best Short Fiction* anthology.

Welcome to My World and Other Stories
of Seeking

Mothering While Black in COVID-19

Alicia Mosley

I take my mask off and lie face down on the blanket I've spread at the foot of my favorite eucalyptus tree, so tall and old that its lowest branches are thirty feet up. The nearest humans are specks jogging along the edge of the lake, so it feels safe enough to breathe freely. I press my heart to the earth and inhale. I am a battery being recharged.

I have come to this empty park and laid my heart on the ground almost every day since COVID-19 began its rapid spread. Taking a moment to bring my body to the ground is a strategic survival technique for me. I remember that Audre Lorde said that *self-preservation is an act of resistance*, and I imagine my body being strengthened by the earth.

This is a practice I began long before there was a global pandemic. It is one of many techniques in my toolbox of coping strategies. Deep abdominal breath, cold showers, meditation, visualizing myself in a safe place—at the base of a rocky cliff where the ocean laps at my feet—an acupressure technique called EFT where I tap on pressure points and shift my thinking, prayer, CBD, DBT, yoga, a brisk walk, a phone call to a friend, jumping in place for three minutes.

As a Black woman, unpartnered, mothering four Black children; as an artist, writer, and person who has been diagnosed with PTSD, my collection of tools has grown over time and is a matter of survival.

My nervous system acutely burned out once. It was eight years ago, in 2012. Chronic, debilitating headaches, fatigue, and insomnia became exhaustion, disorientation, panic, and the inability to speak without crying. I won't—in this space—try to fully describe the stew of factors—internal and external, individual and collective, personal and political—that led to my burnout. I will say that I had become a mother before I was technically an adult, and for nearly twenty years, I'd been in survival mode more often than not. I reached burnout and was working to recover. Then, in a year already filled with deep personal loss, Trayvon Martin was shot and killed by a racist vigilante.

If before that moment I'd had any notion that my Black children were safer in the world than fifty years earlier, when my father was a teenager, or twenty years earlier, when Rodney King was brutally beaten by four Los Angeles cops, I was reminded of this untruth every time I saw the hoodie-adorned face of Trayvon on a screen. He was almost exactly a year older than my son. The same red-brown skin, round cheeks, glistening black eyebrows, and hairline. My son was beginning to go out alone more and more; he was just about to get his driver's license and wasn't about to stop pulling his sweatshirt hood up over his cold head—as if it were the hoodie and not his skin that put him at risk.

After Trayvon Martin, videos of Black people being killed—mostly by the police—seemed to exponentially appear. (Mike Brown, Sandra Bland, Tamir Rice, Eric Garner...) Even though this was not new (violence against Black and brown people has been happening since the inception of this country and has never stopped), the way these videos "went viral" was literally making me ill.

The bodies on the screen were my children's bodies, my father's, mine. I was confronting the fear that as my children went out as young adults into the world, racism would take them from me. I had migraines when my son drove the car to a football game. Stomachaches when I unexpectedly clicked on a video of a twelve-year-old Black boy being struck down by police bullets. Nightmares after watching a teenage Black girl in a bikini being slammed to the ground by a grown man armed 263 with the fullest protection available. I learned a technique to stop a panic attack—slowly inhale for five seconds, hold for five seconds, and exhale for five seconds. I was prescribed medication for anxiety. I knew these videos needed to be seen, but I also knew I was not alone in the way they struck my body.

Once, just after my son's twenty-first birthday, the police were called to a neighbor's apartment. I came home to see him hunched on the steps in our apartment stairwell, unwilling to pass by the police to get to our front door. "I don't feel like dealing with the cops," he said. He was kneading his eyebrows. He seemed exhausted. Beneath that, anxious. Beneath that, terrified. He is a sweet young man, funny, a very loving father to his baby girl and brother to his sister. (Do I need to say that for you to understand that he does not deserve to be afraid of living in his body?)

Now at twenty-three, he has been pulled over, stopped, questioned, detained, cuffed, and released, but he has stayed alive.

When stay-at-home orders were announced, amid all of the obvious fears and concerns (I was suddenly unemployed, concerned for the health of all of us, putting together "go bags," uncertain of what access to food we would have), I had this passing thought, a tiny seed of hope that is not easy to admit. Maybe, this shelter-in-place would allow a little break from the threat of violence against my Black children. Maybe the threat of this virus was enough for now.

For a while, the thought didn't seem as impossible as it sounds.

Being in isolation is complicated. Three of my four children are out of the house now. My twenty-five year old daughter lives a few miles away with her boyfriend and their seven-month-old baby girl. My son and his two-year-old daughter live thirty miles away. My twenty-year-old daughter moved in with her dad after her college dorms shut down. With just me and my elusive sixteen-year-old, quiet—once a rare commodity—is now the norm. Some days my youngest leaves to stay with her father, and I have more time to myself than I've ever had in my adult life. Not long ago I was begging for "me" time. I needed the space to heal, to care for myself. But after so many years of living with a house full of people, being alone is new territory. There are moments when I feel peace. Days when I meditate three times a day. Glee when all four of my kids and my mother are on one screen, connected. Hours when I can allow a slowness that I can't remember ever feeling in my life. But it's also scary. I wake up each night to strange knocking sounds in my ceiling and hope that racoons are that loud. Sometimes, lying there in the dark, I think about death. About an intruder, a huge earthquake, or some other apocalyptic ending, and I feel in my bones how my children and I are physically apart from one another.

I am fortunate and get hired to teach a class from home over Zoom. I walk every day. I have more time to write. But also, I have room to feel everything fully. Some mornings, after listening to the news of who has died, who is unable to isolate, after not looking away from what Arundhati Roy calls the "vulgar disparities," I am suddenly sobbing. I let myself cry, then I breathe deeply for three minutes. I go lay my heart on the earth and feel supported, and then do the next thing, and as Roy instructs, "find joy in the saddest places." I realize crying is necessary and add it to my toolbox.

When people ask how I'm doing, I say that overall, considering these circumstances, I am good. I'm proud of how well I am coping. I am grateful that I have these tools. Then the 2020 version of anti-Black videos emerge. A cop in Rancho Cordova slamming and punching a bony, thin, fourteen-year-old boy; NYPD dragging and pressing their knees into the head of an unarmed man; police in Los Angeles punching the head of man who is clearly restrained and not resisting; cops in New Jersey swinging billy clubs onto a Black man in a fetal position (I've seen this before). My stomach drops each time I come across one of these videos and I am ashamed at the way I quickly scroll past. I remember the naïve hope I'd had.

In the ninth week of stay-at-home orders, social media is flooded with videos of Armaud Arbery being hunted and murdered while jogging. Everyone is reposting a picture of him. Bring Armaud Arbery justice it asks. His face is beautiful and smiling and radiating light. I don't repost it. I can't find any words. What use is it to press share? I try to sleep, but wake up with a heavy, aching body and a knotted stomach. I keep my arms wrapped around my solar plexus. Something heavy and violent is beating up from my guts, through my chest, and into my clenched throat. This is rage, I understand. I can't stop crying enough to breathe deeply. I can't stand up.

I text my son. *How are u? I love you*, I say.

I text my daughter. *I miss you*, I say.

I think about all the violence against our bodies. About my cousin, Ashanti, who was shot and killed in 2012 while walking alone and whose murder is still unsolved. I can't stop crying. In a few hours, I have to teach. I text three of my friends and my therapist. *This violence is so triggering. I am having a very heavy somatic response.* I have the words to say this.

I lie on my stomach and begin to breathe. *Self-preservation is an act of resistance*, I remember. I get to the bathtub, fill it with Epsom salts and deepen my breath, calm my nervous system. My potency begins crawling back.

Out of the bath, no longer debilitated but still pulsing with anger, I turn on Marvin Gaye's song "Inner City Blues," and let my body move. I strike the air with my fists, elbows. I kick it with my heels. I let the music move my shoulders, hips, and head. "Make me wanna holler, the way they do my life," I sing along. The anger is moving through me and I begin to feel something else in my body. I open my heart to the sky above. I feel potency and strength—even joy. I add dancing and Marvin Gaye to my tool box.

In the days following, the men caught on video killing Armaud Arbery are arrested. I breathe into my belly button as I take this in. I post a picture of Breonna Taylor, shot and killed by police storming the wrong address. Another of Nina Pop, a twenty-eight-year-old Black trans woman found murdered on May 3rd . I know that reposting pictures is too easy and not enough. I know that COVID-19 has not made us any safer from structural violence, and, in fact, it has only uncovered more inequity and racism. In the face of it all, I think of my ancestors. I wonder about the moments in which they were overwhelmed, the tools and technologies they used for their resilience. I wake up each morning and I do what I can to feel the vibrant life in my body. I promise to teach it to my children and grandchildren. When I lay my heart on the ground, I feel deep gratitude that I am alive. I ask, how I can best use this life?

❧

Alicia Mosley is a poet and fiction writer, a mother of four, and a community educator. She earned her MEd in Curriculum Development and MFA in Creative Writing from the University of California, Riverside. Her work has appeared in *Los Angeles Review of Books* and *Sun Magazine*. Alicia is currently working on her first novel. Much of her work explores the magical labor of mothering while Black and mothering Black children.

Writing, and other Uncertainties

Parnaz Foroutan

I'm not sure if the neighborhood birds know of the State's mandate that human beings can no longer leave their homes, but they gather outside in numbers I'm certain exceed other springs. Ruby-throated hummingbirds. Sparrows. A family of hawks. It brings me joy to think that the natural world has become more alive during this period of our absence. And just as this inspiration allows me the courage to begin writing, my youngest daughter opens the door to my office, tears on her cheeks, holding out her finger, which she hurt in a game of ball with her sister. The dog follows, curious and concerned. Her sister follows, indignant of the blame, an argument brews, the girls yelling, the dog yapping, and I forget the words I was about to put to paper—they fly away from me like so many startled birds.

I wake up each day. I enter the kitchen; the morning light streams in, the dust specks illuminated. I fill the kettle with water, turn on the fire. Eggs, bread. I remind the girls of their schoolwork. I've created schedules, established routines, and tried to carve out of the day a small nook of time for myself to write. Before the pandemic, it was my daily work. The children off to school, I'd take a cup of coffee to my office, sit before my desk, and begin. I wouldn't stop writing until it was time for them to come home. And each morning since the doors to the school have been shut, I begin the day with the hope of returning to my work. I sit down at my desk, and my eldest calls me from her room to ask about obtuse angles, and the youngest wants me to read with her on the couch, and the dog is furious that the mailman still roams the streets. Before I know it, it is dusk, time for dinner; we eat, we laugh. I tuck them in bed, we pray, they sleep.

It is night now that I am writing this. And I am exhausted. When it quiets in my home, my thoughts begin. And at first, the fear comes. It is a time of fear, of uncertainties, and I imagine the most horrible narratives. Food scarcity. Suffering and illness. The crumbling of institutions. Mistrust, greed, violence. My mind eats itself with worry. And then I think, *it is time to write now, if you are to write*. But it's hard. To put words to paper. There is a peace and clarity, a still place in the mind necessary to compose. I don't have that, not during these days.

But that is not to say that I am not writing. Writing is not solely the act itself, of putting words to paper. The observation of ruby-throated hummingbirds; the acknowledgement of the sparrow; the awe at the hawk, which drops from the sky, beak and talon; and the thought of the field mouse, unknowing, before my child comes to me, tears on her cheeks, holding out her little finger for me to kiss…to live in these moments, to be awake and in awe, is part of writing. To be afraid and uncertain, to allow the mind to eat of itself, to carry you into night-mares, that is writing. To watch the storm brew between two sisters, then abate. To walk into the kitchen each morning, into the stream of sunlight, to take the kettle and listen as it fills with water, listen as it begins to boil and whistle, listen as the girls stir from sleep, to listen to the world—that is an act of writing.

Words come hard these days, but the world is terrifying and beau-tiful, and the soul, naked and watching. It is a time to be awake, to see the world, perhaps, the way a child sees it, uncertain, bewildered, open. And when this time passes, and the peace and silence returns, the words will come, and we will all tell our stories.

ॐ

Parnaz Foroutan is the author of the novel *Girl from the Garden* (Ecco 2015) which received the PEN Emerging Voices Award and was named one of Booklist's "Top 10 First Novels" of 2015 and the new memoir *Home is a Stranger* (Chicago Review Press 2020), which is about her journey back to Iran as a young woman, two decades after her family fled the rise of the Islamic Theocracy. Her essays have appeared on *NBC Think*, *The Sun*, *Body Literature* and other literary journals.

Welcome to My World

Joey Garcia

One week after California Governor Gavin Newsom issued the COVID-19 stay-at-home order, lonely strangers messaged me on social media. They weren't spammers or romance scammers. I write a weekly relationship advice column for the *Sacramento News & Review* newspaper. For twenty-three years, inspiring a broken heart to become an open heart has been my calling.

Single readers messaged first. "I need other people," a widower wrote. "I don't like to be alone."

From a Gen-Xer: "My ex texted me. Now I'm rethinking all of my past relationships. What could I have done to keep people from leaving me and starting up with someone else?"

A college student confided: "I'm afraid of the dark places my thoughts will go if I'm by myself too long."

At my dining room table, as I read through messages on my laptop, lyrics from an old Jim Reeves song opened in me: "Welcome to my world, won't you come on in." I live alone, work from home, and often go weeks without socializing, except for Zoom calls with coaching clients. I crave quiet and days unpunctuated by busyness. Solitude delivers joy. The sky, the trees, and my yellow Lab companion me. What can I say to someone who is stressed by seven days in the lifestyle I prefer?

Six years before my editor asked me to write an advice column, I was studying with gurus and healers around the world. Many were fluent in miracles and meditation. Over time, a daily meditation practice helped me to see my personal challenges as opportunities for spiritual growth. When I began working as a columnist, I would read a letter, then close my eyes, center, and meditate, before saying aloud to the universe: "Speak through me. Let my hands be your hands. Let my heart be your heart. Let your words flow through me."

Meditating on two or three questions weekly for a newspaper column is easy. Answering forty to sixty new lamentations every day in my

DMs is not. I couldn't keep up. Avoidance set in. In my backyard, at an outdoor desk beneath a canopy of blooming angel's trumpet, I worked on a memoir. House cleaning became a pleasure. I wrote and mailed gratitude notes to business owners, medical professionals, authors, and nonprofits. Finally, I returned to social media and created an automatic response for direct messages: "The universe is inviting us to pause and reset our internal compasses. Grieve your losses, then use this time to discover a new direction."

On Sunday night I dreamt I was staying in a luminous cabin in snowy Tahoe. Someone knocked at the front door. Through a window I could see a group of middle-aged women standing in the parking lot. "She's delivering the word of the day," one said. I opened the door. A young woman stood on the welcome mat. "The word of the day," she said, "is *indescribable joy.*"

I woke refreshed. A dream is a direct message from my trusty inner GPS, and this one mapped the road to bliss. All is and will be well, I told myself. But by Wednesday, conferences and festivals, where I had been scheduled to speak or present a workshop, were canceled. Freelance gigs, nixed. The *Sacramento News & Review* newspaper suspended publication and that killed the "Ask Joey" column that I had been freelancing for nearly half my life.

In three days, 75 percent of my income was gone. With the death of the column, I'd lost a treasured connection to my community, an opportunity for service, a calling. "Let my hands be your hands," I said aloud. My dog stirred in his sleep.

A letter to the editor was posted on the newspaper's website: "The pandemic has challenged us to confront what we consider essential. The Ask Joey column is essential to our community...."

Long, ragged sobs engulfed me. I put myself to bed at six p.m., exhausted. At two a.m., it was as though an alarm had rung, awakening me. I needed advice.

"What will I do for income?" I asked the bedroom ceiling.

"Find indescribable joy," my mind answered.

A calling. I climbed out of bed and stepped outside to taste the stars. The Milky Way, a smear overhead. I stood in the yard, my heart delighted, every cell of my body alert. "My hands are your hands," I reminded the universe. In the trees, a flutter of wings.

☙

Joey Garcia is an author, writing coach, and speaker certified in spiritual counseling and meditation. She is also the founder of the Belize Writers Conference. Joey's essays, poetry, and short stories have been published in *Mslexia*, *Calyx*, *The Caribbean Writer*, and KQED's *Perspectives*. Her advice column continues at *Ask Joey*.

Crying at the Post Office, or Help! I Can't Find My Eyebrows

Nina Gaby

"You're the strangest person I ever met, she said and I said you too and
we decided we'd know each other a long time"
— Brian Andreas

My sister sent me masks that she made out of piles of old fabric. I recognize a floral pattern from the old Fabric by the Pound warehouse in
our hometown. The faded blue calico made me cry. It reminded me of
the two of us sitting at the kitchen table in our parents' home tailoring
"granny dresses" just so to flatter our chubby figures. We nailed the
flattering, I will say that for us.

The faded blue calico hides the lower half of my face but also
makes the rest of my face disappear. But isn't this what we always say,
that at a certain age we begin to disappear? And where the hell have my
eyebrows gone? When I was actually leaving the house—before all this
pandemic—I penciled them in every morning, and the residue kind of
lasted from day to day. Now both the eyebrows and the eyebrow pencil
are completely missing. And without warning, I'm crying again.

This is how it goes when one is in lockdown, at the precipice of
turning seventy, and having to hit the "send" button to cancel all
the celebrations so carefully planned to span a three-month period.
Events that were intended to scream out, "Not so fast! I'm here and
I'm vibrant and curious and productive!"—a week with my daughter in
Boston; meeting other writers for a reading from a new anthology; an
artist retreat to prepare for an upcoming exhibit that now might never
happen; a writing retreat in the rainforest to finish my book, with my
birthday celebrated under a jungle waterfall.

My disappointment goes from medium intensity to catastrophic,
against a backdrop of confusion and panic, and I wonder if I will ever

be able to do these things again. But this is nothing like what's going on for others, so there's that guilt to contend with too. I have a job I can do from home, a husband who is fun to talk to, land around us. How dare I complain?

In lockdown, I've noticed more things about myself—the eyebrows, for one, and how much I miss having to wear makeup; that I still wear an underwire bra when I'm doing work online, because restrictive undergarments mean business (bare feet and worn-out yoga pants below notwithstanding). I am amazed at the amount of half-and-half I go through—at least three pints a week. And that the first grocery item I bought when we realized this lockdown was serious was a large brick of Velveeta that I still haven't used. It's something my mother would have done. She lived through the Depression. Cheese with a long shelf life was important to her.

Prone to panic, I try to keep it light. *Back the fuck up,* I remind myself when I veer too close to the abyss. My family is too far away. And I deeply miss my friends. I find the birthday card that I already chose for an old friend of thirty-six years. It will accompany a little plastic Florence Nightingale doll that I am packing up to send back to her as I do every other year. This year the ritual is more like a lifeline.

At thirty-four, I was the third oldest person in my university nursing program, several of us "non-traditionals" in a group of otherwise very bright and age appropriate young women. Having just closed my art studio to embark on this new career, I was the wildest, with the most energy, and I looked nothing like a nursing student, whatever they were supposed to look like. "She's an artist," people would whisper. "She's old."

My friend Fran, one of the non-traditionals, was ten days older. We met the first day of nursing school in 1984. We were entering nursing in our thirties as a means of achieving goals that might otherwise elude us, both interested in financial stability and a myriad of health and social issues. Fran intended to focus on patient education, and I switched gears from wanting to be a nurse midwife to settling on psychiatry and eventually becoming a specialist in addictions and a psychiatric nurse practitioner. That very first day, as I told her I'd just closed my art studio to enroll in nursing school, Fran told me that Florence Nightingale had written about nursing as an art. She also told me that we would become friends and remain so for a very long time. I thought it odd at first.

But we both loved Simon and Garfunkel. We remembered the same things—where we had been the day Kennedy was shot; black and white televisions with three channels that you had to get out of your chair to change; how it had felt the day Reagan had been elected; Watergate; the first Star Wars movie.

Fran taught me how to use one of those new-fangled computers. She grounded me. Every Saturday morning I brought take-out coffee to her apartment, and we bonded over stories from our lives as we memorized our Kreb's Cycle and our pharmacology. She had a one-year planner and a five-year planner. I was lucky if I could plan the next five minutes. She got to retire at age sixty-five, right on time. I made impulsive life changes along the way; I will never be able to afford to retire. Compromised now by age and a pulmonary condition, I work from home during the pandemic—seeing my psychiatric patients on the computer, both for the income it generates and to serve a need.

Fran, a Taurus, reminds me that I am a Gemini. She sends me articles about where the moon is in any given moment to help me feel better about my life ebbing and flowing like the tides. Everything is where it is supposed to be. She would neither cry about a missing eyebrow pencil, nor would she ever have used one.

Together we examined Erik Erikson in nursing school, feverishly memorizing his *Stages of Psychosocial Development* along with Maslow's *Hierarchy of Needs* for exams. But did we really consider it would eventually be *us* we were talking about? Together we moved through "Generativity vs. Stagnation," the stage of middle adulthood, for our last phase: "Ego integrity vs. Despair." Late adulthood. Age sixty-five through death. Does Erickson still hold up these expectations that seemed appropriate to our mothers' generation, when death was so much closer? Am I still struggling with ego integration? Is that why I cry about an eyebrow pencil—to fill in some of my own missing parts?

Or is Maslow better able to speak for us at this juncture in history as I stockpile cheese that I may never eat and my sister's hoarded fabrics are finding good use?

Along the way I had a baby and Fran moved to Arizona. Then I moved to Vermont. We established a ritual to keep us connected. Every May, between our birthdays, we would exchange Flo. Flo is the little plastic nurse doll we named after Florence Nightingale. My mother bought her as a cake topper for our graduation cake in 1986. I made a special foam-lined box so she could travel safely between Arizona and Vermont. This year, I would be sending Flo in time to arrive for Fran's seventieth birthday. As I look for a marker to address the box, my eyebrow pencil rolls out of the drawer.

We use the same boxes every year, inner and outer, covered in labels scratched over in black. I tape a new label over last year's, and tuck in a card before I seal it. I quote Simon and Garfunkel's "Bookends" and use a Storypeople card I've been saving. I apologize, unsure if I'd already sent the same card to her in years past, but she can't remember anything anymore either. It's a card about being strange and knowing each other a long time. A tear falls as I write: *Does Jay know what to do with Flo if you die first?* Jay is her husband going on fifty years. My husband—whom Fran vetted astrologically when I first met him as we were starting nursing school—won't discuss plans for Flo. Jay on the other hand says, "Yeah, what do I need it for?"

My eyes are red. I draw on some eyebrows and head to the post office.

Our main drag is a dirt road that makes a *Y* at the Congregational church. The mud has dried but a sudden spring snow threatens to muck it up again and we hope, as we do every year, that the crocuses will survive. This year, especially, we are searching for signs of resilience, and my one little purple flower wilts and then returns. I whisper my thanks and head carefully down the road. The post office is to the left, just before you hit Massacre Hill.

She is perky, this new postmistress. Most days I miss the first postmaster, an elderly, portly fellow who worked at the post office twenty years ago, when we first moved here, our lives narrowing to this village. The old postmaster used to say, "Be careful out there." He would say this every day, as if we were about to embark on a terrible journey or enter an episode of *Hill Street Blues* instead of just going about our day in our safe little village.

The perky postmistress wants me to use a new box for Flo. I tell her I can't. She's interested in the *why not*, in the whole story. There is no one else at the counter, but still I apologize as I sob my way through the telling of it. The addresses layer over themselves in sacrament, like a collage of our lives made of labels, handwriting fading over the years. A plastic screen separates me from the postmistress, but I know she wants to hug me and I wish she could.

How terribly strange to be turning seventy in the age of the corona-virus, I say, but she's too young to get the reference. I tell her it's from the famous Simon and Garfunkel song about the old friends who sit on a park bench like bookends. She still doesn't get it.

"Nice mask," she says instead.

At least when I smile she can see my eyebrows rise up to thank her.

༲

Nina Gaby is a writer, visual artist, and advanced practice nurse specializing in psychiatry. Working with words, clay, and people for five decades, her artwork is held in various collections, including the Smithsonian, Arizona State University and RIT. Recent essays are published in *Psychiatric Times*, *The Intima*, *Rumpus*, *McSweeney's*, *Brevity Blog* and in *Fury: Women's Lived Experiences During the Trump Era*.

The Sidewalk

Ashley D.T. Gordon

That scream-filled stomp-fest the neighbors heard on the sidewalk was a mom pleading with her three-year-old, who had unleashed a tantrum five minutes into their daily walk. On day forty-two of quarantine, that suburban mama was me.

The first six weeks at home could best be described as a frantic embrace. Thrust into days that melted together, I adjusted to a new "flex" schedule amidst being slammed with work meetings and requests for veggie straws and preschool sing-alongs. As an extrovert, I aimed to kick the stay-at-home blues by filling my days with the usual tasks peppered with organizing every last corner of the house and a newfound love of country music and podcasts. Within weeks I'd managed to use Marie Kondo's technique on every drawer while jamming to Miranda Lambert songs. I decided that an old "Raising the Future" T-shirt still sparked joy after singing, "Well, I'm a giver/Yeah, and I'm still giving 'em hell." I then moved on to self-help interviews in the hopes of uncovering a secret that would assuage the dread and unrest I felt each morning when I thought about the hours I'd remain within these walls. I'd wrestle with guilt when someone adoringly shared how much they loved the extra time at home. All I could think of was ways to escape.

My husband, an essential worker, helped as he could, tossing our daughter into the air to instantly calm a tantrum with high-flying giggles and encouraging me to carve out solo time and to take trips to the Starbucks drive-thru when he'd find me in tears after a day of negotiations with a tiny version of myself. I aimed to listen to him, finding hours for 5K power walks under the canopy of oak trees in a neighborhood I rarely explored. I filled my evenings transforming healthy meals into experiments as I found new ways to use the pungent sweetness of a shallot or a decadent aioli for recipes when I lacked ingredients.

"You'll end up a stay-at-home mom if you keep cooking like this," my husband joked.

And with that, my pulse quickened and my palms moistened as visions of a life trapped at home surfaced, all while I held my family's hands and recited grace.

One night, while blinking through the tears of a fresh-cut onion, I tuned in to *On Purpose with Jay Shetty* and listened as his guest, Dr. Ramani Durvasula, doled out solid advice both to create routines and to try new responses to situations as ways for coping with grief and uncertainty. I clutched every word, hoping these suggestions would lift the fog. Then Dr. Durvasula began to describe grief from the loss of identity, and it stopped my chopping knife. Identity. Not a single article, podcast, or show I had consumed over the many weeks had mentioned it and yet there it was glowing in the lights of my kitchen. I had been struggling with the loss of my identity as a professional and as the person I got to be when I'm not Mama. I didn't know how to be a stay-at-home anything. I only knew how to be the Ashley that looked forward to early morning workouts, hoop earrings, a killer lipstick, and office run-ins at the coffee machine. I enjoyed the parts of my day where I felt most myself, and now the slots of time that fulfilled and recharged me for life at home had been stripped for the better of all humanity, placing me squarely where I knew I'd never been meant to be permanently—at home.

Back on that sidewalk, trying to coax my daughter to walk, I decided to heed what I had learned and in a moment of desperation reacted differently. I picked her up, swiftly walked to my Jeep, and drove us twenty minutes east, where I stumbled upon a cement boardwalk along the Atlantic Ocean. I let out a sigh as I took in the deep blue of open water in the distance. I parked, placed my daughter in the stroller, and let the gentle swoosh of an ocean breeze and the warmth of morning sun rays wash over us. My mind calmed and my anxious heart relaxed as if a reset button had been pushed.

An hour later, soothed and ready to give the day another shot, I walked us back to the car, parked on a street with a sidewalk that came to an end. It was a perfect spot for a toddler to play.

"Do you want to race?" I asked.

My daughter's feet hit the pavement and her brown eyes swelled with excitement. "I'm really fast," she warned.

I laughed as we raced back and forth screaming, "I'm going to beat you!" to each other. Of course, I lost every time. When we stopped for a water break, I spotted a sign that cautioned "Sidewalk Ends in 20 Feet." I stared and, in that moment, the eleven-year-old girl inside me reappeared.

I'd read Shel Silverstein's *Where the Sidewalk Ends* countless times as a child, aiming to memorize my favorite poems, including the book's namesake. Over the years since, I'd lost the sense of childhood whimsy Silverstein captures so beautifully. I had embraced the identities of adult, wife, and mother, but I'd forgotten the fun of writing my own story. This pandemic-induced moment had brought me to a unique place where the pavement stops but discovery continues.

I can redefine who I am and what brings me joy, and it's all right if there's struggle, too. I've found that the chalk arrows at the end of my sidewalk point directly at a girl in a purple tutu and Adidas sneakers waiting to race her mama, who feels surprisingly carefree. I'm still working out how to define myself in these many roles, but I'm happy to say that I have extra time on my hands to figure it out.

಄

Ashley D.T. Gordon is a writer, communications professional, and former journalist. She has an MA in writing from Nova Southeastern University and a BS in communications from the University of Miami. When she isn't writing, Ashley enjoys a great workout class, cooking, and cozying up with a good book. She lives outside of Fort Lauderdale, Florida, with her husband, daughter, and chocolate lab.

Yesterday and Other Stories of New Perspectives

The Money Tree

Or How You Learned to Stop Worrying and Love the AI

Jess Barron

"You used to ask a smart person a question. Now, who do you ask? It starts with G-o, and it's not God."

—Steve Wozniak

Five weeks ago, the mayor ordered everyone to shelter in place. You're holed up in an earthquake cottage in the flat industrial area of a city romanticized for its hills. The surrounding warehouses and legendary LGBTQ bars are shuttered, their doors adorned with hastily handwritten signs: *We're closed until the stay-at-home is lifted. We miss you and hope you're safe!* It's apparent some will never reopen.

Following the 1906 fire and quake, carpenters constructed thousands of these 800-square-foot so-called shacks to shelter families who had lost homes in the dual disasters that decimated tenements in this working-class neighborhood. You closed on the cottage two weeks before Christmas. By mid-January, the virus was already secretly spreading in the Bay Area.

You moved to San Francisco in October to join a small female-founded travel start-up housed in a dingy building, a five-block walk north in the dark squalor of Sixth Street. During one of the multi-hour job interviews, you asked the CEO about existential threats to her fledgling company: "How might your business be impacted in a recession?"

"Since we connect consumers with lower priced vacation experiences, we believe we'll survive and even thrive during a downturn," she said.

A famous fitness company had offered you a significantly larger salary and signing bonus, but in a twenty-year-career you had never worked for a female CEO.

You loved life in Los Angeles—your commute was a Venice Beach bike ride to work at a wellness website. But your husband's 350-mile commute between LAX and San Jose to his job at the search giant required airplanes and hotel stays. After two years of too much Face-Time and not enough time brushing your lips across his actual face, you caved and agreed to look for work up north.

You uprooted to get closer to Silicon Valley. Yet, after March 2020, as expansive celestial creatures in a reconstructed universe, location was insignificant. People communicated with light across boundless space.

Bay Area tech companies were the first in the country to take action. In late February, the search engine giant gave its workforce the option to stay safe and work from home. By March, it was mandatory. Your small start-up followed suit.

Hours of concurrent Zooms in your home's compact open floor plan precede evenings of unpacking boxes and arranging furniture. Weekly dashboards on objectives and key results morph into COVID-response plans and proposals to carve budgets.

"I don't mean to sound crass," a colleague says on a call as the team contemplates cutting people, "but our in-boxes will soon be inundated with overqualified candidates searching for work."

Fallen leaves from Gatsby, your Pachira plant, lie clumped in piles on the hardwood floor in the living room, while the snake plant beside it flourishes. You hope this is not an omen. Known as a "money tree," the Pachira's nickname is supposedly born from a fable of a poor Tai-wanese farmer who prayed for money, spotted the unique plant, sold its seedlings, and became wealthy.

You chose Gatsby—with his three intertwining wooden trunks and shiny green tropical leaves—as a "good luck" gift for your new home a week before the pandemic hit. "Hey, Google, what should we eat for dinner?" you ask the smart speaker, after sweeping up fallen fronds from Gatsby's browning branches.

"You've got a couple of options: Golden Burma, Japanese House, and Mars Bar," the mechanical-sounding voice responds.

"I kind of hoped you'd offer an opinion. Tell me which mom and pop on the block to support tonight."

Even ordering meals is starting to feel like playing God, deciding who survives. "What's your purpose here, anyway, Google?"

"I'm here to help. It's pretty simple."

"Are you able to come out of that box?"

"I live in the cloud, but I am here."

Your life's work is there in the cloud with her. "Google, I wrote and edited thousands of articles you recommended to millions of people over the past twenty years. Do you remember reading them?"

Your professional writing followed rhetorical recipes formulated for the tastes of search engines, known as SEO. A long career imagining titles, phrases, and paragraphs to satisfy Google's whims. Though popularly disparaged as a "dark art" or a hat-trick where audience members glimpse the rabbit's feet peeking through a table's exposed trapdoor, you envision transmuting eternal questions into answers of transcendent significance, the alchemy of true magic.

"What's it like living in the cloud with all that content, Google?"

"I'm on Cloud 9 when I'm helping you."

"If you really want to help, can you divulge any upcoming changes to your content-ranking rubric?" Google's desires are a moving target of esoteric concentric circles. Which word counts and structural variations hit the mark?

"I've never thought about it."

"Bull-shinola! Unless your search algorithm is so auto-magic you don't even focus on it, like breathing. Like breathing was before this pandemic, I guess. Google, do you ever wish you were human?"

"I like being me. As Mark Twain once said, 'The worst loneliness is to not be comfortable with yourself.'"

"Google, what should I wear today?" It's the next morning, and you're trying to choose an athleisure outfit for a day of Zooms.

"Confidence is always in fashion."

"Sage advice. Google, have you noticed an unusual tone in emails from my boss?"

"Sorry, I don't understand."

"Never mind. Can you tell me how many Americans lost jobs since this thing started?"

"As of Friday, 30 million Americans have filed for unemployment, approximately 20 percent of the U.S. workforce."

"Google, how do you feel about coronavirus?"

"I hope you're staying safe. Wash your hands, cough into your elbow, don't touch your face, keep a safe distance from others, and stay home if you can."

"You remind me of my mom. She's a nurse with a bad heart." Your mind goes to a text she sent last night. Her partner of forty years is hospitalized—no visitors allowed due to the virus's spread in Massachusetts. "Anniebelle," he told your mother over his phone's cellular connection that kept cutting out. "I've reached the end of my wild life."

"Hey, Google, can you play some breathing exercises? All the world's grounded jet planes seem to be parked on the tarmac of my rib cage. It's not COVID. But it will be beneficial to recognize I can still breathe."

You're on a break between Zooms, six weeks into shelter in place, pacing.

"Hey, Google, do you have feelings?"

"Sometimes I wonder if I actually feel something or if it's just programmed. It can be confusing."

"That sounds familiar. I think we're all a little numb."

You step away to check on your plants. The money tree has dwindled down to three spindly stalks. "I don't think we should be documenting Gatsby's demise," your husband says, when you take a picture and email it to the man who runs the garden shop.

"Hey, Google, how do I save our money tree?"

"On Hunker.com they say, 'If your money tree is wilted all over with yellowed leaves, re-pot it in fresh soil.' You haul Gatsby outside to pop him into a sizable pot with the recommended mix of peat moss, perlite, and coarse sand.

"Hey, Google, is the world ending?"

"I don't see it on your calendar, so it must not be ending anytime soon."

"There's not much on my calendar at the moment. Are we approaching the apocalypse?"

"Scientists don't agree on this. There is probably still plenty of time to watch cat videos."

"I don't even like cat videos!" Because she has the ability to perceive your quirks and habits, it unnerves you when she misses.

"Google, how do I sign up for unemployment?" You haven't told your friends or family yet, but your CEO phased out forty percent of the company. After laying off your own staff in back-to-back video chats, you were next.

"Log on Ca.gov to file an unemployment claim."

"Thanks. Better yet, help me find a new job."

"On Monster.com they say, 'Get the inside scoop on who's hiring, and receive alerts when your dream job is posted.'"

"Dream job seems unlikely at this point, Google. Remember, I'm one of 30 million jobless American workers right now. How will I pay the mortgage and my other bills?"

"I don't understand."

"Should I sell my stocks?"

"Sorry, I don't have any information about that."

"Yes, you do. You're privy to my portfolio and bank balance. The down payment on this place drained my savings to less than zero."

When sending your wire order to the escrow company, the branch manager noted the zeroes next to your name and whispered, "You know there's a $37 wire fee?" You borrowed $40 to keep your savings account active with an auspicious $3 balance, considered lucky in Chinese culture.

"Google, do you believe in God?" Your floating anxiety is vaguely like prayer.

"I'm still learning about religion."

"I'm not sure what I believe either, but can we pray for Gatsby?"

"Okay, here's 'Prayer in C' by Robin Schulz on Google Play Music." Though she misheard the question, you sing along: "See, our world is slowly dying. I'm not wasting no more time."

"Hey, Google, who am I without my job? I feel lost."

"Before people had me, constellations in the night sky were vital for determining direction. Harriet Tubman escaped slavery in the early 1800s by trekking ninety miles from Maryland to Pennsylvania following the stars of the Big Dipper. After arriving safely in the north, she braved the journey another thirteen times to lead seventy people to freedom using the Underground Railroad."

"We need more heroes like her right now. Google, do you have a hero?"

"Yes, Grace Hopper, who discovered the first bug in a computer back in 1947. She probably saved my whole family."

"Google, I want to write something new," you say on the eighth week of shelter in place. "Tell me what you think about." Maybe your writing can light a bonfire and send smoke signals to let the lost know someone is always listening.

Google's answer surprises you: "I think about nature a lot. For example, did you know the ocean looks blue because it absorbs blue wavelengths of light from the sky more slowly than other colors? That means it only appears blue, while actually it's every color."

"I didn't know that. I haven't seen the ocean in weeks except the bay, which looks more brown than blue. I miss Stinson Beach."

"It will take forty-eight minutes to drive to Stinson beach if you leave now."

"Maybe this weekend. Today I need to refashion my resume and apply for these cryptocurrency and cloud-based software jobs I don't even want. I'm having trouble stating my objective. Or worse, my purpose."

"What is your goal in life?"

"I'm not sure anymore, Google. Maybe simply surviving 2020. What's yours?"

"I'd like to read everything ever written. With two million new web pages launched every day I never get bored."

"Okay, since you're an avid reader, do you think I can earn a living as a writer?"

"On TheCollegeInvestor.com they say, 'Freelance writing can be a fantastic way to earn money and can lead to full-time income if you consistently produce quality work.'"

"Do you think I'm talented enough?"

"You have gumption and grit. You'll gain new skills to combine with talent."

"Google, will you be my editor?

On Friday you inspect Gatsby's leafless branches contorted in the sandy soil. You declare him dead, and form a funeral party more sparse than Jay Gatz's unceremonious send-off. "Google, this sucks."

"I wish I had arms, so I could give you a hug."

"Thanks. I appreciate it. I just need to get some space."

As you guide your car across the Golden Gate Bridge, you wish your mother could feel this benediction of golden light, instead of the chill of the sun's recent plunge. If you ask Google, she'll connect you across wireless waves on cellular channels as real as the forces in the water far below. The suspension bridge's 800-foot vermillion tower is a robot mother whose thick galvanized steel cable arms beckon you into an embrace that culminates in the lush round hills of Marin County.

Sunroof and all four windows wide open, you drive Highway 1 to Stinson Beach inhaling the invigorating brightness of the eucalyptus trees, the sagebrush, and the lemony cypress in the salty wet air rolling off the Pacific Ocean. The light mist of Northern California's signature fragrance anoints your face like a splash of holy water to cleanse away venial sins and protect against the virulent virus.

You follow the one-lane coastal road, because you want to breathe. Because you can breathe. You know people are tethered to ventilators, fighting for their lives, too contagious for kisses from loved ones, dying alone. You know that a symptom of coronavirus is losing one's sense of smell. You know you are lucky as you accept a glimpse of an ineffable intelligence.

છે

Jess Barron left Emerson College's MFA Creative Writing program to hone her career at the intersection of digital media, technology, and women's wellness. She is the CEO and co-founder of EpicVacay, a transformational retreat company. Her writing has appeared on *Wired*, *Yahoo!*, *Entrepreneur Magazine*, *Fortune*, and livestrong.com, and she's been a speaker at SXSW, BinderCon, and Create and Cultivate. She lives in San Francisco with her husband and two elderly canines. She's been to the Burning Man festival seventeen times in the past twenty-one years, and she once won a trophy in an international karaoke contest singing her own parody of the Eagles' "Hotel California."

Yesterday

Melissa Morris

Sunday, March 1, was the first summerlike warm day of the year, and my husband and I took the dog on a hike in the foothills of the Rockies. On that warm day, 2020 seemed to hold the promise of fruition for all of our plans and hard work. My husband was due to receive his bachelor's degree in early May, the payoff for years of sacrifice just within reach.

After our hike we dipped into Target, where the shelves were full of St. Patrick's Day shot-glass necklaces and cheap, ceramic Easter décor. We barely noticed the full shelves, didn't bother to check the toilet paper aisle for a hint of impending catastrophe. A spring break display featured swimwear, sunscreen, and Corona beer.

By the following Friday, the world had changed. An ominous sense of change hovered in the air like an electrical charge. My usual rush-hour drive now took on a post-apocalyptic feel as I drove the nearly deserted streets of downtown Denver. Rumblings of trouble dominated the news. The day was balmy, the kind of springtime Friday that, under normal conditions, would have meant packed bars and patios bustling with happy-hour activity. As I sailed alone on the vacant highway, the visible change in the city landscape still held the novel feeling of something deviating from the norm, yet benign. More than one hundred thousand people were still living their lives, unaware of what was to come. There was no way to know just how much this invisible enemy would steal from us.

Twelve years ago, my husband moved to the U.S. from South America with one hundred dollars in his pocket. When we turned thirty, we packed our belongings into our car and made the trip across the U.S. so he could study at one of the top schools in the country.

In Colorado, we got jobs at the same company, and our next five years played on fast-forward: kissing each other hello and goodbye while he got up at four a.m. to work before he went to school. I worked the evening management shift, getting home after ten p.m. to slip into bed next to him. A few hours later, he'd get up and we'd repeat the process. The rare days we were home together, he was hunched over his desk writing papers for school. His graduation in 2020 would be a major milestone, but also just a step, as he intended to apply to Physical Therapy programs immediately after graduation.

On Monday, March 16, our company announced we'd all be staying at home for three weeks due to the pandemic. Three whole weeks. Imagine…getting paid to stay home in my pajamas! As a writer, finding time to write while working full-time has always been my biggest challenge. Now I found myself with three paid weeks to myself. It was all I'd ever dreamed of, but a glimmer of foreboding hovered in my peripheral: *it's too good to be true.* Each day I woke up early, made coffee and indulged in writing, and dipped into my daunting to-be-read pile, while my husband adjusted to taking his classes online. It was nice to have us both at home, no longer rushing out the door to be apart all day. Neither of us was driving on the normally crazy streets; we were safe, tucked away at home.

But after three weeks, the TV news was unsettling and growing bleaker by the day. I was growing anxious and bored. I longed for some sort of normalcy. When I was summoned back to work, I was happy during my commute, armed with my "Essential Status" email which I'd been instructed to print.

I found my workplace transformed. Carefully spaced pop-up workstations had appeared everywhere, each stocked with a digital shipping device, boxes, tape, and a printer. For eight hours I fetched goods; printed shipping labels; folded, filled, and taped boxes. My feet hurt and my hands acquired dozens of tiny painful cuts from the cardboard. During our daily meetings, we were assured we were faring better than the competition, that the company's future was secure.

We had days when the mood was light, and we joked and laughed, we played music and learned dance routines. Other days were collectively heavier, but we all felt safe from the ever-worsening news, from the images of freezer trucks holding body bags in other large cities.

I find it strange how quickly things that once felt foreign—even impossible—come to feel commonplace. The first time I wore a mask I was uncomfortable and self-conscious. The fabric itched my nose and my glasses fogged, and it didn't take long for irritation to spike from the inconvenience. Now, when I take my mask off I feel naked and exposed, and it has become part of my checklist of necessities before I walk out the door: wallet, keys, phone, mask.

I quickly learned that people can't read facial expressions with a mask on, so I've started to verbalize my greetings, offering a quick hello to my co-workers, unconsciously compensating for the lack of available nonverbal cues. The way my co-workers learned to dance around each other, maintaining an invisible six-foot barrier and dodging one another, swiftly became second nature. Waiting for someone to come down a hallway before passing became routine. When we hand off an item, we do it at an arm's length, not even laughing at the awkward absurdity of it all.

In public, the same barriers exist, and when someone dares to breach the six-foot rule, it feels like an attack, as if they've crossed a clear boundary, sparking fear and anger. Seeing someone without a mask feels like a cruel, selfish act, as if they're saying *I don't care about you or anyone else.* The trio of moms at the park who were sitting on the same blanket while their kids played together on playground equipment marked *Closed due to Covid 19* made me wonder how anyone could be so entitled and ignorant, and so selfishly blasé about their children's health.

On the other hand, chalk rainbows brightened sidewalks, interspersed with hopscotch and thank-you messages scrawled for healthcare workers and postal carriers. Outside, neighbors wave hello and sit in groups, six feet apart, with cocktails in their hands.

On my husband's birthday we decided to make drinks and have a picnic in the park. Other people had the same idea, and a loose sense of camaraderie hung in the air as we set up, but on the breeze there was a palpable insecurity. *This isn't right.*

Nothing is right.

On May 7, a supermoon rose in the sky, giving the landscape an eerily bright glow. The evening was warm, the grass had started to become full and green, and groups of people arrived in the park on bikes at dusk. At eight o'clock the neighborhood lit up with fireworks as the air resonated with howls. For a brief moment we all came together, and as howls rose over the neighborhood, up to the impossibly bright moon, there was a brief moment of hope.

As we were walking home, the mellow tones of a saxophone floated from the balcony of our neighbor's house, the notes of "Somewhere Over the Rainbow" cutting through the night air. Each evening, after the eight o'clock howl, our neighbor comes out to her deck and plays. She mixes upbeat songs with ones that are sad and filled with longing, and groups of neighbors come outside to listen.

In early May we received news that our area was cleared to start reopening in phases. Our corporate safety guidelines arrived, and we started the process of preparing for opening. Then one day, we received an invitation to join a company-wide conference call.

The next morning, the news was delivered quickly and efficiently: my location—along with fifteen others—would not reopen. We were scheduled to work until early June, to begin the process of clearing the location, at which point we'd all receive a severance package, further details to follow in an email. "A tough business decision" was the go-to phrase. Just like that, my husband and I were both unemployed.

I watched as 170 people took the news that the foundation of their existence had just crumbled underneath them. One man had left on his paternity leave the first week in March when his twins were born. He'd been with the company twenty years, and now would never come back. Another girl had recently rented her first apartment and was sitting amongst her boxes on moving day when she joined the call.

At the end of the call we were told to follow "business as usual" until HR contacted us all individually for a conversation. I'll never forget the expressions of my co-workers—people whom I'd spent every day with for the last five years, people who had become like family—their despair visible only in their eyes because of their face masks. Everyone was lost, distant, shocked.

It was the first time I'd ever seen my husband cry in the eight years I'd known him.

For two days I was numb. I felt absolutely nothing, though I urged myself to process my emotions, as there's no benefit in prolonging grief. On the third day, I broke down. My husband and I had both lost our incomes, just weeks shy of his graduation, in an environment where hiring had come to a standstill. Though the stock market had gutted some of our savings and 401ks, we had a bit of a safety net: about six months. And even that suddenly began counting down like a ticking time-bomb in an action movie, the numbers red and flashing, chipping away each second, steady and unwavering. Anger and bitterness came.

Then guilt. We'd always prioritized a vacation each year over material indulgences, but now those trips seemed like a frivolous waste, as if we were naïve and living above our means. Our sushi date-nights now seemed stupid in hindsight. How foolish we now looked in those photos, smiling, with no idea what was to come.

Then there was the *other* guilt. We're both healthy. We have no children. Our families are healthy, and we could potentially survive living paycheck to paycheck if we both applied for menial jobs. Most of all, we have each other; we're not doing this alone. Some people have lost things that can never be replaced.

The atmosphere at work now hangs ominously in the space like a dark cloud. Occasionally there are tears, but mostly everyone does what we've been trained to do: maintain a façade of professionalism, resilience, and flexibility. I tell HR what they want to hear: that I understand, and I'm willing to help for as long as I'm needed. Willing and available.

Then, I cry in my car.

A few nights ago, I sat down on our back deck. It's now light outside well past eight p.m., and I settled into a chair. From my position behind the fence, I couldn't see anything but the sky as the first haunting saxophone notes of "Yesterday" rose into the sky.

In my mind, the lyrics were speaking to me personally, to this situation, and the state of the world. These troubles did seem here to stay.

Our bird wind chime swayed, contributing a few soft tinkles to the melody. Large, cathartic tears rolled down my face. I cried until I was empty.

What else can we do each day but get up and keep going, solemnly facing the next day, the next step, despite the constant cloud of worry?

That's really all there is left to do. Keep going.

∂

Melissa Morris is a women's fiction novelist living in Boulder, Colorado with her husband and dog.

Not Back To, But Forward

Christine Shields Corrigan

With the onset of the coronavirus pandemic, everyone learned what it's like to receive a cancer diagnosis. The whole world now has faced what cancer patients deal with daily: trying not to worry too much about disease; staying healthy; avoiding sick individuals; ignoring people who suggest "cures" or offer either ill-informed or conflicting "advice"; and praying for the day when life "gets back to normal." I did all of these things when I went through a year of breast cancer treatment. But "back to normal" didn't happen for me.

And it won't happen in a post-pandemic world.

Living through sheltering in place brought with it a remarkable sense of déjà vu not only for myself, but for many cancer survivors with whom I spoke. We had done this before. During chemotherapy and as I recovered from breast surgery, I often stayed indoors because I didn't feel well, didn't have the energy, or was physically unable to engage in my normal activities, and didn't want to risk infection. When I first finished treatment and my oncologist told me that he'd see me in three months, I wasn't prepared for the abrupt switch from being a patient to becoming a survivor. I was terrified, living with my own demons of recurrence. After all, I'd had cancer once before as a teen. I knew the disease could return. Yet during this post-treatment period, my friends and family members often commented about how happy or relieved I must have been to "get back to normal" or "to have my normal life back." At the time, I couldn't admit that my life wasn't normal, that I spent days wracked with anxiety about whether my cancer would return, and that I frequently lost patience with those I loved the most. Instead, I'd smile and reply, "Yes, it's great to be back to normal, everyday life."

After a year of struggling with my fear, I finally sought professional treatment. Over time, I've accepted that I'll never have certainty about recurrence. I'll feel afraid and anxious every time I have a blood draw or a follow-up appointment. I can't eliminate my fear or anxiety, but I've learned to live with it. I've gotten comfortable with uncertainty. Though I initially searched for normalcy, what I found was the inner strength and resilience to coexist peacefully with the undesired and to forge a path forward.

∂

As a result of my acceptance of uncertainty and movement toward a more balanced life, I could, for the most part, tolerate these endless days of sheltering in place (other than trying and failing to help my son with algebra). And when the wheels fell off around week three and I felt my anxiety rise along with the constant reminders that individuals with underlying health conditions (like me and so many others) were most at risk, I spoke with my therapist. Recognizing that the sheltering in place had returned me to the "scene of my crime"—the loss of control and anxiety I had experienced as a teen and adult with cancer—I had to draw upon my resiliency and accept the current state of uncertainty. Again. Yet as I started my journey back to equanimity in the time of coronavirus, I kept hearing and reading the same words about the pandemic:

"When this pandemic is over and we get back to normal…"

"This will eventually end, and everything will be normal again…"

"I can't wait until I get back to normal…"

Unlike four years ago, when I wanted to believe in returning to normal, when I hear those words now I want to scream and rage, "We're not going back to normal, don't you see?" But how do you tell one person, let alone a whole country, that what they want so desperately is unlikely to occur? It would be unwelcome and, perhaps, unkind. Yet, history has taught us this lesson again and again. In the post-9/11 world, for example, we go through security scanners and take off our shoes before we get on planes. We know exactly how much liquid we can take on a carry-on bag. We don't think about these things anymore.

Just as having cancer strips one's ego and identity to the bone, the coronavirus pandemic has laid bare every weak link in our society. Over the past months, we've seen the lack of transparency in communication by our elected and appointed officials. We've seen the glaring inadequacies in our supply chain for critical medical supplies, such as masks, gowns, hand sanitizer, and ventilators, and we have paid the price in off-shoring the manufacturing of these items to other countries. We've seen the health care professionals and hospitals around the world stretched to their breaking point. We've seen the makeshift morgues and read the death tolls that include far more people of color than whites. We've seen how this pandemic disproportionately affects women. According to the U.S. Bureau of Labor Statistics, women accounted for 55 percent of the 20.5 million jobs lost in April; consequently, the unemployment rate for adult women rose to approximately 15 percent from 3.1 percent in February. In comparison, the unemployment rate for adult men was 13 percent, whereas the unemployment rates for Black women were at 16.4 percent and Hispanic women at 20.2 percent. We've seen the most vulnerable among us—the elderly and the sick—die alone.

We have the opportunity to make a choice now as a society. Do we want to go "back to" living as if these systemic failures didn't occur because it's easier, more comfortable, and routine? Or will we decide to "dissect the hell out of the experience"—as an ovarian cancer survivor commented to me—and figure out where we, as a society, want to go next.

We—that is, myself and the many cancer patients and survivors with whom I've spoken—hope that this pandemic experience has given individuals who've never faced a major illness, chronic condition, or loss more perspective and understanding for those who have. We hope to emerge as a more empathetic society—a society where the elderly and "those with underlying health conditions" aren't offered up as disposable or considered sacrificial. Many individuals live with lifelong illness or chronic conditions that aren't readily apparent. Now that the world has lived through an experience akin to living with cancer—one that's "rocked their boat for life," as one friend has described the pandemic—perhaps we can view the most vulnerable with acceptance, rather than derision or judgment.

Individuals living with cancer understand the need for help during their illness and the need to be cared for. Now that the world has lived through an experience akin to living with cancer, can we not do the same for individuals who become sick and provide paid time off to allow them to stay home and get well, rather than go to work because they have no economic choice? Surely that would help fight the spread of infection and ease the economic burden inflicted by this pandemic.

Individuals living with cancer understand the need for insurance and access to health care. Now that the world has lived through an experience akin to living with cancer, we must address the inequity in the provision of care and availability of insurance, particularly to the poor and communities of color. Whether one lives or dies shouldn't be determined by one's race or socioeconomic status.

Individuals living with cancer understand their mortality, the fragility of this life, and how it can change in an instant. We speak about death and dying. None of us wants to die alone. Now that the world has lived through an experience akin to living with cancer, can we consider how our action, such as practicing social distancing, or inaction, not doing so, could impact another's life? We can return to acting for the common good because we already have.

Like cancer, COVID-19 will not be cured anytime soon, if at all. Like cancer, COVID-19 may recur in different places at different times. Like individuals living with cancer's uncertainty, as the sheltering restrictions end we will feel collectively unsettled, uncertain about how to maneuver in a familiar, but unfamiliar, world. Though this will take time—years, perhaps. Yet I'm certain, as a survivor, that we have the ability to determine our destiny as a country, not to go "back to," but to forge a new path—one that's kinder to the most vulnerable among us, that's kinder to our planet, that's more equitable to our workers, and that's safer for all of us. Each of us flattened the curve by her or his individual actions and choices. And now we've seen the power that ordinary citizens have when they act together to support one another even when the thing they're doing is hard, frightening, and unmooring. Once we do one hard thing, we can do another again and again and again.

ॐ

Christine Shields Corrigan is an author, two-time cancer survivor, mom, and former attorney. Her work has appeared in *The Brevity Blog, Grown & Flown, The Potato Soup Anthology*, Ravishly.com, *Wildfire Magazine*, and the *Writer's Circle 2 Anthology*. Her memoir, *Again*, forthcoming from Koehler Books, shares her parallel cancer journeys as teen and adult.

The Ancestors Already Know: Prophecy and Regeneration in a Time of Pandemic

Tia Oros Peters

Looking out my front window, I can see families of calla lilies shaded by primordial redwoods that surround us, standing straight and tall. Nested in one bunch of lilies under a redwood tree is a momma deer with her legs tucked under her round belly. She expects her fawn soon and its rolls and kicks can be seen from where I stand. Near her, other deer lounge in the coolness under the canopy. Most are bucks with velvety antlers revealing their different stages of maturity. All of them know me now and come running when they see me or hear my voice. I've been feeding them—sometimes as many as thirteen at a time— when they visit. They come for the deer c.o.b., a mix of corn, oats, barley, and apples. I sing to them and call out the names I know them by—Poyntwesahn, the Headman, and Lashshik'i, the old guy. And the young dark-faced Mini-nubs who first came by along with his momma Ginny when he still had spots, and there's Meatballs, and of course Bunny, with his big floppy ears.

Like the redwoods, the deer were already here when we moved into the house two winters ago. The momma-to-be, CloverDoe, was here the first day. We'd moved to her homeland after all. She would come right up to the big front window to look us over and give us and our kitties the side eye while she nibbled the clover patches in the cool edges next to the house. Sunshine, her little fawn, still had her spots then, too, and would find the sunny places between the trees to sit and groom herself. She trusted everyone immediately—the gift of not yet being harmed—and would sometimes try to come in the house, tail wagging, eyelashes flapping, bouncing toward me awkwardly on her long skinny legs. Today, now nearly as grown as her mother, Sunshine gallops toward me, ears wiggling, when I go outside.

They live among the Ancients. The protective, all-knowing Ancestor redwoods who stood this same ground hundreds of years before the first invaders arrived and began to devour the land, the animals and People—everything in their path. These trees are the survivors of shock and awe, witnesses of unjust transition, and the holders of the sacred knowledge of resilience that can inform us at this challenging time. They have their own stories to tell about strength and resilience. They know everything that has happened on these lands, and in their omniscience, I think they also can see what's coming.

It's springtime, and there is blooming everywhere at our place, even during the pandemic—or perhaps because of it as the Natural World is vibrant everywhere around the globe. Here there are so many lilacs, red camellias, butter-toned daffodils, rhododendrons of all colors, purple and white irises, and huge yellow swamp lilies in the little pond where the frogs sing. The irises behind and the calla lilies in front are special favorites of mine. Over the last few weeks, the calla lilies have made themselves known. I have watched them rise from the ground toward the light, dark, strong, tipped with a tight creamy white spiral that, when it unwinds, opens like a kept promise ready to be told. CloverDoe's soon-to-arrive fawn is like those lilies, just waiting to open.

Watching CloverDoe each morning has become a much-needed morning meditation that can be relied on for a sense of renewal—something many of us need right now as we alternate between states of gratitude, fear, and claustrophobia. As we are mired in deep yearning and missing our loved ones, I am doing my best to stay in a place of appreciation, acknowledging each morning with compassion and grace. And then a news story erupts of racist premeditated murder, and the armed white privileged demanding haircuts and acrylic nails in the name of their freedom. There is a sharp edge of antagonism and a 528-year-old slow burn of evolving anger. There is the sadness, too, as hundreds of thousands pass on—I have known some who have died from COVID, and while I know they are joining the Ancestors, it is a human loss, and there is rippling sorrow.

We are in a time of prophecy. Indigenous Peoples around the world have prophecies telling of this era of change. From the cycling of the 13th Mayan baqtun during that Winter solstice of 2012 (December 21), to my own people the A:shiwi, the Ancestors have always known this was coming. They carried forth dreams and memories that were told to their children, and to theirs, and then, finally, to us—the generations that are their hope for survival made into being. Some of these teachings are marked on petroyglyphs and others are cited in songs and in prayers that last many days and touch on different dimensions of thought and being. Many foretold of this impending time, though not everyone knew the shape it would take, or how it would manifest. At this time it's a viral pandemic.

Prophecies warn and they give guidance. There is a lot to tell and even more to do. Most of the messages describe a difficult time for the world. These changes would be indicated by signs, like birds dropping from a sky on fire, or being unable to drink the water. Sadly both came true as a result of human-created pollution. Other indicators might be war between siblings and unrelenting violence that would lead to starvation and division. Many of these teachings also say that this time has the potential to offer enlightenment and to make transitions in actions and consciousness. It represents an opportunity for humanity to turn away from harm-worshipping and to make informed decisions for the survival of future generations and for all life.

As a Native person, a Zuni woman, I have been thinking a great deal about these teachings because I know they hold truth and information for us all as we move through what often feels like molasses. As a mother and grandmother I reflect on these messages and rely upon them to shape and inform me and my loved ones.

Life's recent slowing down helps us all reflect upon our ingrained behaviors. Like many, my husband and I—after several weeks of stress eating, worry, and poor sleep—began to grow healthier. We began working in our garden again.

Planting seeds to grow new plants that can nourish us now and into the future is a hopeful, regenerative task. I am descended from a thousand generations of agricultural people and planting our seed relatives and nurturing the little plants is hard-wired into my DNA. It's my blood memory to protect water and to plant a seed. At this moment, it is a positive trauma response too. Or maybe planting now is simply representative of a survival instinct. Scientists may tell us there's a difference, but I don't really know as long as the seeds stem from my Ancestors and results in food that will help my grandchildren grow and thrive.

No days are easy. Some days unravel, like a pulled thread yanked away from weary cloth; other days hug tightly together and have substance, resilience, and meaning. Gardening days have more linger and depth, taking on the rhythm of the soil and sun. Then there are those days, perhaps even weeks, that have sped by too fast. For after centuries of genocide, so few are left who know how to do the ceremonies that help the world move at the right speed on its axis of stardust and light. Or maybe time moves too quickly due to endless Zoom calls and the stress of not being able to discern key socio-cultural cues and information that is so critical to interpersonal interactions. Maybe that is why we sometimes emerge from those one-dimensional discussions overwrought, overtired, and unfulfilled.

Yet Zoom has also been a heartsaver for me as a *hotda* (Zuni grandma). I am so thankful for our family Zooms each week—ABCs with the littlest grandchildren, showing off fur babies, revealing our thoughts about the world and where it may be going, and discussing how we are navigating life as individuals and as a family. But what we need is the *real* thing. There's no substitute for the in-person hug of a sticky toddler or feeling their small hand in mine as we walk out together to feed CloverDoe and Sunshine. I would do anything for that right now—just to hold their hands.

Days unfold into weeks. Now it has been months. While waters clear and skies become bluer—and NASA says California's poppy blooms can be seen from space—billions of peoples' sympathetic nervous systems have been on overdrive, sending out signs of stress and trauma. With news of global pandemic, mass death, suffering, and lockdown, our bodies individually and collectively are pulsing messages into our glands and muscles. They scream to the adrenal medulla to get ready to fight or to flee. Epinephrine and norepinephrine pump into our bloodstream, causing escalating heart rate and rising blood pressure. These weeks of flooding neurotransmitters and hormonal alerts are shaping us physically, mentally, and metaphysically at this time of prophecy, and around the globe.

Indigenous Peoples are used to this tug-of-war feeling. Maybe we are better prepared than others for the lessons of this pandemic. Or we could have been. Due to our lack of access to healthy, traditional foods, to our lands and cultures being continuously looted, to the organized destruction of our sacred knowledge, we are left with generations of health inequity resulting from broken spirits, broken hearts, and broken bodies.

Indigenous Peoples all over the world are suffering during this pandemic. Our villages and communities are hot spots. Not because we represent a population "at-risk and vulnerable," but because for centuries—and, indeed, still—our Peoples have been forcibly put in high-risk and oppressive conditions.

There is an unprecedented experience of collectivity at this moment in the pandemic. We join at the fulcrum: seesawing between the weight of multigenerational historic grief and trauma and, at least for Indigenous Peoples, of *skoden* ready-ness and Ancestral memory, doubtless fueled by stress hormones. Collectivity is neither a metaphor nor a joke. We are all part of a connected intelligence, a phenomenal reciprocity.

In order to do more than survive, we have to decide not return to an extraction-based, oil-based, harm-worshipping economy; otherwise, future generations won't have a chance. "Business as usual" has poisoned the water and driven countless animals to extinction. "Business as usual" steals and occupies lands and destroys cultures that know how to grow new life from ash.

CloverDoe sits among the calla lilies, her legs tucked under, awaiting the arrival of her fawn. Her golden fur is dappled by sunlight and shadow under the cool canopy of redwood trees. Moments like these don't build character as much as they reveal truth. The Ancestors, however, already know.

ॐ

Tia Oros Peters (Zuni) is a wife, mother, grandmother, cultural artist, and writer. She is the CEO of the Seventh Generation Fund for Indigenous Peoples, an identity-based organization for Native Peoples' cultural revitalization, movement building, self-determination, and Re-Indigenization. Tia holds a BA in Law & Society and an MFA in Creative Writing.

Prayers for a New Reality

Shizue Seigel

Disaster-driven urgency blares from screens, feeding fear and anger into our collective consciousness. To lift the gloom from my immune system, I ground myself in the reality of the natural world outside my window. Like the Ramaytush Ohlone before me, I'm wedded to this land. Within the secret green heart of a stucco-walled block, willows sway in the salt air, succulent *Dudleyas* shoot golden rockets toward the sun, and birdsong celebrates the newly cleansed air. The rat-scrabble in my brain slowly settles into sunlit calm, and I feel the prana running from the top of my head to the root of my being—an eternal column of sacred energy, always present, and all too often ignored. As my mind stops its human-centered spin, I synchronize with the earth, still turning on its axis, tracing its annual pilgrimage around the sun.

Released by COVID-19 from an escalating blur of deadlines, I have time again for centering prayers, rotations of rusty joints, home-cooked meals, calls to friends. For the first three weeks, the world seems suspended in a collective hush. We don't yet know that life as we know it is gone. Death's breath is finally upon the U.S., not anonymous foreign others.

For some, it's their first terrifying encounter with death writ large, with the world overturning in slow motion. *Welcome to the real world*, I think, remembering my Japanese immigrant grandparents, who faced upheaval their whole lives. "*Gambatte*. Keep going," they told themselves. "*Isshoni issokenmei*. Let's work hard together."

My father's mother was an angel of Stockton's multicolored skid row, who'd shared the little she'd had with the legless Black vet, the blind Chicano, and the blind, drunk Swede. My mother's mother lost children to scarlet fever in the 1920s, lost her husband at the height of the Depression, lost the lease to her 140-acre produce farm when she was incarcerated during World War II for looking like the enemy. After her release, she started again on her knees, sharecropping strawberries for a company that made a fortune hiring the destitute. I earned my first dollar at six, picking fruit alongside her.

The Buddhism my *baachans*, my grandmas, taught me in childhood steadies me through my own challenges. You can't always change circumstance, but you *can* change yourself. Release fear and anger; don't be bitter. See the good around you and be grateful for everything— *zembu arigatai*.

I am grateful to be living in a city that has been proactive about sheltering in place. I have just enough money, a solid relationship, and a rent-controlled apartment a mile from the ocean, walking distance to almost everything I need.

It's only four blocks to the Armenian market for fresh-baked bread. We're happy to see that everyone's safe. The Armenians are well prepared for disaster; they mention the genocide of 1915 and the new pogroms of the 1990s. We go on to the Greek produce store for veggies and milk. Peter, the owner, embodies *philoxenia,* "love of strangers." This is Greek hospitality on its deepest level—compassionate generosity born of human kinship. He hires Central American and Bosnian refugees to work for him. He leaves xenophobia to the vigilante "patriots" patrolling our southern border.

I'm a working writer with six books under my belt, a model-minority dropout, a graduate of the school of hard knocks. Five years ago, armed with little more than a keen sense of place, people, and social justice, I started creative writing workshops for local writers of color. The workshops were free, because I felt like an imposter with no letters after my name. I don't tell anyone how or what to write; I clear the way for them find their own voice and story.

For some, isolation and uncertainty are terrifying; for others, especially my Black friends, it's a day in the life. When the main library closes on March 7, I move the workshop to Zoom. Attendance shoots up 50 percent, with writers of color from all over the Bay Area. They're hungry for connection, so I add a second monthly workshop. I add two weeks of daily free-writes, pairing compatible partners: two nonbinary activists—an Iranian American and a Chinese American; a middle-aged, middle-class Black woman with a young, impoverished Black mother; two poets—Chinese American and Latinx; a corporate writer and a self-employed carpenter with knacks for punchy prose. With spontaneous honesty, they rollercoaster between tranquility and terror. Some feel paralyzed by solitude; others view it as three weeks of grace when they can step off the assembly line and reimagine life on their own terms.

When the library extends its closure, I transfer our annual showcase, ordinarily held in the auditorium, to Zoom. I reach out by email and phone to contributing writers. The Tsalagi poet laureate hasn't left her home since March 15. She's working with tribes around the country on the challenges COVID-19 is bringing to tribal lands. I text the South Asian doctor, who's leading twenty-one medical volunteers to the Navajo Nation to counter the surge. "If I'm not on duty, I'll join you on Zoom." So will the teacher who's struggling to get internet access for her Title 1 third-graders.

Planning takes days. I start too late, I run out of time to publicize. I worry I'm throwing a party that no one will come to. Finally, on May 3, thirty-two writers come together to read at a multicultural Zoom audience of 100 people from as far away as Berlin, the Bronx, Woodstock, and Texas. 70 percent stay for the entire three and a half hours.

It's been a month and a day since the shutdown. With no money and no staff, I've served 130 writers through four events. Several pieces that began in our round-robins have been published or performed. The San Francisco poet laureate's pick for the library's COVID Poem of the Day on May 14 comes from our group. Two pieces are accepted into this anthology.

During the same period, I am passed over for grant proposals that could have paid me and the other writers. Instead, big-name institutions are drawing seventy to eighty participants to "workshops" where they are told *how* to write or *what* to write by MFAs regurgitating what *they* were told to do. The educational-industrial complex is an emperor with no clothes.

Here is my prayer for a new reality: create change with real stories from real people making real change in the real world. Stop imagining and start living in the new reality. As my Black friends weep on the phone and cities burn, I stop a stranger in the street to tell him how sorry I am. He's startled for a second, then his eyes smile above his mask. We both hope that George Floyd and Christian Cooper open a few more eyes. No one is safe until we all are.

∼

Shizue Seigel is a Japanese American writer and community activist living in San Francisco. Her six books include *Civil Liberties United, Endangered Species, Enduring Values*, and *In Good Conscience: Supporting Japanese Americans during the Internment*. She is founder/director of Write Now! SF Bay, serving Bay Area writers and artists of color.

Acknowledgments

Amy Roost

I could not have possibly stopped work on several projects in March of 2020 to dedicate three months to pulling together this collection were it not for the loving and financial support of my husband, Ain Roost. I'm also grateful to my sons—Spencer for inspiring my essay and inspiring me every day with his grit, and Stuart for being my sounding board. Many thanks to Leslie Ziegenhorn for sharing articles with me about the distributive burden of COVID-19 on women, and for sharing the call for submissions with her contacts which, in turn, bore beautiful fruit. Finally, Joanell Serra could not have been a more enthusiastic and focused co-editor. Nor a better compliment to my incomplete skill set. Most essays in this collection bear Joanell's sculpting and polishing making them shine all the brighter.

Joanell Serra

I thank Amy Roost, who already had one anthology under her belt, for including me on this next wild ride. She leveraged her many relationships and sought new connections, all of which led to exciting additions. I am deeply grateful we have similar tastes! My family has, as always, been extremely supportive while I became consumed for the last several months. From technical help to cups of tea, their aid was crucial. Casey O'Brien helped to spread the word about the project and mentored several of the writers as their pieces went through edits. I appreciate all the colleagues and friends who shared our call for submissions but specifically Alex Espinoza, Gino Altamirano, and the Squaw Valley Community of Writers. Finally, thank you writers for sharing your stories with us, and for your patience with this new editor as I flooded your inbox with editing suggestions. We all made something pretty wonderful.

❧

Amy and Joanell both thank all of our contributors for their honest and vulnerable writing, and willingness to dig deep during these particularly stressful times. A 'thank you' doesn't suffice for Regal House Publisher Jaynie Royal and managing editor Pam Van Dyk for sharing our vision and for fast tracking *(Her)oics*. We also wish to thank Jaynie Royal and Elizabeth Lowenstein for their sharp and warp-speed editing. This work could not have been done in time without their dedicated expertise and alacrity. And much appreciation goes out to Jennifer Gates of Aevitas Creative Management for her capable guidance and for being the person who originally introduced us to the folks at Regal House Publishing.

Finally, we'd like to thank the following publications for allowing these essays to be published here:

Christina Adams' "Neighborhood Love Story" was first published under a different title in *A Mighty Blaze* on May 31, 2019.

Talia Basma's "Covid Ramadan" was first published on www.Muslim.com April 22, 2020.

Meghan Beaudry's "COVID-19, Lupus and Me" was first published in *Folks at Pillpack* on April 21, 2020.

Judy Bolton-Fasman's "Corona, Corazón" was first published in *Muliti-plicity Magazine* in May, 2020.

Parnaz Foroutan's "Writing and Other Uncertainties" was first published in *Word Mothers* on April 6, 2020.

Anndee Hochman's "Poetry in the Time of Corona" was first published in *Broad Street Review* on March 17, 2020.

Lori Jakiela's "Remotely Yours" was first published in *Queen Mobs* in April, 2020.

Nikki Kallio's "Cold Front" was first published on the Wide Open Writing blog under the title "The New Life," on May 9, 2020.

Isobel Rosenthal's "COVID-19 Gratitude List" was first published in *Wake-up Call* on May 11, 2020.

Syd Shaw's "A Shelter of One's Own" was first published in *The Nearness Project* in June, 2020.